目录

亲爱的读者 ---------- 5
承诺 ---------- 7
米其林指南历史 ---------- 10
如何使用本指南 ---------- 12

▪餐厅及街头小吃列表

星级餐厅 ---------- 27
必比登美食推介 ---------- 30
以地区分类 ---------- 32
以菜式分类 ---------- 39
熟食小贩中心 ---------- 46
街头小吃 ---------- 51
供应优质酒品的餐厅 ---------- 52
有景观的餐厅 ---------- 55

▪餐厅及街头小吃

餐厅-以英文字母顺序排列 ---------- 58
熟食小贩中心-以英文字母顺序排列 ---------- 208
街头小吃-以英文字母顺序排列 ---------- 238

▪酒店

酒店列表-以舒适程度分类 ---------- 242
酒店列表-以英文字母顺序排列 ---------- 244

▪地图

地图 ---------- 284

DEAR READER

It's our great pleasure to present the first edition of the MICHELIN Guide Singapore.

In Singapore, there are amazing dining choices at every turn. The city's multi-ethnic culture serves up a host of cuisines, each with its own unique aroma and flavour. Our recommendations within these pages bring you a selection of the best across all styles, nationalities and price bands, with every establishment chosen first and foremost for the quality of its cooking.

We are delighted to include a selection of hawker centres in the guide, since this national icon plays such a central role in the daily lives of so many Singaporeans.

Every entry in the guide has been selected by our team of full-time Michelin inspectors who are the eyes and ears of our readers. They always pay their own bills and their anonymity is key to ensuring that they receive the same treatment as any other guest. Entry into the guide is free of charge.

Our famous Michelin Stars ✣ are awarded to restaurants with exceptional cooking, but look out too for the Bib Gourmands ⊛ – these are places offering a carefully prepared but simpler style of cooking for under SG$45 and they represent excellent value for money.

Our independent inspectors have also chosen a selection of the best hotels that Singapore has to offer, ranging from intimate townhouses to grand palaces.

We are always very interested to hear what you, our readers, think of the establishments listed in the MICHELIN guide. Your opinions and suggestions matter enormously to us and help shape the guide, so please do get in touch.

You can email us at michelinguide.singapore@michelin.com

We hope you enjoy all your dining and hotel experiences in Singapore.

Bon appétit!

亲爱的读者

很高兴首本新加坡米其林指南诞生了！

新加坡是美食汇聚之都，多元种族的背景让本地的饮食文化丰富多彩，呈现独一无二的风味。获得本指南推荐的餐厅，其食材素质与食物水平全属优秀之列；餐厅种类涵盖各种类型、价钱。

每个地方均有其独特饮食风貌，论新加坡美食，不得不提价廉物美的熟食小贩中心，故此，指南内当然少不了熟食小贩中心推介。

本指南内推荐的餐厅全部由全职米其林评审员团队严格挑选，只有最优秀的食店才获推介。为确保体验到与一般顾客同等的服务待遇，让评审结果更客观公正，我们的评审员会以匿名身份到访各大食肆。

除了闻名遐迩的米其林星级❀食肆推介那些食物素质特佳的食店外，还有必比登美食推介☺，获推荐的是装潢简单、烹调和选料用心却价钱实惠，个人消费额不到$45的食店。

与餐厅食肆一样，米其林评审员团队在芸芸酒店中挑选了一系列优质酒店，推荐给广大读者。从时尚型格到优雅舒适，以至豪华典雅，各个级别和风格的酒店，那怕是新开幕者，只要服务水平高、房间舒适及设备完善，也会获本指南推荐。

我们向来重视读者的回馈，渴望聆听阁下的意见。如对本指南有任何意见或提议，观迎电邮至下列电子邮箱：

michelinguide.singapore@michelin.com

祝阁下在新加坡拥有愉快的美食和住宿体验！

Bon appétit!

THE MICHELIN GUIDE'S COMMITMENTS

"This volume was created at the turn of the century and will last at least as long".

This foreword to the very first edition of the MICHELIN Guide, written in 1900, has become famous over the years and the guide has lived up to the prediction. It is read across the world and the key to its popularity is the consistency of its commitment to its readers, which is based on the following promises:

Anonymous inspections:
Our inspectors make regular and anonymous visits to restaurants and hotels to gauge the quality of the products and services offered to an ordinary customer. They settle their own bill and may then introduce themselves and ask for more information about the establishment. Our readers' comments are also a valuable source of information, which we can then follow up with another visit of our own.

Independence:
Our choice of establishments is a completely independent one, made for the benefit of our readers alone. The decisions to be taken are discussed around the table by the inspectors and the editor. Inclusion in the guide is completely free of charge.

Selection and choice:
Our guide offers a selection of the best restaurants and hotels. This is only possible because all the inspectors rigorously apply the same methods.

Annual Updates:
All the practical information, the classifications and awards are revised and updated every single year to give the most reliable information possible.

Consistency:
The criteria for the classifications are the same in every country covered by the MICHELIN Guide.

...And our aim:
To do everything possible to make travel, holidays and eating out a pleasure, as part of Michelin's ongoing commitment to improving travel and mobility.

承诺

「这册书于世纪交替时创办,亦将继续传承下去。」

这是1900年首册米其林指南的前言,多年来享负盛名,并一直传承下去。指南在世界各地均大受欢迎,关键在其秉承一贯宗旨,履行对读者的承诺。

匿名评审

我们的评审员以匿名形式定期到访餐厅和酒店,以一般顾客的身份对餐厅和酒店的食品和服务素质作出评估。评审员自行结账后,在需要时会介绍自己,并会详细询问有关餐厅或酒店的资料。读者的评语和推荐也是宝贵的资讯来源,我们会跟据读者的推荐到访该餐厅。

独立性

餐厅的评选完全是我们独立的决定,纯以读者利益为依归。经评审员和编辑一同讨论后才作出决定,并不会向收录在指南内的餐厅和酒店收取任何费用。

选择

全赖一众评审员使用一致且严谨的评选方法,本指南才能向读者推介一系列优秀餐厅和酒店。

每年更新

每年都会修订和更新所有实用资讯、分类及评级,务求为读者提供最可靠的资料。

一致性

每个国家地区的米其林指南均采用相同的评审和分类准则。

我们的目标

尽全力令旅游、度假及在外用膳成为一大乐事,实践米其林一贯优化旅游和生活的承诺。

ONCE UPON A TIME, IN THE HEART OF FRANCE...

It all started way back in 1889, in Clermont-Ferrand, when the Michelin brothers founded the Manufacture Française des Pneumatiques Michelin tyre company – this was at a time when driving was considered quite an adventure!

In 1900, fewer than 3,000 cars existed in France. The Michelin brothers hit upon the idea of creating a small guide packed with useful information for the new pioneers of the road, such as where to fill up with petrol or change a tyre, as well as where to eat and sleep. The MICHELIN Guide was born.

The purpose of the guide was obvious: to track down the best hotels and restaurants across the country. To do this, Michelin employed a veritable armada of anonymous professional inspectors to scour every region – something that had never before been attempted.

Over the years, bumpy roads were replaced by smoother highways and the company continued to develop, as indeed did the country's cuisine: cooks became chefs, artisans developed into artists, and traditional dishes were transformed into works of art. All the while, the MICHELIN Guide, by now a faithful travel companion, kept pace with – and encouraged – these changes. The most famous distinction awarded by the guide was created in 1926: the "étoile de bonne table" – the famous star which quickly established itself as the reference in the world of gastronomy.

Bibendum — the famous tyre-clad Michelin Man — continued to widen his reach and by 1911, the guide covered the whole of Europe.

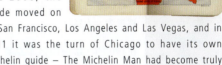

In 2006, the collection crossed the Atlantic, awarding stars to 39 restaurants in New York. In 2007 and 2008, the guide moved on to San Francisco, Los Angeles and Las Vegas, and in 2011 it was the turn of Chicago to have its own Michelin guide — The Michelin Man had become truly American!

In November 2007, The Michelin Man took his first steps in Asia: in recognition of the excellence of Japanese cuisine, stars rained down on Tokyo, which was gripped by culinary fever; a guide to Kyoto, Kobe, Osaka and Nara followed, with Yokohama and Shonan then joining Tokyo. Thereafter the Michelin Man set his feet down in Southern China, with the publication in 2009 of a guide to Hong Kong and Macau.

The Red Guide was now firmly on the map in the Far East. The Michelin Man then explored Southeast Asia and in 2016 the first edition of MICHELIN Guide Singapore was published. The MICHELIN guides collection now covers 27 titles in 27 countries, with over 30 million copies sold in a century. Quite a record!

Meanwhile, the search continues... Looking for a delicious pot-au-feu in a typical Parisian bistro, or some mouth-watering Singapore street food? The Michelin Man never stops spanning the globe, making new discoveries and selecting the very best that the culinary world has to offer!

从前,在法国中部……

这一切始于1889年,米其林兄弟在法国克莱蒙费朗(Clermont-Ferrand)创办Manufacture Française des Pneumatiques Michelin 轮胎公司 - 当年驾驶汽车仍被视为一大冒险。

在1900年,法国的汽车总数量少于3,000辆。米其林兄弟灵机一触,想到为道路驾驶的先驱提供含实用资讯的小指南,如补充汽油或更换轮胎,以至用餐和睡觉的好去处。米其林指南就这样诞生了!

指南的宗旨非常清晰:搜罗全国各地最好的酒店和餐厅。为达目的,米其林招揽了一整队专业的神秘评审员,走遍全国每一个角落寻找值得推介的酒店和餐厅,这在当时是前所未有的创举。

多年来,崎岖不平的道路早已被平顺的高速公路取代,米其林公司持续茁壮成长。同时间,全国各地餐饮业的发展亦一日千里:厨子成为大厨、传统手艺成为艺术,传统菜肴亦转化成为艺术杰作。现今米其林指南已成为广受信赖的旅游伙伴,不仅与时并进,更致力推动这些转变。指南中最著名的是早在1926年面世,并迅即成为美食界权威指标的「星级推介」。

由米其林轮胎人必比登为代言人的米其林指南,不断拓展其版图,到1911年已覆盖全欧洲。

2006年,米其林指南系列成功跨越大西洋,授予纽约39家餐厅星级推介。在2007及2008年,米其林指南在三藩市、洛杉矶和拉斯维加斯出版,2011年已拓展至芝加哥,米其林轮胎人必比登也正式落户美国。

2007年11月,米其林轮胎人首次踏足亚洲,在东京广发星级推介,以表扬日本料理的卓越成就,同时亦掀起美食热潮。其后,旋即推出京都、神户、大阪及奈良指南,并继东京之后推出横滨和湘南指南。香港和澳门指南亦于2009年推出。

今年必比登更涉足新加坡,推出首本米其林新加坡指南,令这本以红色为标志的指南,在远东地区的覆盖范围更广泛。

时至今日,米其林指南系列共计27本,涵盖27个国家,一个世纪以来总销量超过三千万。这是个令人感到鼓舞的纪录!

此时此刻,我们仍然继续对美食的追寻……是巴黎餐厅的美味杂菜锅还是令人回味无穷的新加坡街头小吃?必比登将会努力不懈,发掘全球美食,为读者挑选最出色的佳肴美馔!

11

HOW TO USE THIS RESTAURANT GUIDE
如何使用餐厅指南

Map number / coordinates
地图号码 / 座标

Cuisine type
菜式种类

Name of restaurant
餐厅名称

Stars for good food
星级美食

❀ to ❀❀❀

**Bib Gourmand
(Inspectors' favourite
for good value)**
(必比登美食推介)

☺

**Restaurant classification
according to comfort**
餐厅 — 以舒适程度分类

Particularly pleasant if in red
红色代表上佳

ᵡ	Simple shop	简单的食店
X	Quite comfortable	颇舒适
XX	Comfortable	舒适
XXX	Very comfortable	十分舒适
XXXX	Top class comfort	高级舒适
XXXXX	Luxury	豪华

12

CANTONESE 粤菜   MAP 地图 18/D-1

Summer Pavillion
夏苑

Start with a cool drink in the Chihuly lounge before you're ushered into this sumptuous dining room which proves the ideal environment in which to enjoy the high quality Cantonese cooking. The polished service and stunning porcelain merit a mention, as does the wonderfully fluid choreography of the tea service. Look out for the roasted duck and the double-boiled sea whelk soup and fish maw which is presented in a whole coconut.

翻新后重开的夏苑，点心异常出色，作为配角的中国茶以典雅多样的瓷质茶具感衬，赏心悦目，每喝一口尖鼎沐浴在如丝般润滑的美茶中，服务员适时添茶，值得一赞。点心以外，椰皇花胶响螺炖鸡汤、北京片皮鸭、大红片皮乳猪或自制参巴酱同样值得一试。不论你以乌龙茶或杨枝甘露作结，都是难忘的体验。

TEL. 6434 5286　　　　　■ PRICE 价钱
The Ritz-Carlton, Millenia, Level 3,　Lunch 午膳
7 Raffles Ave　　　　　à la carte 点菜 $ 100-400
莱佛士道7号　　　　　Dinner 晚膳
丽思卡尔顿美年酒店 Level 3　à la carte 点菜 $ 100-400
www.ritzcarlton.com
　　　　　　　　　　　■ OPENING HOURS 营业时间
　　　　　　　　　　　Lunch 午膳 11:30-14:15 (L.O.)
　　　　　　　　　　　Dinner 晚膳 17:30-22:15 (L.O.)

175

Restaurant symbols
餐厅图标

$ Cash only
只接受现金

♿ Wheelchair access
轮椅通道

🍽 Terrace dining
阳台用餐

≼ Interesting view
上佳景观

🅿 Valet parking
代客泊车

🅿 Car park
停车场

⌸ Private room with maximum capacity
私人厢房及座位数目

☰ Counter
柜台式

☎ Reservations required
需订座

☏ Reservations not accepted
不设订座

🍇 Interesting wine list
供应优质酒品

13

HOW TO USE THIS HAWKER CENTRE / STREET FOOD GUIDE
如何使用熟食小贩中心及街头小吃指南

Map number / coordinates
地图号码 / 座标

Hawker Centre name
熟食小贩中心名称

Address
地址

Stall name
店铺名称

Stars for good food
星级美食

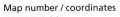 to

Bib Gourmand
(Inspectors' favourite for good value)
（必比登美食推介）

127 Toa Payoh West Market & Food Centre
大巴窑大牌127
Blk 127, Lorong 1 Toa Payoh 大巴窑1巷大牌127   Map 地图: 3/A-1

This small hawker centre consists of only 40 stalls, yet the food on offer is more than satisfying. One must-try item is the handmade Teochew pau - bite-sized and full of amazingly delicious fillings. The very tasty carrot cake is also worth having.

即使这中心只有40家店子，还是值得远道而来。潮式包点是其中一种必尝美食，别看它子子小小，松软的包皮裹着各式诱人馅料。一口大小正好可多尝几款。而菜头粿亦值得一试，裹着蛋浆的菜头粿煎得外脆内软，一试难忘。

🚚 Chey Sua Carrot Cake
青山菜頭粿

The pan-fried cake is popular. They'll deliver the food to your table when there's no queue at the stall
煎萝卜糕非常受欢迎。下单时报上桌子号码，店方会把食物送到你的桌上。

Stall 铺 #02-30

08:00-15:00
$ 2-4

🚚 Teochew Handmade Pau
潮洲自制飽點

Lotus seed paste pau; steamed chicken pau; and Shou Tao bao...all handmade
莲蓉包、大鸡包及寿桃包等潮式包点全部人手炮制。

Stall 铺 #02-02

06:00-14:00
$ 2-3
Closed Monday 周一休息

231

Street Food 街头小吃
Popular places for local dishes
馳名小吃店

———— Stall name
店铺名称

Bismillah Biryani

Biryani with fish or meat inside and flavoured with various Indian herbs.
以多种香料烹调的印度香饭像小山般堆在碟上，鱼和肉藏在其中，色香味美。

$ 6-20 11:00-15:00, 17:30-22:00
MAP 地图 8/C-2
50 Dunlop Street
南洛街 50号

———— Stars for good food
星级美食
✿ to ✿✿✿

Bib Gourmand
(Inspectors' favourite for good value)
（必比登美食推介）
✿

Hill Street Tai Hwa Pork Noodle 大華豬肉粿條麵 ✿

Using fresh ingredients, the noodles are cooked to order and every bowl comes with its own instantly-made sauce and soup.
材料新鲜，每碗面均是独立烹煮，酱汁也是即时调和，常见人龙。

$ 5-10 09:30-21:00
Closed 1st and 3rd Monday of the month
每月第一及第三个周一休息
MAP 地图 9/A-2
#01-12 Blk 466, Crawford Lane
哥罗福街 466座 #01-12

———— Map number / coordinates
地图号码 / 座标

Jalan Sultan Prawn Mee 惹蘭蘇丹蝦麵

A famous noodle stall with over 70 years of history; pork rib prawn mee is the most popular dish.
逾七十年历史的街头面档，经常满座，最有名的是汤底鲜甜的排骨虾面。

$ 5-10 08:00-15:30
Closed Tuesday
周二休息
MAP 地图 9/B-2
2 Jalan Ayer, Lorong 1 Geylang
芽笼 1巷惹兰亚逸 2号

HOW TO USE THIS HOTEL GUIDE
如何使用酒店指南

Map number / coordinates
地图号码／座标

Hotel style
酒店风格

Name of hotel
酒店名称

Hotel classification according to comfort
酒店 — 以舒适程度分类

Particularly pleasant if in red
红色代表上佳

 Quite comfortable
颇舒适

 Comfortable
舒适

 Very comfortable
十分舒适

 Top class comfort
高级舒适

 Luxury
豪华

Restaurants recommended in MICHELIN Guide
米其林指南内的推荐餐厅

TRADITIONAL 传统   MAP 地图 18/C-1

Raffles
莱佛士

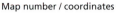 

It may have changed hands many times over the last decade but Raffles, with its striking colonial architecture, remains an essential part of Singaporean identity. The gardens may need some TLC and the public areas of shops, restaurants and boutiques are packed with visitors but, once ensconced in the areas reserved for hotel guests, the mood changes and the pace slows.

这幢获列为国家历史文物的酒店在过去十年曾多次易手，犹幸其经典的殖民建筑风格仍得以完整保存。走过绿草如茵的花园，步入富丽堂皇的大堂，惬人的建筑和历经变迁的怀旧布置都叫人目眩神驰。所有房间均为套房。屋顶泳池是放松身心的上佳之选。购物廊行人如鲫，数十家商店叫人流连忘返。

TEL. 6337 1886
1 Beach Road
美芝路1号
www.raffles.com/singapore

Suites 套房 = $ 740-12,000
Suites 套房 103

RECOMMENDED RESTAURANTS 餐厅推荐
Long Bar Steakhouse ✕✕
Raffles Grill ✕✕✕

268

LUXURY 豪华 MAP 地图 17/B-2
Parkroyal on Pickering
皮克林宾乐雅

One of the more original looking hotels in Singapore is made up of three glass towers linked by Sky Gardens. Its eco-credentials are very much in evidence throughout, with its use of natural materials and living walls of plants. All the stylish bedrooms have views of the city skyline. If you don't suffer from vertigo ask for a room on one of the Sky Garden floors.

装潢以木、石、水和植物等大自然元素作主题,更显环保意念。设计现代兼具个性的客房能观赏一望无尽的天际;水疗中心内的无边际泳池,景色更是扣人心弦。建议选择空中花园楼层的房间。闲来在房外的小径散步解郁,煞是美好。南面楼层的Lime环境舒适写意,供应多国美食,疲急懒动时也是不错的进餐选择。

TEL. 6809 8888
3 Upper Pickering Street
皮克林街上段3号
www.parkroyalhotels.com

♦ = $ 300-460
♦♦ = $ 300-460
Suites 套房 = $ 480-1,800
□ = $ 38

Rooms 客房 338
Suites 套房 29

267

Hotel symbols
酒店图标

  Wheelchair access
  轮椅通道

  Interesting view
  上佳景观

  Valet parking
  代客泊车

  Car park
  停车场

  Garage
  室内停车场

  Non smoking rooms
  非吸烟房

  Conference rooms
  会议房

  Outdoor/Indoor swimming pool
  室外/室内游泳池

  Spa
  水疗服务

  Exercise room
  健身房

  Casino
  娱乐场所

MICHELIN IS CONTINUALLY INNOVATING FOR SAFER, CLEANER, MORE ECONOMICAL, MORE CONNECTED... BETTER ALL-ROUND MOBILITY.

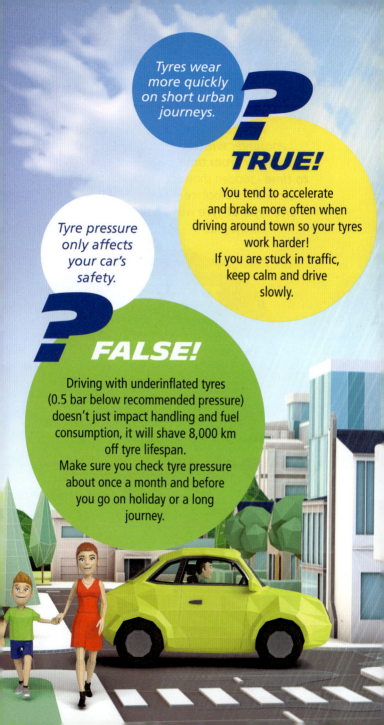

MICHELIN IS COMMITTED

▶ MICHELIN IS **GLOBAL LEADER IN FUEL-EFFICIENT TYRES** FOR LIGHT VEHICLES.

▶ **EDUCATING OF YOUNGSTERS IN ROAD SAFETY**, NOT FORGETTING TWO-WHEELERS. LOCAL ROAD SAFETY CAMPAIGNS WERE RUN IN **16 COUNTRIES** IN 2015.

QUIZ

1 TYRES ARE BLACK SO WHY IS THE MICHELIN MAN WHITE?

Back in 1898 when the Michelin Man was first created from a stack of tyres, they were made of natural rubber, cotton and sulphur and were therefore light-coloured. The composition of tyres did not change until after the First World War when carbon black was introduced. But the Michelin Man kept his colour!

2 FOR HOW LONG HAS MICHELIN BEEN GUIDING TRAVELLERS?

Since 1900. When the MICHELIN guide was published at the turn of the century, it was claimed that it would last for a hundred years. It's still around today and remains a reference with new editions and online restaurant listings in a number of countries.

3 WHEN WAS THE "BIB GOURMAND" INTRODUCED IN THE MICHELIN GUIDE?

The symbol was created in 1997 but as early as 1954 the MICHELIN guide was recommending "exceptional good food at moderate prices". Today, it features on the MICHELIN Restaurants website and app.

If you want to enjoy a fun day out and find out more about Michelin, why not visit the l'Aventure Michelin museum and shop in Clermont-Ferrand, France:
www.laventuremichelin.com

SINGAPORE
新加坡

RESTAURANTS
餐厅

Starred restaurants — 27
星级餐厅

Bib Gourmand restaurants — 30
必比登美食推介
(Inspectors' favourites for good value)
(评审员推介)

By area — 32
以地区分类

By cuisine type — 39
以菜式分类

Hawker Centres — 46
熟食小贩中心

Street Food — 51
街头小吃

Restaurants with interesting wine lists — 52
提供优质餐酒的餐厅

Restaurants with views — 55
有景观的餐厅

Restaurants in alphabetical order — 58
餐厅 - 以英文字母顺序排列

Hawker Centres in alphabetical order — 208
熟食小贩中心 - 以英文字母顺序排列

Street Food in alphabetical order — 238
街头小吃 - 以英文字母顺序排列

25

Don't confuse the rating ✗ with the Stars ✲! The first defines comfort and service, while Stars are awarded for the best cuisine.

千万别混淆了餐具 ✗ 和星星 ✲ 图标！餐具图标表示该餐厅的舒适程度和服务素质，而星星图标代表的是食物素质和味道非常出色而获授予米其林星级的餐馆。

Enjoy good food without spending a fortune! Look out for the Bib Gourmand symbol ⓐ to find restaurants offering good food at great prices!

要省钱又想品尝美食，便要留心注有 ⓐ 必比登图标的食店，此类店子提供的是价钱实惠且素质高的美食。

STARRED RESTAURANTS
星级餐厅

Within this selection, we have highlighted a number of restaurants for their particularly good cooking. When awarding one, two or three Michelin Stars there are a number of factors we consider: the quality and compatibility of the ingredients, the technical skill and flair that goes into their preparation, the clarity and combination of flavours, the value for money and above all, the taste. Equally important is the ability to produce excellent cooking not once but time and time again. Our inspectors make as many visits as necessary, so that you can be sure of the quality and consistency.

A two or three star restaurant has to offer something very special that separates it from the rest. Three stars – our highest award – are given to the very best.

Cuisines in any style of restaurant and of any nationality are eligible for a star. The decoration, service and comfort levels have no bearing on the award.

在这系列的选择里，推荐的是食物素质特别优秀的餐厅。给予一、二或三颗米其林星时，我们考虑到以下因素：材料的素质和搭配、烹调技巧和特色、气味浓度和组合、价钱是否相宜及味道层次。同样重要的是该餐馆的食物能恒常保持高水平。阁下对我们的推荐绝对可以放心！我们的评审员会因应需要多次到访同一家餐馆，以确认其食物品质恒常保持在高水平。

二或三星餐厅必有独特之处，比同类型其他餐厅更出众。最高评级 - 三星 - 只会给予最优秀的餐厅。

星级评定不会受到餐厅风格、菜式、装潢陈设、服务及舒适程度影响。只要烹调技巧出色，食物品质特别优秀，都有机会获得米其林星星。

Exceptional cuisine, worth a special journey.
卓越的烹调,值得专程造访!

Our highest award is given for the superlative cooking of chefs at the peak of their profession. The ingredients are exemplary, the cooking is elevated to an art form and their dishes are often destined to become classics.

获得最高级别的餐馆,其厨师的烹调技巧卓绝,选才用料堪称典范,并将烹饪提升至艺术层次,菜式大多会成为经典。

| Joël Robuchon | XxXxX | French contemporary 时尚法国菜 | 112 |

Excellent cooking, worth a detour.
烹调出色,不容错过!

The personality and talent of the chef and their team is evident in the refined, expertly crafted dishes.

主厨的个人风格与烹饪天赋及其团队的优秀手艺完全反映在精巧味美的菜式上。

André	XxX	Innovative 创新菜	61
L'Atelier de Joël Robuchon	XX	French contemporary 时尚法国菜	119
Les Amis	XxX	French 法国菜	121
Odette	XxxX	French contemporary 时尚法国菜	143
Shisen Hanten 四川飯店	XxX	Chinese 中国菜	166
Shoukouwa 小康和	XX	Sushi 寿司	168

High quality cooking, worth a stop!
优质烹调，不妨一试！

Within their category, these establishments use quality ingredients and serve carefully prepared dishes with distinct flavours.

此名单上的餐馆，在同类型餐馆中，其食材较具素质，烹调细致用心、味道出色。

Alma	XX	European contemporary 时尚欧陆菜	60
Béni	X	French contemporary 时尚法国菜	66
Candlenut	X	Peranakan 娘惹菜	70
Corner House	XX	Innovative 创新菜	78
Crystal Jade Golden Palace 翡翠金阁	XXX	Chinese 中国菜	79
Cut	XXXX	Steakhouse 扒房	80
Forest 森	XXX	Chinese contemporary 时尚中国菜	90
Hill Street Tai Hwa Pork Noodle 大華豬肉粿條麵	🍴	Street food 街头小吃	238
Hong Kong Soy Sauce Chicken Rice & Noodle 香港油鸡饭面	🍴	Street food 街头小吃	216
Jaan	XXX	French contemporary 时尚法国菜	107
Lei Garden 利苑	XXX	Cantonese 粤菜	120
Osia 澳西亚	XX	Australian contemporary 时尚澳洲菜	146
Putien (Kitchener Road) 莆田 (吉真那路)	X	Fujian 福建菜	153
Rhubarb	XXX	French 法国菜	156
Shinji (Beach Road)	XX	Sushi 寿司	162
Shinji (Tanglin Road)	XX	Sushi 寿司	163
Summer Pavillion 夏苑	XXX	Cantonese 粤菜	175
Sushi Ichi 鮨一	X	Sushi 寿司	176
Terra	XX	Italian 意大利菜	182
The Kitchen at Bacchanalia	X	Innovative 创新菜	184
The Song of India	XXX	Indian 印度菜	186
Waku Ghin	XXX	Japanese 日本菜	197

BIB GOURMAND RESTAURANTS
必比登美食推介

This symbol indicates our inspectors' favourites for good value. These restaurants offer quality cooking for $45 or less (price of a 3 course meal excluding drinks).

必比登图标表示该餐厅提供具素质且经济实惠的美食：费用在 45 元或以下（三道菜式但不包括饮料）。

A Noodle Story 超好面	🍴	Street food 街头小吃	212
Alaturka	X	Turkish 土耳其菜	58
Alliance Seafood 聯合海鮮燒烤	🍴	Street food 街头小吃	229
Balestier Road Hoover Rojak 豪華羅雜	🍴	Street food 街头小吃	236
Bismillah Biryani	🍴	Street food 街头小吃	238
Chey Sua Carrot Cake 青山菜頭粿	🍴	Street food 街头小吃	231
Claypot Laksa 德普路真善美驰名砂煲叻沙	🍴	Street food 街头小吃	210
Famous Crispy Curry Puff 驰名香脆咖喱卜	🍴	Street food 街头小吃	212
Famous Sungei Road Trishaw Laksa 驰名结霜橋三輪車叻沙	🍴	Street food 街头小吃	224
Hjh Maimunah (Jalan Pisang)	🍴	Malaysian 马来西亚菜	97
Hong Heng Fried Sotong Prawn Mee 鴻興炒蘇東蝦麵	🍴	Street food 街头小吃	234
Hong Kee Beef Noodle 桐記牛肉粿條	🍴	Street food 街头小吃	213
Hoo Kee Rice Dumpling 和記肉粽	🍴	Street food 街头小吃	213
JB Ah Meng 新山亞明	🍴	Street food 街头小吃	239
Ka Soh 家嫂	X	Singaporean 新加坡菜	113
Kok Sen 国成球记	🍴	Singaporean 新加坡菜	116
Lagnaa	X	Indian 印度菜	118
Liang Zhao Ji 梁照記	🍴	Street food 街头小吃	237
Na Na Curry 南南咖喱	🍴	Street food 街头小吃	230
New Ubin	🍴	Singaporean 新加坡菜	140

Peony Jade (Keppel) 玉河畔 (吉宝)	XX	Cantonese 粤菜	151
Shi Hui Yuan 實惠園	🍴	Street food 街头小吃	228
Shish Mahal	X	Indian 印度菜	167
Sin Huat Eating House 新發	🍴	Street food 街头小吃	239
Song Fa Bak Kut Teh (New Bridge Road) 松發肉骨茶 (新桥路)	🍴	Singaporean 新加坡菜	171
The Fishball Story 魚緣	🍴	Street food 街头小吃	221
328 Katong Laksa (Joo Chiat) 328加東叻沙 (如切路)	🍴	Singaporean 新加坡菜	187
Tian Tian Hainanese Chicken Rice 天天海南雞飯	🍴	Street food 街头小吃	227
Tiong Bahru Hainanese Boneless Chicken Rice 中峇魯海南起骨雞飯	🍴	Street food 街头小吃	235
True Blue Cuisine	X	Peranakan 娘惹菜	192
Wedang	🍴	Street food 街头小吃	221
Whole Earth 環界	X	Vegetarian 素菜	199
Yhingthai Palace 銀泰	XX	Thai 泰国菜	202
Zaffron Kitchen (East Coast)	X	Indian 印度菜	205

RESTAURANTS BY AREA
餐厅 - 以地区分类

Ang Mo Kio 宏茂桥

Mellben Seafood (Ang Mo Kio) 龍海鮮螃蟹王(宏茂桥)		X	Seafood 海鲜	130
New Ubin	🍴	⌂	Singaporean 新加坡菜	140

Bayfront 海湾舫

Cut	✿	XxxX	Steakhouse 扒房	80
Daniel Boulud Bistro & Oyster Bar		XX	French 法国菜	81
Long Chim		XX	Thai 泰国菜	125
Majestic Bay 冠華		XX	Cantonese 粤菜	128
Punjab Grill		XxX	Indian 印度菜	152
Sky on 57		XxX	Innovative 创新菜	170
Spago		XxX	Pan Fusion 混合菜	172
Waku Ghin	✿	XxX	Japanese 日本菜	197

Botanic Gardens 植物园

Corner House	✿	XX	Innovative 创新菜	78
Open Farm Community		X	International 国际菜	145

Bras Basah 百胜

Garibaldi		XxX	Italian 意大利菜	92
Gunther's		XxX	French 法国菜	95
Shinji (Beach Road)	✿	XX	Sushi 寿司	162
Yhingthai Palace 銀泰	🍴	XX	Thai 泰国菜	202

Bugis 武吉士

Alaturka	🍴	X	Turkish 土耳其菜	58
Ash & Elm		X	European 欧陆菜	62
Chikuyotei 竹葉亭		XX	Japanese 日本菜	75

Hjh Maimunah (Jalan Pisang) 🌶	😋	Malaysian 马来西亚菜		97
Man Fu Yuan 满福苑	XxX	Cantonese 粤菜		129

Bukit Merah 紅山

Alkaff Mansion	XX	Italian 意大利菜	59
Keng Eng Kee 瓊榮記	😋	Singaporean 新加坡菜	114

Chinatown 牛车水

Ding Dong	X	South East Asian 东南亚菜	82
Luke's (Gemmill Lane)	XX	Steakhouse 扒房	126
Nam Seng Noodles 南生	😋	Noodles 面食	137

City Hall 政府大厦

Aura		XxX	Italian 意大利菜	63
Jaan	✿	XxxX	French contemporary 时尚法国菜	107
Lei Garden 利苑	✿	XxX	Cantonese 粤菜	120
Long Bar Steakhouse		XxX	Steakhouse 扒房	124
Mikuni		XxX	Japanese 日本菜	134
National Kitchen		XX	Singaporean 新加坡菜	139
Odette	✿✿	XxxX	French contemporary 时尚法国菜	143
Raffles Grill		XxxX	French contemporary 时尚法国菜	154
Saha		XX	Indian 印度菜	158
Shahi Maharani		XX	Indian 印度菜	160
Wah Lok 華樂		XX	Cantonese 粤菜	195
Whitegrass		XxX	Australian contemporary 时尚澳洲菜	198

Clarke Quay 克拉码头

FOC		X	Spanish 西班牙菜	89
Song Fa Bak Kut Teh (New Bridge Road) 松發肉骨茶 (新桥路)	😊	😋	Singaporean 新加坡菜	171
The Kitchen at Bacchanalia	✿	X	Innovative 创新菜	184
Tian Tian Fisherman's Pier Seafood 天天渔港		XX	Seafood 海鲜	188

RESTAURANTS BY AREA 餐厅 - 以地区分类

Tunglok Signatures 同樂经典	XX	Chinese 中国菜	193

Dhoby Ghaut 多美歌

Tim Ho Wan (Plaza Singapura) 添好運 (Plaza Singapura)	🍴	Dim Sum 点心	189
Wild Rocket	X	Innovative 创新菜	200

Farrer Park 花拉公园

Char 叉		X	Cantonese 粤菜	73
Putien (Kitchener Road) 莆田（吉真那路）	✿	X	Fujian 福建菜	153

Fort Canning Park 福康宁公园

Lewin Terrace		XX	French Contemporary 时尚法国菜	122
True Blue Cuisine	⊛	X	Peranakan 娘惹菜	192

Geylang 芽笼

Geylang Claypot Rice 芽籠瓦煲飯	🍴 Cantonese 粤菜	93

Joo Chiat 如切

Chilli Padi (Joo Chiat) 辣椒香(如切)		X	Peranakan 娘惹菜	76
Roland 東皇		X	Singaporean 新加坡菜菜	157
328 Katong Laksa (Joo Chiat) 328 加東叻沙 (如切路)	⊛	🍴	Singaporean 新加坡菜菜	187
Zaffron Kitchen (East Coast)	⊛	X	Indian 印度菜	205

Keppel Bay 吉宝湾

Peony Jade (Keppel) 玉河畔 (Keppel)	⊛	XX	Cantonese 粤菜	151

Little India 小印度

Lagnaa	⊛	X	Indian 印度菜	118
Shish Mahal	⊛	X	Indian 印度菜	167

Marina Square 滨海广场

Cherry Garden 樱桃園	XX	Cantonese 粤菜	74
Colony	XXX	International 国际菜	77
Dolce Vita	XX	Italian 意大利菜	83
Labyrinth	XX	Innovative 创新菜	117
Melt Café	XX	International 国际菜	131
Peach Blossoms 鸿桃轩	XX	Cantonese 粤菜	149
Rang Mahal	XXX	Indian 印度菜	155
Shiraishi 白石	XX	Sushi 寿司	165
Summer Pavillion 夏苑	✽ XXX	Cantonese 粤菜	175
Umi + Vino	XX	Seafood 海鲜	194

Newton 纽顿

Buona Terra	XX	Italian 意大利菜	68
Indocafe	XX	Peranakan 娘惹菜	106
Ki-sho 葵匠	X	Japanese 日本菜	115
Li Bai 李白	XXX	Cantonese 粤菜	123
The Song of India	✽ XXX	Indian 印度菜	186

Orchard 乌节

Alma	✽ XX	European contemporary 时尚欧陆菜	60
Basilico	XX	Italian 意大利菜	65
Béni	✽ X	French contemporary 时尚法国菜	66
Crystal Jade Golden Palace 翡翠金閣	✽ XXX	Chinese 中国菜	79
Fat Cow	X	Japanese steakhouse 日式扒房	86
Gordon Grill	XXX	Steakhouse 扒房	94
Hashida	X	Sushi 寿司	96
Hua Ting 華廳	XXX	Cantonese 粤菜	99
Iggy's	XXX	Innovative 创新菜	100
Il Cielo	XX	Italian 意大利菜	101
Imperial Treasure Shanghai Cuisine 御園	XX	Shanghainese 沪菜	103

RESTAURANTS BY AREA 餐厅 - 以地区分类

Imperial Treasure Super Peking Duck (Paragon) 御寶至尊烤鴨店 (百利宮)		XX Cantonese 粤菜	104
Imperial Treasure Teochew Cuisine 御寶閣		XX Teochew 潮州菜	105
Jade Palace 金湖		XX Cantonese 粤菜	109
Jiang-Nan Chun 江南春		XxX Cantonese 粤菜	111
Les Amis	✿✿	XxX French 法国菜	121
Mezza9		XX International 国际菜	133
Min Jiang 岷江川菜馆		XxX Chinese 中国菜	135
Nadaman 灘万日本料理		XX Japanese 日本菜	136
Shang Palace 香宮		XxX Cantonese 粤菜	161
Shinji (Tanglin Road)	✿	XX Sushi 寿司	163
Shisen Hanten 四川飯店	✿✿	XxX Chinese 中国菜	166
Summer Palace 夏宮		XxX Cantonese 粤菜	174
Sushi Ichi 鮨一	✿	X Sushi 寿司	176
Tambuah Mas (Tanglin)		X Indonesian 印尼菜	180
Yan Ting 宴庭		XxX Cantonese 粤菜	201

Outram Park 欧南园

Ka Soh 家嫂	ⓐ	X Singaporean 新加坡菜	113

Raffles Place 莱佛士坊

Forlino		XxX Italian 意大利菜	91
Jade 玉楼		XxxX Chinese 中国菜	108
Palm Beach Seafood 棕榈滩海鲜		XX Seafood 海鲜	148
Saint Pierre		XxX French contemporary 时尚法国菜	159
Shoukouwa 小康和	✿✿	XX Sushi 寿司	168
Straits Chinese		X PERANAKAN 娘惹菜	173
The Clifford Pier		XX Singaporean 新加坡菜	183
The Lighthouse		XX Italian 意大利菜	185
Zafferano		XxX Italian 意大利菜	203

36

River Valley 里峇峇利

Imperial Treasure Cantonese Cuisine (Great World City) 御寶軒(世界城)		XxX Cantonese 粤菜	102
Toritama Shirokane 酉玉白金		X Japanese 日本菜	191

Sentosa 圣淘沙

Feng Shui Inn 风水廷		XxX Cantonese 粤菜	87
Forest 森	❀	XxX Chinese contemporary 时尚中国菜	90
Joël Robuchon	❀❀❀	XxXxX French contemporary 时尚法国菜	112
L'Atelier de Joël Robuchon	❀❀	XX French contemporary 时尚法国菜	119
Ocean		XX American contemporary 时尚美国菜	142
Osia 澳西亚	❀	XX Australian contemporary 时尚澳洲菜	146
Syun 春		XX Japanese contemporary 时尚日本菜	179
Tangerine 天滋林		X Contemporary 时尚菜	181

Tanjong Pagar 丹戎巴葛

André	❀❀	XxX Innovative 创新菜	61
BAM!		X Spanish 西班牙菜	64
Burnt Ends		X BBQ 烧烤	69
Candlenut	❀	X PERANAKAN 娘惹菜	70
Capital 首都		XX Cantonese 粤菜	71
Esquina		X Spanish 西班牙菜	85
Fleur de Sel		XX French 法国菜	88
Kok Sen 国成球记	☻	🍴 Singaporean 新加坡菜	116
Majestic 大華		XX Cantonese 粤菜	127
Meta		X Innovative 创新菜	132
Nicolas		XX French 法国菜	141
Otto		XxX Italian 意大利菜	147
Rhubarb	❀	XxX French 法国菜	156
Sushi Mitsuya		XX Sushi 寿司	177
Terra	❀	XX Italian 意大利菜	182
Tippling Club		XX Innovative 创新菜	190
Whole Earth 環界	☻	X Vegetarian 素菜	199

RESTAURANTS BY AREA 餐厅 - 以地区分类

Tiong Bahru 中峇鲁

| Open Door Policy | X | European contemporary 时尚欧陆菜 | 144 |
| Sin Hoi Sai (Tiong Bahru) 新海山(中巴鲁) | X | Seafood 海鲜 | 169 |

Toa Payoh 大巴窑

| Boon Tong Kee (Balestier Road) 文東記(马里士他路) | X | Singaporean 新加坡菜 | 67 |

RESTAURANTS BY CUISINE TYPE
餐厅 - 以菜式分类

American contemporary 时尚美国菜

Ocean		XX	Sentosa 圣淘沙	142

Australian contemporary 时尚澳洲菜

Osia 澳西亚	✹	XX	Sentosa 圣淘沙	146
Whitegrass		XXX	City Hall 政府大厦	198

BBQ 烧烤

Burnt Ends		X	Tanjong Pagar 丹戎巴葛	69

Cantonese 粤菜

Capital 首都		XX	Tanjong Pagar 丹戎巴葛	71
Char 叉		X	Farrer Park 花拉公园	73
Cherry Garden 樱桃园		XX	Marina Square 滨海广场	74
Feng Shui Inn 风水廷		XXX	Sentosa 圣淘沙	87
Geylang Claypot Rice 芽籠瓦煲飯		🍴	Geylang 芽笼	93
Hua Ting 華廳		XXX	Orchard 乌节	99
Imperial Treasure Cantonese Cuisine (Great World City) 御寶軒(世界城)		XX	River Valley 里峇峇利	102
Imperial Treasure Super Peking Duck (Paragon) 御寶至尊烤鸭店(百利宫)		XX	Orchard 乌节	104
Jade Palace 金湖		XX	Orchard 乌节	109
Jiang-Nan Chun 江南春		XXX	Orchard 乌节	111
Lei Garden 利苑	✹	XXX	City Hall 政府大厦	120
Li Bai 李白		XXX	Newton 纽顿	123
Majestic 大華		XX	Tanjong Pagar 丹戎巴葛	127
Majestic Bay 冠華		XX	Bayfront 海湾舫	128
Man Fu Yuan 满福苑		XXX	Bugis 武吉士	129
Peach Blossoms 鸿桃轩		XX	Marina Square 滨海广场	149
Peony Jade (Keppel) 玉河畔(吉宝)	🚇	XX	Keppel Bay 吉宝湾	151

RESTAURANTS BY CUISINE TYPE 餐厅 - 以菜式分类

Shang Palace 香宫		XxX	Orchard 乌节	161
Summer Palace 夏宫		XxX	Orchard 乌节	174
Summer Pavillion 夏苑	✿	XxX	Marina Square 滨海广场	175
Wah Lok 華樂		XX	City Hall 政府大厦	195
Yan Ting 宴庭		XxX	Orchard 乌节	201

Chinese 中国菜

Crystal Jade Golden Palace 翡翠金閣	✿	XxX	Orchard 乌节	79
Jade 玉楼		XxxX	Raffles Place 莱佛士坊	108
Min Jiang 岷江川菜馆		XxX	Orchard 乌节	135
Shisen Hanten 四川飯店	✿✿	XxX	Orchard 乌节	166
Tunglok Signatures 同樂經典		XX	Clarke Quay 克拉码头	193

Chinese contemporary 时尚中国菜

Forest 森	✿	XxX	Sentosa 圣淘沙	90

Contemporary 时尚菜

Tangerine 天滋林		X	Sentosa 圣淘沙	181

Dim Sum 点心

Tim Ho Wan (Plaza Singapura) 添好運 (Plaza Singapura)		🍽	Dhoby Ghaut 多美歌	189

European 欧陆菜

Ash & Elm		X	Bugis 武吉士	62

European contemporary 时尚欧陆菜

Alma	✿	XX	Orchard 乌节	60
Open Door Policy		X	Tiong Bahru 中峇鲁	144

French 法国菜

Daniel Boulud Bistro & Oyster Bar		XX	Bayfront 海湾舫	81
Fleur de Sel		XX	Tanjong Pagar 丹戎巴葛	88

Gunther's			XxX	Bras Basah 百胜	95
Les Amis		✿✿	XxX	Orchard 乌节	121
Nicolas			XX	Tanjong Pagar 丹戎巴葛	141
Rhubarb		✿	XxX	Tanjong Pagar 丹戎巴葛	156

French contemporary 时尚法国菜

Béni		✿	X	Orchard 乌节	66
Jaan		✿	XxxX	City Hall 政府大厦	107
Joël Robuchon		✿✿✿	XxxxX	Sentosa 圣淘沙	112
L'Atelier de Joël Robuchon		✿✿	XX	Sentosa 圣淘沙	119
Lewin Terrace			XX	Fort Canning Park 福康宁公园	122
Odette		✿✿	XxxX	City Hall 政府大厦	143
Raffles Grill			XxxX	City Hall 政府大厦	154
Saint Pierre			XxX	Raffles Place 莱佛士坊	159

Fujian 福建菜

Putien (Kitchener Road) 莆田 (吉真那路)		✿	X	Farrer Park 花拉公园	153

Indian 印度菜

Lagnaa		ⓐ	X	Little India 小印度	118
Punjab Grill			XxX	Bayfront 海湾舫	152
Rang Mahal			XxX	Marina Square 滨海广场	155
Saha			XX	City Hall 政府大厦	158
Shahi Maharani			XX	City Hall 政府大厦	160
Shish Mahal		ⓐ	X	Little India 小印度	167
The Song of India		✿	XxX	Newton 纽顿	186
Zaffron Kitchen (East Coast)		ⓐ	X	Joo Chiat 如切	205

Indonesian 印尼菜

Tambuah Mas (Tanglin)			X	Orchard 乌节	180

Innovative 创新菜

André		✿✿	XxX	Tanjong Pagar 丹戎巴葛	61

RESTAURANTS BY CUISINE TYPE 餐厅 - 以菜式分类

Corner House	✪	XX	Botanic Gardens 植物园	78
Iggy's		XXX	Orchard 乌节	100
Labyrinth		XX	Marina Square 滨海广场	117
Meta		X	Tanjong Pagar 丹戎巴葛	132
Sky on 57		XXX	Bayfront 海湾舫	170
The Kitchen at Bacchanalia	✪	X	Clarke Quay 克拉码头	184
Tippling Club		XX	Tanjong Pagar 丹戎巴葛	190
Wild Rocket		X	Dhoby Ghaut 多美歌	200

International 国际菜

Colony	XXX	Marina Square 滨海广场	77
Melt Café	XX	Marina Square 滨海广场	131
Mezza9	XX	Orchard 乌节	133
Open Farm Community	X	Botanic Gardens 植物园	145

Italian 意大利菜

Alkaff Mansion		XX	Bukit Merah 红山	59
Aura		XXX	City Hall 政府大厦	63
Basilico		XX	Orchard 乌节	65
Buona Terra		XX	Newton 纽顿	68
Dolce Vita		XX	Marina Square 滨海广场	83
Forlino		XXX	Raffles Place 莱佛士坊	91
Garibaldi		XXX	Bras Basah 百胜	92
Il Cielo		XX	Orchard 乌节	101
Otto		XXX	Tanjong Pagar 丹戎巴葛	147
Terra	✪	XX	Tanjong Pagar 丹戎巴葛	182
The Lighthouse		XX	Raffles Place 莱佛士坊	185
Zafferano		XXX	Raffles Place 莱佛士坊	203

Japanese 日本菜

Chikuyotei 竹葉亭	XX	Bugis 武吉士	75
Ki-sho 葵匠	X	Newton 纽顿	115
Mikuni	XXX	City Hall 政府大厦	134

Nadaman 滩万日本料理		XX	Orchard 乌节	136
Toritama Shirokane 酉玉白金		X	River Valley 里峇峇利	191
Waku Ghin	✿	XxX	Bayfront 海湾舫	197

Japanese contemporary 时尚日本菜

Syun 春	XX	Sentosa 圣淘沙	179

Japanese steakhouse 日式扒房

Fat Cow	X	Orchard 乌节	86

Malaysian 马来西亚菜

Hjh Maimunah (Jalan Pisang)	☺	自	Bugis 武吉士	97

Noodles 面食

Nam Seng Noodles 南生	自	Chinatown 牛车水	137

Pan Fusion 混合菜

Spago	XxX	Bayfront 海湾舫	172

Peranakan 娘惹菜

Candlenut	✿	X	Tanjong Pagar 丹戎巴葛	70
Chilli Padi (Joo Chiat) 辣椒香(如切)		X	Joo Chiat 如切	76
Indocafe		XX	Newton 纽顿	106
Straits Chinese		X	Raffles Place 莱佛士坊	173
True Blue Cuisine	☺	X	Fort Canning Park 福康宁公园	192

Seafood 海鲜

Mellben Seafood (Ang Mo Kio) 龍海鲜螃蟹王(宏茂桥)	X	Ang Mo Kio 宏茂桥	130
Palm Beach Seafood 棕榈滩海鲜	XX	Raffles Place 莱佛士坊	148
Sin Hoi Sai (Tiong Bahru) 新海山(中峇鲁)	X	Tiong Bahru 中峇鲁	169

RESTAURANTS BY CUISINE TYPE 餐厅 - 以菜式分类

Tian Tian Fisherman's Pier Seafood 天天漁港		XX	Clarke Quay 克拉码头	188
Umi + Vino		XX	Marina Square 滨海广场	194

Shanghainese 沪菜

Imperial Treasure Shanghai Cuisine 御園		XX	Orchard 乌节	103

Singaporean 新加坡菜

Boon Tong Kee (Balestier Road) 文東記 (马里士他路)		X	Toa Payoh 大巴窑	67
Ka Soh 家嫂	☺	X	Outram Park 欧南园	113
Keng Eng Kee 瓊榮記		占	Bukit Merah 紅山	114
Kok Sen 国成球记	☺	占	Tanjong Pagar 丹戎巴葛	116
National Kitchen		XX	City Hall 政府大厦	139
New Ubin	☺	占	Ang Mo Kio 宏茂桥	140
Roland 東皇		X	Joo Chiat 如切	157
Song Fa Bak Kut Teh (New Bridge Road) 松發肉骨茶 (新桥路)	☺	占	Clarke Quay 克拉码头	171
The Clifford Pier		XX	Raffles Place 莱佛士坊	183
328 Katong Laksa (Joo Chiat) 328加東叻沙 (如切路)	☺	占	Joo Chiat 如切	187

South East Asian 东南亚菜

Ding Dong		X	Chinatown 牛车水	82

Spanish 西班牙菜

BAM!		X	Tanjong Pagar 丹戎巴葛	64
Esquina		X	Tanjong Pagar 丹戎巴葛	85
FOC		X	Clarke Quay 克拉码头	89

Steakhouse 扒房

Cut	✪	XxxX	Bayfront 海湾舫	80
Gordon Grill		XxX	Orchard 乌节	94
Long Bar Steakhouse		XxX	City Hall 政府大厦	124

Luke's (Gemmill Lane)		XX	Chinatown 牛车水	126

Sushi 寿司

Hashida		X	Orchard 乌节	96
Shinji (Beach Road)	✿	XX	Bras Basah 百胜	162
Shinji (Tanglin Road)	✿	XX	Orchard 乌节	163
Shiraishi 白石		XX	Marina Square 滨海广场	165
Shoukouwa 小康和	✿✿	XX	Raffles Place 莱佛士坊	168
Sushi Ichi 鮨一	✿	X	Orchard 乌节	176
Sushi Mitsuya		XX	Tanjong Pagar 丹戎巴葛	177

Teochew 潮州菜

Imperial Treasure Teochew Cuisine 御寶閣		XX	Orchard 乌节	105

Thai 泰国菜

Long Chim		XX	Bayfront 海湾舫	125
Yhingthai Palace 銀泰	⊛	XX	Bras Basah 百胜	202

Turkish 土耳其菜

Alaturka	⊛	X	Bugis 武吉士	58

Vegetarian 素菜

Whole Earth 環界	⊛	X	Tanjong Pagar 丹戎巴葛	199

HAWKER CENTRES
熟食小販中心

ABC Brickworks Market & Food Centre
ABC红砖巴刹及熟食中心

| Lao Jian Cheng 老堅成 | | Bukit Merah 紅山 | 208 |
| Y. R Ahmad | | Bukit Merah 紅山 | 208 |

Albert Centre 雅柏中心

| Pondok Makan Indonesia | | Bugis 武吉士 | 209 |
| Singapore Famous Rojak 新加坡啰嗻 | | Bugis 武吉士 | 209 |

Alexandra Village Food Centre
亞历山大村美食中心

Claypot Laksa 德普路真善美馳名砂煲叻沙	⊕		Bukit Merah 紅山	210
Leon Kee Claypot Pork Rib Soup 諒記砂鍋當歸肉骨茶			Bukit Merah 紅山	210
Tiong Bahru Lien Fa Shui Jing Pau 中峇鲁联发水晶包			Bukit Merah 紅山	211
Xiang Jiang Soya Sauce Chicken 香江豉油鸡			Bukit Merah 紅山	211

Amoy Street Food Centre 廈门街熟食中心

A Noodle Story 超好面	⊕		Tanjong Pagar 丹戎巴葛	212
Famous Crispy Curry Puff 馳名香脆咖喱卜	⊕		Tanjong Pagar 丹戎巴葛	212
Hong Kee Beef Noodle 桐記牛肉粿條	⊕		Tanjong Pagar 丹戎巴葛	213
Hoo Kee Rice Dumpling 和記肉粽	⊕		Tanjong Pagar 丹戎巴葛	213
Lian He Shao La Fan Mian 聯合燒臘飯•麵			Tanjong Pagar 丹戎巴葛	213
Yuan Chun Famous Lor Mee 源春馳名鹵麵			Tanjong Pagar 丹戎巴葛	213

Ang Mo Kio 724 Food Centre
宏茂桥724座巴刹与熟食中心

Hup Hup Minced Meat Noodle
合合香菇肉脞麵   Ang Mo Kio 宏茂桥   215

Chinatown Complex Market & Food Centre
牛车水

Hong Kong Soy Sauce Chicken Rice & Noodle 香港油鸡饭面	Chinatown 牛车水	216
168 CMY Satay 168春满圆沙爹	Chinatown 牛车水	216
The 50s 五十年代	Chinatown 牛车水	217
Zhong Guo La Mian Xiao Long Bao 中国拉面小笼包	Chinatown 牛车水	217

85 Redhill Food Centre
红山巷第85座巴刹与熟食中心

Lor Duck Rice and Noodle 卤鸭饭面	Bukit Merah 红山	218
Shi Le Yuan 實叻圏	Bukit Merah 红山	218

Empress Market 皇后巴刹与熟食中心

Seng Kee Porridge 成記粥品   Farrer Road 花拉路   219

Golden Mile Food Centre 黄金熟食中心

Chung Cheng 崇正	Lavender 劳明达	220
91 Fried Kway Teow Mee 91翠绿炒粿條麵	Lavender 劳明达	220
The Fishball Story 魚緣	Lavender 劳明达	221
Wedang	Lavender 劳明达	221

Haig Road Market & Food Centre
海格路巴刹与熟食中心

Traditional Haig Road Putu Piring   Tanjong Katong 丹戎加东   223

HAWKWE CENTRES 熟食小贩中心

Hong Lim Market and Food Centre
芳林巴刹与熟食中心

Ah Heng Curry Chicken Bee Hoon Mee 亚王咖喱鸡米粉面		Chinatown 牛车水	224
Famous Sungei Road Trishaw Laksa 驰名结霜橋三輪車叻沙		Chinatown 牛车水	224
Hokkien Street Bak Kut Teh 福建街肉骨茶		Chinatown 牛车水	225
Ji Ji Wonton Noodle 基記麵家		Chinatown 牛车水	225
Outram Park Fried Kway Teow 歐南園炒粿條麵		Chinatown 牛车水	225
Tai Wah Pork Noodle 大華肉脞麵		Chinatown 牛车水	225

Maxwell Food Centre 麦士威熟食中心

Lim Kee (Orchard) Banana Fritters 林記油炸芎蕉		Tanjong Pagar 丹戎巴葛	226
Rojak•Popian & Cockle 囉嚦•薄餅•鮮蛤		Tanjong Pagar 丹戎巴葛	226
Tian Tian Hainanese Chicken Rice 天天海南雞飯		Tanjong Pagar 丹戎巴葛	227

Mei Ling Market & Food Centre
美玲巴刹与熟食中心

Lao Jie Fang 老街坊		Queenstown 女皇镇	228
Shi Hui Yuan 實惠園		Queenstown 女皇镇	228

Newton Food Centre 纽顿熟食中心

Alliance Seafood 聯合海鮮燒烤		Newton 纽顿	229

115 Bukit Merah View Market & Hawker Centre
红山景大牌115

Na Na Curry 南南咖喱		Bukit Merah 紅山	230

127 Toa Payoh West Market & Food Centre
大巴窑大牌127

| Chey Sua Carrot Cake 青山菜頭粿 | Toa Payoh 大巴窑 | 231 |
| Teochew Handmade Pau 潮洲自制飽點 | Toa Payoh 大巴窑 | 231 |

People's Park Complex Food Centre 珍珠坊

| Hong Peng La Mian Xiao Long Bao 洪鵬拉面小籠包 | Chinatown 牛车水 | 232 |
| People's Park Hainanese Chicken Rice 珍珠坊海南鸡饭 | Chinatown 牛车水 | 232 |

Tekka Centre 竹脚中心

| Allauddin's Briyani | Little India 小印度 | 233 |
| Heng Gi Goose and Duck Rice 興記鵝·鴨飯 | Little India 小印度 | 233 |

Tiong Bahru Market 中峇鲁市场

Hong Heng Fried Sotong Prawn Mee 鴻興炒蘇東蝦麵	Tiong Bahru 中峇鲁	234
Jian Bo Shui Kueh 楗柏水粿	Tiong Bahru 中峇鲁	234
Lor Mee 178 鹵麵178	Tiong Bahru 中峇鲁	235
Teochew Fish Porridge 潮洲魚粥	Tiong Bahru 中峇鲁	235
Tiong Bahru Hainanese boneless Chicken Rice 中峇鲁海南起骨雞飯	Tiong Bahru 中峇鲁	235

Whampoa Makan Place 黄埔熟食中心

Balestier Road Hoover Rojak 豪華羅雜	Balestier 马里士他	236
China Whampoa Home Made Noodle 中國黃埔麵粉粿	Balestier 马里士他	236
Huat Heng Fried Oyster 發興炒蚝煎	Balestier 马里士他	237
Liang Zhao Ji 梁照記	Balestier 马里士他	237

The best way to immerse yourself in local life is by trying street food 🚋. To find great food and local specialities, check out our selection of hawker centres and street food vendors.

认识一个地方和体验当地文化的最佳渠道是品尝道地的街头小吃，跟着我们的熟食小贩中心及街头小吃推介 🚋 去寻找最经典、最受欢迎的美点吧！

The symbol 🍇 denotes a particularly interesting wine list.

🍇 这个图标表示该餐厅提供一系列优质餐酒。

STREET FOOD
街头小吃

Bismillah Biryani	Little India 小印度	238
Hill Street Tai Hwa Pork Noodle 大華豬肉粿條麵	Lavender 劳明达	238
Jalan Sultan Prawn Mee 惹蘭蘇丹蝦麵	Geylang 芽笼	238
JB Ah Meng 新山亞明	Geylang 芽笼	239
Lor 9 Beef Kway Teow 九巷牛河	Geylang 芽笼	239
Nasi Lemak Kukus	Little India 小印度	239
Sin Huat Eating House 新發	Geylang 芽笼	239

RESTAURANTS WITH INTERESTING WINE LISTS
供应优质酒品的餐厅

Alma	✤	XX	European contemporary 时尚欧陆菜	60
André	✤✤	XxX	Innovative 创新菜	61
Aura		XxX	Italian 意大利菜	63
Béni	✤	X	French contemporary 时尚法国菜	66
Buona Terra		XX	Italian 意大利菜	68
Cherry Garden 樱桃園		XxX	Cantonese 粤菜	74
Colony		XxX	International 国际菜	77
Corner House	✤	XX	Innovative 创新菜	78
Cut	✤	XxxX	Steakhouse 扒房	80
Daniel Boulud Bistro & Oyster Bar		XX	French 法国菜	81
Fleur de Sel		XX	French 法国菜	88
Forlino		XxX	Italian 意大利菜	91
Garibaldi		XxX	Italian 意大利菜	92
Gunther's		XxX	French 法国菜	95
Iggy's		XxX	Innovative 创新菜	100
Jaan	✤	XxxX	French contemporary 时尚法国菜	107
Joël Robuchon	✤✤✤	XxXxX	French contemporary 时尚法国菜	112
Ki-sho 葵匠		X	Japanese 日本菜	115
L'Atelier de Joël Robuchon	✤✤	XX	French contemporary 时尚法国菜	119
Les Amis	✤✤	XxX	French 法国菜	121
Odette	✤✤	XxxX	French contemporary 时尚法国菜	143
Osia 澳西亚	✤	XX	Australian contemporary 时尚澳洲菜	146
Otto		XxX	Italian 意大利菜	147

Shang Palace 香宫		XxX	Cantonese 粤菜	161
Spago		XxX	Pan Fusion 混合菜	172
Summer Pavillion 夏苑	❀	XxX	Cantonese 粤菜	175
Umi + Vino		XX	Seafood 海鲜	194
Waku Ghin	❀	XxX	Japanese 日本菜	197
Zafferano		XX	Italian 意大利菜	203

An important business lunch? The symbol ✥ indicates restaurants with private rooms.

需要一个合适的地点享用商务午餐？可从注有这个 ✥ 图标的餐厅中选一家有私人厢房且合你心意的餐馆。

Read 'How to use this guide' for an explanation of our symbols, classifications and abbreviations.

请仔细阅读"如何使用餐厅/酒店指南",当中的图标、分类等简介助你掌握使用本指南的诀窍,作出智慧的选择。

RESTAURANTS WITH VIEWS
有景观的餐厅

Dolce Vita	XX	Italian 意大利菜	83
Forlino	XxX	Italian 意大利菜	91
Majestic Bay 冠華	XX	Cantonese 粤菜	128
Ocean	XX	American contemporary 时尚美国菜	142
Palm Beach Seafood 棕榈滩海鲜	XX	Seafood 海鲜	148
Saint Pierre	XxX	French contemporary 时尚法国菜	159
Shisen Hanten 四川飯店 ❀❀	XxX	Chinese 中国菜	166
Sky on 57	XxX	Innovative 创新菜	170
Spago	XxX	Pan Fusion 混合菜	172
Tangerine 天滋林	X	Contemporary 时尚菜	181
The Clifford Pier	XX	Singaporean 新加坡菜	183
The Lighthouse	XX	Italian 意大利菜	185
Tian Tian Fisherman's Pier Seafood 天天渔港	XX	Seafood 海鲜	188
Tunglok Signatures 同樂经典	XX	Chinese 中国菜	193
Zafferano	XxX	Italian 意大利菜	203

RESTAURANT
餐厅

In alphabetical order —————— 58
以英文字母顺序排列

TURKISH 土耳其菜　　　　　　　　　　　　　　MAP 地图　8/D-3

Alaturka

There's always something appealing about finding a good little restaurant tucked away in an area more usually associated with the notion of tourist traps. The Turkish atmosphere here is helped along by the carpets hanging on the walls and all the colourful lamps. Start by sharing some meze – you'll find the hummus and baba ganoush particularly good. Vegetarians will find much to savour, while carnivores can plump for the delicious grilled kebabs.

邻近苏丹回教堂和亚拉街，老旧的小屋中，是这家土国乡土气息浓郁的餐馆。小小的店子只能容纳约二十人。墙上的吉卜赛地毯、天花上深棕色的木横梁，感觉一如店内的菜式般质朴。豆泥(hummus)、烤优格乳蒜泥茄子(babakunus)及旋转烤肉(kebabs)是土国传统菜式，值得一试。店内还供应素菜菜式。

TEL. 6294 0304
16 Bussorah Street
巴梭拉街 16 号
www.alaturka.com.sg

■ PRICE 价钱
Lunch 午膳
à la carte 点菜 $ 36-53
Dinner 晚膳
à la carte 点菜 $ 36-53

■ OPENING HOURS 营业时间
12:00-22:15 (L.O.)
Friday and Saturday 周五及周六
12:00-22:45 (L.O.)

58

ITALIAN 意大利菜

MAP 地图 14/D-3

Alkaff Mansion

120

Built in 1918 by a family of Yemeni traders, this mansion in the Telok Blangah Hill Park lay derelict for some years before being restored to the charming, romantic spot it is today. Its current owner hired an Italian chef whose cooking is largely classical but with his own added little twists. He imports much of the produce directly from Italy and pays special attention to the homemade pasta; other standouts include Sardinian-style suckling pig.

来自撒丁岛的意大利厨师烹调的传统意大利菜，带有个人风格，意大利进口的材料令菜式味道更正宗，然而，自制意大利面才是厨师最得意作品。Cartoccio 风格墨鱼汁海鲜意大利面、火焰盐粒烤鲈鱼是其拿手菜。在满眼翠绿园景的平台进餐，气氛浪漫。宽广的私人厢房和活动室，可用作举办商务或私人派对。

TEL. 6510 3068
10 Telok Blangah Green
布兰雅绿道 10号
www.alkaff.com.sg

■ PRICE 价钱
Lunch 午膳
set 套餐 $ 36-98
à la carte 点菜 $ 62-130
Dinner 晚膳
set 套餐 $ 98
à la carte 点菜 $ 62-130

■ OPENING HOURS 营业时间
Lunch 午膳 11:30-14:15 (L.O.)
Dinner 晚膳 18:00-22:30 (L.O.)

59

EUROPEAN CONTEMPORARY 时尚欧陆菜

MAP 地图　6/B-2

Alma

　　　　　　　　　10

In 2015 the internationally acclaimed eponymous chef took over the space at the Goodwood Park hotel previously occupied by Gaia. While the soul of the restaurant may be Spanish, his kitchen focuses on contemporary European cuisine with plenty of Asian influences – ingredients are carefully selected and preparations are sophisticated and well thought-through. The atmosphere is nicely relaxed and helped along by the good-natured service.

这里划分为几部分：主要用餐区以深色木家具配以橙黑色餐椅，柔和舒适；酒窖后为私人厢房；另设户外用餐区，可以边喝酒边享用Tapas。主餐牌供应时尚欧陆菜，法国主厨曾于法国的星级食店服务，食材都经精挑细选，加上巧妙的配搭和精心处理，令人回味无穷。酒单选择丰富，包罗了超过四百个品牌。

TEL. 6735 9937
Goodwood Park Hotel, 22 Scotts Road
史各士路22号良木园酒店
www.alma.sg

■ PRICE 价钱
Lunch 午膳
set 套餐 ＄48-108
Dinner 晚膳
set 套餐 ＄68-148

■ OPENING HOURS 营业时间
Lunch 午膳　12:00-14:30 (L.O.)
Dinner 晚膳　18:30-22:30 (L.O.)

■ ANNUAL AND WEEKLY CLOSING 休息日期
Closed Monday lunch, Tuesday lunch, Saturday lunch and Sunday
周一、周二、周六午膳及周日休息

INNOVATIVE 创新菜   MAP 地图 17/A-3

André

On three floors of a discreet 1922 townhouse is a restaurant that has been meticulously designed down to the very last detail by its passionate owner. His cuisine is founded on 8 philosophies (texture, terroir etc) that form the basis of a set menu. It's French in essence, but is also creative and sophisticated although not without some playful elements. The stylish space is complemented by excellent service which is occasionally led by his wife.

富经验的店主兼厨师，不光对于烹调食物严仅细致，连餐馆的室内布置也一丝不苟，一砖一瓦均由他悉心设计与布置，三层高的屋子空间虽不算宽敞，环境却甚是舒适。八个套餐分别由八个特色主题组成，供应的全是创意与传统精髓并重、不落俗套且卖相精致的法国美食。服务团队的优秀服务更是锦上添花。

TEL. 6534 8880
41 Bukit Pasoh Road
武吉巴梳路 41号
www.restaurantandre.com

■ PRICE 价钱
Lunch 午膳
set 套餐 $ 128
Dinner 晚膳
set 套餐 $ 298

■ OPENING HOURS 营业时间
Lunch 午膳 12:00-14:30 (L.O.)
Dinner 晚膳 19:00-21:30 (L.O.)

■ ANNUAL AND WEEKLY CLOSING 休息日期
Closed Tuesday, Thursday and Weekend lunch; Monday and Public Holidays 周二、周四及周末午膳，周一及公众假期休息

EUROPEAN 欧陆菜

MAP 地图 8/C-3

Ash & Elm

There aren't many restaurants that are as good at hosting business lunches as they are for entertaining large family tables, but then this restaurant, within the InterContinental hotel, is unlike most. It serves a mix of dishes from across Europe, from three kitchens: one for cheese and charcuterie, one for wood-fired dishes and one for charcoal-grilled meats. The high ceiling adds grandeur to the large, contemporary and thoughtfully-lit room.

高高的天花、时尚舒适的布置、柔和温暖的灯光和开放式厨房，筑构出温馨写意的空间。餐馆供应混合了法国、意大利、西班牙等欧洲各地风味和扒房概念的菜式。在这儿，你可以品尝到来自欧洲各国的冻肉、法式蛋黄酱拌蟹饼、凯撒沙拉、碳火烤肉、精选乳酪等等。

TEL. 6825 1008
Intercontinental Hotel, Level 1,
80 Middle Road
密驼路 80号洲际酒店地面层
www.intercontinental.com/singapore

■ PRICE 价钱
Lunch 午膳
set 套餐 $ 38- 58
à la carte 点菜 $ 60-120
Dinner 晚膳
à la carte 点菜 $ 60-120

■ OPENING HOURS 营业时间
Lunch 午膳　12:00-14:30 (L.O.)
Dinner 晚膳　18:00-22:30 (L.O.)

ITALIAN 意大利菜

MAP 地图 17/B-1

Aura

If nourishment is needed after a contemplative tour of the National Gallery, then Aura and its breezy Sky Lounge sister are right on hand. Beppe de Vito and co have gathered together a seasoned team who understand the concept of hospitality and who deliver eminently satisfying Italian dishes like trofie with crab and porcini, scallops crudo with avocado and truffles, and grilled sea bream with pistachio salsa.

亲切专业的服务。装潢时尚高雅,长长的巨幅落地琉璃窗,街上景色尽收眼帘。餐馆新开业不久,烹饪团队由数位意大利厨师组成,为食客烹调美味的意大利菜。香菌蟹肉trofie、松露牛油果带子(scallop crudo) ,光想想便已让人食指大动。精心挑选的红酒单带给你意外惊喜。

TEL. 6866 1977
National Gallery Singapore, #05-03,
1 St. Andrews Road
圣安德烈路1号国家美术馆 #05-03
www.aura.sg

■ PRICE 价钱
Lunch 午膳
à la carte 点菜 $ 88-188
Dinner 晚膳
set 套餐 $ 88
à la carte 点菜 $ 88-188

■ OPENING HOURS 营业时间
Lunch 午膳 12:00-14:30 (L.O.)
Dinner 晚膳 18:30-22:30 (L.O.)

SPANISH 西班牙菜 MAP 地图 17/A-3

BAM!

There is no shortage of fashionable eateries with counter seating in Singapore so the challenge is how to stand out from the crowd. The USP here is the pairing of tapas with sake. The have over 80 different types, with a team trained to recommend the perfect one. When it comes to the tapas, the Spanish ingredients are prepared with modern techniques to deliver dishes with a degree of originality, and that includes some Japanese influences too.

装潢简约西化，配以开放式小厨房，令人感到轻松自在。然而，此店独特之处是以日本清酒搭配西班牙美食。这里供应逾八十款清酒，经训练的团队会为食客搭配最完美的清酒美食。厨师以现代烹调手法处理食材，不难发现一些自创菜式中带有日本风味，颇为特别。欲将挑选菜式的大权交予厨师可试试Omakase餐单。

TEL. 6226 0500
38 Tras Street
道拉实街38号
www.bamtapassake.com

■ PRICE 价钱
Lunch 午膳
set 套餐 $ 120-180
à la carte 点菜 $ 35-80

Dinner 晚膳
set 套餐 $ 120-180
à la carte 点菜 $ 35-80

■ OPENING HOURS 营业时间
Lunch 午膳 12:00-14:00 (L.O.)
Dinner 晚膳 18:00-22:30 (L.O.)

■ ANNUAL AND WEEKLY CLOSING 休息日期
Closed Monday and Saturday lunch; and Sunday 周一及周六午膳，周日休息

ITALIAN 意大利菜 MAP 地图 6/A-3

Basilico

By concentrating on quality not quantity, Basilico proves that buffets and good food are not mutually exclusive. The main course at dinner is served at the table but everything else is from the various stations – all regions of Italy are covered and the dessert counter is especially good. The handsome room, on the 2nd floor of the luxurious Regent hotel, comes with an impressive walk-in wine cellar, an open kitchen and an outdoor terrace.

简约的设计，巨幅的落地琉璃窗引领你去到连着泳池旁的露台，气氛柔和舒适。餐馆中央的偌大自助餐柜台上放着的冻肉、乳酪、前菜等琳琅满目，令垂涎禁不住淌下。来自意大利北部的厨师烹调的前菜、意大利面及炖饭和甜品等，全是正宗意国菜，品味皆优。店内供应的意大利佳酿用作佐餐适合不过。

TEL. 6725 3232
Regent-Four Seasons Hotel, Level 2,
1 Cuscaden Road
卡斯加登路1号丽晶酒店 Level 2
www.regenthotels.com

■ PRICE 价钱
Lunch 午膳
set 套餐 $55
à la carte 点菜 $60-100
Dinner 晚膳
set 套餐 $88
à la carte 点菜 $60-100

■ OPENING HOURS 营业时间
Lunch 午膳 12:00-14:30 (L.O.)
Dinner 晚膳 18:30-22:00 (L.O.)

FRENCH CONTEMPORARY 时尚法国菜

MAP 地图　6/B-3

Béni

Under the same ownership as Hashida a couple of floors below, this small, elegant restaurant offers contemporary French cuisine. The minimalist décor is designed so as not to detract from the food and the counter allows guests to watch the chefs go about their work. The top quality seasonal ingredients come largely from France and Japan and the two set menus change on a weekly basis. The wine list is well chosen, as are the wine pairings.

在柔弱的灯光下，十四个座位围绕着中空的黑色花岗岩柜台整齐排列，身处中央的厨师就在食客面前即席烹调。这儿不设点菜，只提供两款餐牌，日籍主厨会每周更新其中一款菜式，多选用时令高级食材，有来自日本海的鱼获、意大利的松露、宫崎县的和牛等。酒单丰富多样，更提供Royal Blue Tea。

TEL. 6235 2285
Mandarin Gallery, #02-37,
333A Orchard Road
乌节路333A号文华购物廊#02-37
www.beni-sg.com

■ PRICE 价钱
Lunch 午膳
set 套餐 $ 128-228
Dinner 晚膳
set 套餐 $ 238-358

■ OPENING HOURS 营业时间
Lunch 午膳　12:00-15:00 L.O. 14:00
Dinner 晚膳　19:00-23:00 L.O. 21:00

■ ANNUAL AND WEEKLY CLOSING 休息日期
Closed Sunday 周日休息

SINGAPOREAN 新加坡菜

MAP 地图 4/B-1

Boon Tong Kee (Balestier Road)
文東記 (马里士他路)

What started with a small stall is now a group of eight restaurants – this two-storey operation with a large kitchen was the first branch to open and has been going for nearly 40 years. At the beginning it just offered chicken rice, fish head and deep-fried tofu but now it provides a variety of cze char dishes. Singaporeans know their chicken and they know that this is the place to come for it.

文東記的鸡饭在本地久负盛名，由最初的小摊档发展到现在共有八间店子，这家位于马里士他路的是首家店铺、在三十八年前开业，起初店面面积和厨房都很细小，只供应鸡饭、鱼头和炸豆腐，慢慢发展成为现在拥有两层楼层的餐馆并设有大型厨房，为食客提供更多煮炒菜式。风味道地的海南鸡值得一试。

TEL. 6254 3937
399, 401 & 403 Balestier Road
马里士他路 399, 401 & 403 号

■ PRICE 价钱
Lunch 午膳
à la carte 点菜 $ 10-20
Dinner 晚膳
à la carte 点菜 $ 10-20

■ OPENING HOURS 营业时间
11:00-03:45 (L.O.)

ITALIAN 意大利菜

Buona Terra

MAP 地图 6/B-2

The entrance to this sophisticated and intimate Italian restaurant, housed within a refurbished colonial house, is flanked by an imposing glass display of bottles from its impressive wine collection. Lunch sees a good value set menu while at dinner the flexible menu allows for any combination of appetiser, pasta or main course. Signature dishes include scallop tartare, squid ink tonnarelli, lamb loin with pistachio crust, and nougat parfait.

这意大利餐厅置身于殖民地建筑的一隅，穿过放满餐酒的走廊，先映入眼廉的是缤纷雅致的画作，二十四个座位分成两行分布在内，予人舒适之感。午膳可点选套餐；晚间可从餐单选取三至五道菜，自由组合头盘、意大利面、主菜及甜点。酒单中能找到不少罕见的限量或年份佳酿，嗜杯中物者绝不能错过。

TEL. 6733 0209
29 Scotts Road
史各士路 29 号
www.scotts29.com

■ PRICE 价钱
Lunch 午膳
set 套餐 $ 38
Dinner 晚膳
set 套餐 $ 88-128

■ OPENING HOURS 营业时间
Lunch 午膳 12:00-14:30 (L.O.)
Dinner 晚膳 18:30-22:30 L.O. 22:15

■ ANNUAL AND WEEKLY CLOSING 休息日期
Closed Saturday and Public Holiday lunch; Sunday 周六及公众假期午膳及周日休息

BBQ 烧烤　　　　　　　　　　　　　　　MAP 地图　17/A-3

Burnt Ends

It's all about the grill and the wood-fired oven here – as well as keeping flavours true and unadulterated. The wonderful sourdough sets the tone, as do simple but highly effective dishes like garlic shoots with gremolata; their own smoked quail eggs with caviar are renowned and the sweet beef marmalade with pickles is particularly delicious. Chunks of meat and whole roast fish are what they do best – so don't bother saving room for dessert.

以600度高温的碳炉及木碳烧烤食物是这儿的特点。看似简单的菜式，透过食材的选配和一丝不苟的烹调显出心思与技巧。鱼子酱烟熏鹌鹑蛋是此店名菜；橘子酱烟熏甜牛肉令你没齿难忘，原条烤鱼和烤肉块更是不能错过。狭长的餐室只以木制餐柜台将客人和厨师分隔开，食客能边享用美食边观赏厨师工作时的风采。

TEL. 6224 3933
20 Teck Lim Road
德霖路 20号
www.burntends.com.sg

■ PRICE 价钱
Lunch 午膳
à la carte 点菜 $ 42-74
Dinner 晚膳
à la carte 点菜 $ 42-84

■ OPENING HOURS 营业时间
Lunch 午膳　11:45-14:00 (L.O.)
Dinner 晚膳　18:00-00:00 (L.O.)

■ ANNUAL AND WEEKLY CLOSING 休息日期
Closed Tuesday lunch, Sunday and Monday
周二午膳、周日及周一休息

PERANAKAN 娘惹菜　　　　　　　　　　MAP 地图　17/A-3

Candlenut

The Singaporean chef here started young, learning from his mother and grandmother. Since then he's widened his skills and broadened his experience, resulting in a repertoire which is modern and interesting yet respectful of tradition. Lunch is à la carte, while dinner offers a set menu of little dishes and is a great way of experiencing the various tastes and textures of this skilfully prepared cuisine. Service is sweet and eager to please.

年轻的新加坡籍主厨自小受到母亲和祖母熏陶，烹调风格带着印尼特色，主理的是既有新意亦不失传统风味的娘惹菜。晚餐只供应由三道小菜组成的套餐，小菜份量不多却胜在能尝试不同味道和质感的娘惹菜式。位于酒店内的餐馆没有华丽的装潢，但服务团队待客的热诚还是会令你对她好感加倍。

TEL. 8121 4107
Dorsett Residences, #01-03,
331 New Bridge Road
新桥路 331号 Dorsett Residences #01-03
www.candlenut.com.sg

■ PRICE 价钱
Lunch 午膳
à la carte 点菜 $ 20-60
Dinner 晚膳
set 套餐 $ 50

■ OPENING HOURS 营业时间
Lunch 午膳　12:00-14:30 (L.O.)
Dinner 晚膳　18:00-21:15 (L.O.)

■ ANNUAL AND WEEKLY CLOSING 休息日期
Closed Saturday lunch and Sunday
周六午膳及周日休息

CANTONESE 粤菜　　　　　　　　　　　　　　　　MAP 地图　17/A-3

Capital
首都

When you can claim to have been the first restaurant in Singapore to have served hairy crabs then it's little wonder you have plenty of customers and lots of regulars. The third generation of the Cheong family run the show these days, with Dad cooking, Mum serving and assorted relatives assisting. Classic Cantonese cooking is what they offer, but if it's the season go for the great value hairy crab menu – or just pop in and grab some to take home.

这家历史悠久的粤菜酒家，主要供应经典粤菜及烧味如香脆如烧鹅的烧鸭，已传至第三代。掌厨的是东主的父亲，其母则带领一众亲戚在店面服务客人。每到大闸蟹季节，这家号称本地首家供应大闸蟹的酒家，都会食客不绝，为的是享用大闸蟹套餐。食客亦可将蟹买回家按自己喜欢的方式烹调。

TEL. 6222 3938
323 New Bridge Road
新桥路 323号

■ **PRICE** 价钱
Lunch 午膳
à la carte 点菜 $ 30-70
Dinner 晚膳
à la carte 点菜 $ 30-70

■ OPENING HOURS 营业时间
Lunch 午膳　11:30-14:00 (L.O.)
Dinner 晚膳　17:30-22:00 (L.O.)

■ ANNUAL AND WEEKLY CLOSING 休息日期
Closed Lunar New Year 农历新年休息

71

Don't confuse the rating ✖ with the Stars ✿! The first defines comfort and service, while Stars are awarded for the best cuisine.

千万别混淆了餐具 ✖ 和星星 ✿ 图标！餐具图标表示该餐厅的舒适程度和服务素质，而星星图标代表的是食物素质和味道非常出色而获授予米其林星级的餐馆。

Enjoy good food without spending a fortune! Look out for the Bib Gourmand symbol 🙂 to find restaurants offering good food at great prices!

要省钱又想品尝美食，便要留心注有 🙂 必比登图标的食店，此类店子提供的是价钱实惠且素质高的美食。

CANTONESE 粤菜　　　　　　　　　　　MAP 地图　8/D-1

Char
叉

Cantonese roast meats prepared in a traditional way (with just a hint of Western style) lure plenty of customers to this relaxed and friendly restaurant. There's roast duck and crispy pork belly but it's the meltingly tender BBQ pork that really stands out; other Cantonese dishes on offer include seafood and stir-fried noodles. It occupies two floors – the ground floor's large round tables make it better suited to family gatherings.

设计简约随意并富现代感，地面层设有大圆桌适合家庭用餐，楼上一层有小酒吧和方桌，适合年轻人聚会。主打广式烧味，传统做法混合西式烹调法或调味料。一定要试叉烧，外观和味道都有浓浓的怀旧气息，色深带多肥脂，入口即溶却不油腻。餐厅还供应广式小菜、海鲜和粉面。午市套餐精简而价钱合理。

TEL. 9661 3578
363 Jalan Besar
惹兰勿刹 363号

■ PRICE 价钱
Lunch 午膳
set 套餐 $ 12
à la carte 点菜 $ 20-25
Dinner 晚膳
à la carte 点菜 $ 20-25

■ OPENING HOURS 营业时间
Lunch 午膳　11:30-14:00 (L.O.)
Dinner 晚膳　18:00-21:30 (L.O.)

■ ANNUAL AND WEEKLY CLOSING 休息日期
Closed Monday 周一休息

CANTONESE 粤菜　　　　　　　　　　　　　　MAP 地图　18/C-1

Cherry Garden
樱桃园

Grace, style and opulence are the hallmarks of this revered Cantonese restaurant within the Mandarin Oriental. A wall of windows lets natural light flood the room at lunch, while at night the well-spaced tables ensure plenty of privacy for intimate dinners. The dishes, from velvety congee to delicious dumplings, are prepared with considerable care. A well-priced weekend dim sum menu offers a great way of experiencing the kitchen's ability.

粗糙的石砖墙、高悬着的红灯笼，中式古典木门后，是布置富丽堂皇、古意盎然的中菜馆。一道通往花园的琉璃门、一列列偌大的琉璃窗，直接透射进内的自然光令房间生气盎盎。皮薄如透明、内馅汁丰味浓的意式西葫芦水晶饺滋味无穷，黑椒鳕鱼金网卷令人回味。周末和公众假期设有两组点心早午餐时段。

TEL. 6338 0066
Mandarin Oriental Hotel, Level 5,
5 Raffles Avenue, Marina Square
莱佛士道 5号文华东方酒店 Level 5

■ PRICE 价钱
Lunch 午膳
set 套餐 $ 68-78
à la carte 点菜 $ 80-100
Dinner 晚膳
à la carte 点菜 $ 80-170

■ OPENING HOURS 营业时间
Lunch 午膳　12:00-14:30 (L.O.)
Dinner 晚膳　18:30-22:30 (L.O.)

JAPANESE 日本菜   MAP 地图 8/C-3

Chikuyotei
竹葉亭

The InterContinental hotel's Japanese restaurant is geared unapologetically to the fiscally unencumbered and offers a comprehensive selection of various cuisine styles, from soba and sushi to tempura and sukiyaki. However, it is the delicious unagi (eel) that really stands out. The delightful serving team, wearing traditional kimono, provide charming and helpful service and there's a good selection of sake on offer too.

花岗岩石特色墙、木板屏风、红木地板，感觉非常朴实。穿着传统和服的女服务生，会否令你有置身日本的感觉？鳗鱼是此餐馆最有人气的食品。当然，寿司、天妇罗、乔麦面、和牛等是一家日本餐馆不能或缺的食物。经过悉心挑选的清酒单非常吸引。

TEL. 9725 5311
Intercontinental Hotel, Level 1,
80 Middle Road
密驼路 80号洲际酒店地面楼层
www.facebook.com/Chikuyotei-
Singapore-1474220579468830

■ **PRICE** 价钱
Lunch 午膳
set 套餐 $ 38-148
à la carte 点菜 $ 60-200
Dinner 晚膳
set 套餐 $ 118-178
à la carte 点菜 $ 60-200

■ **OPENING HOURS** 营业时间
Lunch 午膳 12:00-14:30 (L.O.)
Dinner 晚膳 18:30-22:30 (L.O.)

PERANAKAN 娘惹菜　　　　　　　　　　　　　　　　MAP 地图　12/C-1

Chilli Padi (Joo Chiat)
辣椒香(如切)

For anyone wishing to explore the Peranakan culture, coming to Joo Chiat is a must – while you're there, you'll find this restaurant is the ideal place in which to taste authentic Peranakan dishes. The friendly staff are on hand to offer helpful advice, with the standout dishes being kueh pai ti, ikan assam and ayam rendang. The red-hued walls, Chinese furnishings and ceiling fans add to the atmosphere.

如切区是探索娘惹文化的必到之地，而位于区内的这家店子便是品尝娘惹菜的理想地。红墙壁与大红印花桌布、中式摆设和木吊扇，充满浓浓的南洋气息。图文并茂的餐单，方便食客点选菜式，友善的店员也乐于为食客效劳。惹味开胃的娘惹花篮饼、酸辣阿参鱼和香浓的鸡仁当均是不能错过的经典菜肴。

TEL. 6275 1002
11 Joo Chiat Place, Joo Chiat
如切坊 11號

■ PRICE 价钱
Lunch 午膳
à la carte 点菜 $ 15-30
Dinner 晚膳
à la carte 点菜 $ 15-30

■ OPENING HOURS 营业时间
Lunch 午膳　11:00-14:30 (L.O.)
Dinner 晚膳　18:30-21:30 (L.O.)

INTERNATIONAL 国际菜

MAP 地图 18/D-1

Colony

What sets this buffet apart from the plethora scattered around the city is that items can be prepared 'à la minute' and even customised to individual's preferences. There are seven stations catering for all tastes, from fresh oysters and roast meats to myriad cheeses and cured meats – the selection of patisserie is especially impressive. The smart room comes with a certain poise and is refreshingly free of pretension.

精致的美食源源不绝出场，七大开放式厨房应有尽有，从供应生蚝的ice bar、传来阵阵肉香的烧烤区、以至供应印度菜式的印度厨房，厨师即场展示技艺，并可按食客要求烹煮，这也是其优胜之处。乳酪多达三十多种；甜品区令人眼花撩乱，在这装潢典雅而满是诱惑的餐厅，你会感到选择是如此困难。

TEL. 6434 5288
The Ritz-Carlton, Millenia, Level 3,
7 Raffles Avenue
莱佛士道 7 号丽思卡尔顿美年酒店 Level 3

■ PRICE 价钱
Lunch 午膳
set 套餐 $58
Sunday brunch 周日早午餐 $188
Dinner 晚膳
 set 套餐 $78

■ OPENING HOURS 营业时间
Lunch 午膳　12:00-14:30 (L.O.)
Sunday brunch 周日早午餐　12:00-15:30 (L.O.) Dinner 晚膳　18:30-22:30 (L.O.)

INNOVATIVE 创新菜　　　　　　　　　　　　MAP 地图　5/B-2

Corner House

When your restaurant occupies a colonial house, dating from 1910, within the Botanic Gardens, it stands to reason the kitchen will have an in-depth understanding of how best to use herbs and plants in the cooking process – indeed, the chef himself describes his contemporary cuisine as 'gastro-botanica'. There's a choice of three rooms: Claret Corner, The Verandah or Whispering Corner which overlooks the patio and is ideal for a romantic dinner.

餐厅位于新加坡植物园、一幢两层高的黑白色殖民地平房内，窗外一片绿油油，餐碟亦仿如一盘盛放的鲜花，因为年轻的主厨喜以香草和食用花卉入馔。不设点菜，套餐均采用来自法国和日本的顶级时令食材，定时更换菜式，例如珍珠洋葱 (Oignon doux des Cévennes) 会制成烤松露洋葱杯、洋葱茶等。酒单令人目不暇给。

TEL. 6469 1000
1 Cluny Road,
Singapore Botanic Gardens
(Nassim Gate entrance)
克伦尼路 1号新加坡植物园（那森路入口）
www.cornerhouse.com.sg

■ PRICE 价钱
Lunch 午膳
set 套餐 $ 48-98
Dinner 晚膳
set 套餐 $108-248

■ OPENING HOURS 营业时间
Lunch 午膳　12:00-15:00 L.O. 14:30
Dinner 晚膳　18:30-23:00 L.O. 22:00

■ ANNUAL AND WEEKLY CLOSING 休息日期
Closed Monday 周一休息

CHINESE 中国菜

MAP 地图 6/B-3

Crystal Jade Golden Palace
翡翠金阁

♿ 🅿 ⏷15 📞

Opened in 2002, this is most comfortable branch of this restaurant group and the only one which specialises in Teochew dishes, like cold crab and sugar-coated yam. Look out too for the Cantonese barbecue meat and assorted seafood dishes; more contemporary offerings include chilled foie gras with sake and roasted suckling pig with black truffle. Their wine cellar includes a good international selection.

集团内唯一一间有潮州菜供应的食府，餐单上大部分均是传统潮州菜如冻蟹、反沙芋等，还有粤式烧味、海鲜菜式和午市的即制点心，此外，还有一些较新派的菜式如清酒鹅肝、黑松露乳猪卷等，不妨一试。

TEL. 6734 6866
Paragon Shopping Centre, #05-22,
290 Orchard Road
乌节路 290号百利宫 #05-22
www.crystaljade.com

SPECIALITIES TO PRE-ORDER 预订食物
Roasted suckling pig rolled with black truffle rice 黑松露乳猪饭卷

■ PRICE 价钱
Lunch 午膳
set 套餐 $ 48
à la carte 点菜 $ 50-100
Dinner 晚膳
à la carte 点菜 $ 70-150

■ OPENING HOURS 营业时间
Lunch 午膳   11:30-14:30 (L.O.)
Dinner 晚膳 18:00-22:00 (L.O.)

■ ANNUAL AND WEEKLY CLOSING 休息日期
Closed 2 days Lunar New Year
农历新年 2 天休息

STEAKHOUSE 扒房　　　　　　　　　　　MAP 地图　18/D-2

Cut

　　　　　&　P　🍽40

The original West Coast celebrity chef is winning over Singaporeans one Hokkaido Snow beef rib-eye at a time. While the bone marrow flan at this luxurious steakhouse is just as good as the LA original, don't forget you're really here for the eating of beef. The meat is perfectly seasoned and grilled over charcoal before being finished off under a 1200 degree broiler to leave it succulent and juicy – and the side dishes are pretty good too.

以1,200度炭火烤炙的牛肉，汁丰肉嫩；恰到好处的调味，进食后齿颊仍留有余香！想吃美国和牛、英国红牛或日本和牛？不用坐飞机远渡重洋，只需安坐于座位上让殷勤的服务员为你下单，便能品尝其滋味。前菜如杂菌酱香草牛骨髓沙拉 (bone marrow flan，mushroom marmalade，parsley salad)也很美味。

TEL. 6688 8517
Marina Bay Sands Hotel,
Galleria Level, B1-71,
2 Bayfront Avenue
贝弗兰道2号宾海湾金莎酒店 B1-71
www.wolfgangpuck.com

■ PRICE 价钱
Dinner 晚膳
à la carte 点菜 $ 150-600

■ OPENING HOURS 营业时间
18:00-21:30 (L.O.)
Friday and Saturday 周五及周六
18:00-22:30 (L.O.)

FRENCH 法国菜　　　　　　　　　　　　　　　　MAP 地图　18/D-2

Daniel Boulud Bistro & Oyster Bar

Daniel Boulud's bistros are synonymous with stylish surroundings, slick service and great burgers – especially his special foie gras creation! You can also expect top quality fish and shellfish from around the world and a menu with its spotlight on the best seasonal produce. The restaurant comes with three distinct areas: an oyster bar at the front, a circular bar area with booths, and a dining room with upper and lower sections.

设计时尚的餐馆,掺杂了巴黎地下车通道的装潢风格,感觉隋意舒适。此店的烹调和美食概念源自法国小酒馆的风格,朴实而不卖弄花巧;海鲜柜台上的生蚝和贝壳类海产,还有美味的汉堡包,令人回味无穷!建议尝尝主厨原创、加了鹅肝的汉堡包。

TEL. 6688 8525
Marina Bay Sands Hotel,
Galleria Level, B1-48,
2 Bayfront Avenue
贝弗兰道 2号宾海湾金莎酒店 B1-71
www.dbbistro.com/singapore/

■ PRICE 价钱
Lunch 午膳
set 套餐 $42-68
à la carte 点菜 $70-150
Dinner 晚膳
à la carte 点菜 $70-150

■ OPENING HOURS 营业时间
12:00-23:00 (L.O.)
Sunday and Monday 周日及周一
12:00-22:00 (L.O.)

SOUTH EAST ASIAN 东南亚菜　　　　　MAP 地图　17/A-3

Ding Dong

Spread over two floors of a shophouse, this relaxed eatery from the Ryan Clift stable attracts a fashionable crowd, especially at night when the atmosphere is boosted by a cocktail list and a loud soundtrack. The kitchen puts its own spin on assorted classics from across SE Asia and uses plenty of modern techniques so although traditional flavour combinations underpin the dishes, don't be surprised to see the occasional bit of dry ice too.

简约的装饰、黑白色调的配搭总予人时尚感觉，墙上的中式剪纸挂饰，添上一点东南亚风味，恰恰带出了餐厅的主题：东南亚菜。大部分东南亚国家的美食都有供应，唯烹调手法却未必跟随传统，厨师选择以新颖的烹调方式演译东南亚风味，例如以干冰配食物，虽令人感到意外却蛮有趣。晚上到此光喝酒的客人也不少！

TEL. 8333 9652
23 Ann Siang Road
安祥山路 23号
www.dingdong.com.sg

■ PRICE 价钱
Lunch 午膳
set 套餐 $ 25
à la carte 点菜 $ 51-73
Dinner 晚膳
set 套餐 $ 80
à la carte 点菜 $ 51-73

■ OPENING HOURS 营业时间
Lunch 午膳　12:00-14:30 (L.O.)
Dinner 晚膳　18:00-23:30 (L.O.)

■ ANNUAL AND WEEKLY CLOSING 休息日期
Closed Saturday lunch and Sunday
周六午膳及周日休息

ITALIAN 意大利菜 MAP 地图 18/C-1

Dolce Vita

Next to the hotel's swimming pool is this authentic Italian restaurant. It has an appealing Mediterranean feel and through the floor-to-ceiling windows you can see the pool and the bay beyond. The cooking has its roots in traditional recipes but the kitchen adds its own little touches. The bright surroundings, relaxing atmosphere and charming service make it a good choice for family gatherings, with weekend brunches being particularly popular.

位于露天泳池旁的这家意大利餐厅，供应的是带点现代风味的正宗意大利菜。室内布置洋溢着浓浓的地中海气息，气氛轻松，开放式落地琉璃窗，让你饱览池畔和海湾景色。这里绝对是与亲朋共聚品尝美食的上佳之处。何不找个周末，与至亲挚爱来尝尝早午合餐，顺道欣赏一下蓝天白云、碧水绿荫？

TEL. 6885 3500
Mandarin Oriental Hotel, Level 5,
5 Raffles Avenue, Manina Square
莱佛士道5号滨海广场
文华东方酒店 Level 5

■ PRICE 价钱
Lunch 午膳
set 套餐 ＄75-118
à la carte 点菜 ＄85-190

Dinner 晚膳
set 套餐 ＄128
à la carte 点菜 ＄85-190

■ OPENING HOURS 营业时间
Lunch 午膳　12:00-14:15 (L.O.)
Weekends lunch 周末午膳
12:00-13:30 (L.O.)
Dinner 晚膳　18:30-22:15 (L.O.)

The symbol 🍇 denotes a particularly interesting wine list.

🍇 这个图标表示该餐厅提供一系列优质餐酒。

The best way to immerse yourself in local life is by trying street food 🍜. To find great food and local specialities, check out our selection of hawker centres and street food vendors.

认识一个地方和体验当地文化的最佳渠道是品尝道地的街头小吃，跟着我们的熟食小贩中心及街头小吃推介 🍜 去寻找最经典、最受欢迎的美点吧！

SPANISH 西班牙菜　　　　　　　　　　　　　MAP 地图　17/A-3

Esquina

On an 'esquina' just off Keong Saik Road is an old shophouse that lends itself very nicely to this hip Spanish restaurant. Grab one of the tractor seat stools at the counter and watch the chefs in action. Their small plates are original and confidently prepared; the flavours are distinct and the imported ingredients excellent. The great soundtrack adds to the vibe and there's a very good value menu offered at lunchtime.

充满西欧时尚风情的餐厅，以动听的音乐筑构出和谐舒适的气氛。坐在吧台前的吧椅上看着厨师烹调食物，感觉悠闲写意。主厨虽年轻，烹调及呈上小碟美食予食客时却是信心充足。带有个人风格、外型精致的西班牙菜式，选用优质食材，加上细腻的烹调技巧，味道很棒。中午套餐物有所值，值得一试。

TEL. 6222 1616
16 Jiak Chuan Road
若泉路 16 号
www.esquina.com.sg

■ PRICE 价钱
Lunch 午膳
set 套餐 $ 28
à la carte 点菜 $ 37-75
Dinner 晚膳
à la carte 点菜 $ 37-75

■ OPENING HOURS 营业时间
Lunch 午膳　12:00-14:00 (L.O.)
Dinner 晚膳　18:00-22:30 (L.O.)

■ ANNUAL AND WEEKLY CLOSING 休息日期
Closed Saturday lunch and Sunday
周六午膳及周日休息

JAPANESE STEAKHOUSE 日式扒房　　MAP 地图　6/A-3

Fat Cow

Start with nigiri or sushi before the main event – beef. The restaurant specialises in various grades of Wagyu from three prefectures in Japan, along with breeds from Australia and the US. The meat is charcoal grilled but you can also opt for subiyaki or shabu-shabu. Service is delightful and the layout of the intimate, immaculate room lets you watch the team in action. The one surprise is the location – it's on the ground floor of a medical centre.

日本大厨和其团队就在餐柜台后为你预备食物。从处理刺身到如何裁切牛肉的各个部位，都能一览无遗。这儿的和牛来自日本、澳洲、美国的著名农场。食客选择和牛的级别后，厨师会以木炭烤煮，当然，你可以选择以寿喜烧或火锅形式烹调和牛。日本清酒和威士忌酒单看着蛮吸引，何妨浅尝一杯？

TEL. 6735 0308
Camden Medical Centre,
Ground Level,
1 Orchard Boulevard
乌节林荫道1号地面楼层
www.fat-cow.com.sg

■ PRICE 价钱
Lunch 午膳
set 套餐 $ 30-50
à la carte 点菜 $ 50-275
Dinner 晚膳
à la carte 点菜 $ 50-275

■ OPENING HOURS 营业时间
Lunch 午膳　12:00-15:00 L.O. 14:30
Dinner 晚膳　18:00-23:00 L.O. 22:30

CANTONESE 粤菜

MAP 地图　1/A-1

Feng Shui Inn
风水廷

It may be hidden away on the ground floor of Crockfords Tower but this Cantonese restaurant is well worth seeking out. The large dining room is elegantly decorated with superb lacquered panels and great granite walls. The signature dishes include highly nutritious double-boiled soups, Canadian geoduck clams, crispy fish skin, and pan-fried tiger prawns. At lunch, don't miss the baked yam pastry or the steamed prawn dumplings on the list of dim sum.

由在香港从事厨师多年的经验老师傅掌厨，以极新鲜食材炮制的粤菜味道令人垂涎。青柠黄金脆鱼皮、豉油皇干煎老虎虾、古法牛柳粒等均为其拿手菜。说到粤菜，当然少不了老火汤，天天新款的风水廷老火汤是必试之选。午市点心的风水鲜虾饺和香芋黄金角同样不能错过。

TEL. 6577 6599
Crockfords Tower, G2,
Resorts World Sentosa,
8 Sentosa Gateway
圣淘沙桥门8号圣淘沙名胜世界
康乐福豪华酒店 G2
www.rwsentosa.com

■ PRICE 价钱
Lunch 午膳
à la carte 点菜 $ 50-130
Dinner 晚膳
à la carte 点菜 $ 50-130

■ OPENING HOURS 营业时间
11:30-22:30 (L.O.)
Friday to Sunday 周五及周末
11:30-01:00 (L.O.)

FRENCH 法国菜　　　　　　　　　　　　　　　　MAP 地图　17/A-3

Fleur de Sel

　　　　　　　　　　　　　　🍽12 🍴 🕐 🍇

You'll find the artisan French salt from which the restaurant gets its name on each table – but you won't need it because the owner-chef has worked for some of the world's greatest chefs and knows what he's doing. At this 'bistro de luxe' he delivers classical French cuisine prepared in a modern, lighter style – and that makes it easy to save room for his signature Baba. There's a good choice of clarets and burgundies to accompany the dishes.

盐之花是法国顶级海盐，店主以此为餐厅命名，有何特别喻意?高级法国小馆格调的餐馆，由富经验的主厨兼店主Alexandre亲自领导，提供以现代方法烹调、外型带点时尚的经典法国美食。以高级食材组成的餐单和一系列波尔多、孛艮第美酒，足证餐馆走的确是高格调之风。甜点La Baba是主厨的招牌美食。

TEL. 6222 6861
64 Tras Street
道拉实街64号
www.fleurdesel.com.sg

■ PRICE 价钱
Lunch 午膳
set 套餐 $38-48
Dinner 晚膳
set 套餐 $88-108

■ OPENING HOURS 营业时间
Lunch 午膳　12:00-14:30 (L.O.)
Dinner 晚膳　18:30-22:00 (L.O.)

■ ANNUAL AND WEEKLY CLOSING 休息日期
Closed Saturday lunch and Sunday
周六午膳及周日休息

SPANISH 西班牙菜　　　　　　　　　　　　MAP 地图　17/B-2

FOC

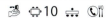

'Fine fun food from Barcelona' is how the eponymous chef describes his Singaporean outpost. He's brought along the flavours of Catalonia which he blends with modern cooking techniques to create original and exciting dishes. The surroundings are relaxed and always furiously busy, with the principal players in the operation represented by huge papier mâché heads. Ask for a seat at the counter to get the most out of the experience.

打着精致有趣的巴塞罗那美食的旗号，此餐馆是西班牙一星厨师Nandu Jubany在这儿的据点。时尚、繁忙、朝气勃勃，是不苟泥的格调。小碟西班牙菜式，在传统的基调上注入了新元素，味道与口感的融合创造出独特的原创风味，让味觉得到不一样的体验。酒吧台顶以店主和主厨的大型黏土头像作装饰，煞是有趣。

TEL. 6100 4040
40 Hong Kong Street
香港街 40号
www.focrestaurant.com

■ PRICE 价钱
Lunch 午膳
à la carte 点菜　$ 40-70
Dinner 晚膳
à la carte 点菜　$ 40-70

■ OPENING HOURS 营业时间
Lunch 午膳　12:00-14:00 (L.O.)
Dinner 晚膳　18:00-22:00 (L.O.)

■ ANNUAL AND WEEKLY CLOSING 休息日期
Closed Sunday 周日休息

CHINESE CONTEMPORARY 时尚中国菜　　　MAP 地图　1/A-1

Forest
森

To best experience the modern, innovative dishes of celebrity chef Sam Leong, come here to the Equarius hotel for dinner rather than lunch. Signature dishes include milky chicken broth with morel mushrooms and bamboo; Sichuan-style mapo tofu with crab meat; and pan-fried foie gras with smoked duck breast. Service in this airy, high-ceilinged dining room with its forest motif is courteous and eager.

高高的天花上全是淡棕色树叶绘图，落地琉璃窗和门，让露台和店外的花园景致一览无遗。大厨以新颖的烹调手法处理来自亚洲各地的食材，透过反传统的烹饪概念替中国菜进行革新。午餐菜单较简单，欲品尝美味中菜，便要于晚饭时间到访。野生竹笙羊肚菌牛奶鸡汤、川式麻婆豆腐蟹肉蒸饭是其特色食品。

TEL. 6577 6688
Equarius Hotel, Lobby,
8 Sentosa Gateway
圣淘沙桥门 8号圣淘沙名胜世界
逸濠酒店大堂楼层
www.rwsentosa.com

■ PRICE 价钱
Lunch 午膳
set 套餐 $ 42-62
à la carte 点菜 $ 50-65
Dinner 晚膳
set 套餐 $ 138-268
à la carte 点菜 $ 65-130

■ OPENING HOURS 营业时间
Lunch 午膳　12:00-14:15 (L.O.)
Dinner 晚膳　18:00-22:15 (L.O.)

ITALIAN 意大利菜 MAP 地图 18/C-2

Forlino

Italian flair, Japanese precision and super-fresh ingredients combine to create delicious dishes in this plush dining room with great views. At lunch most are in for the quick business menu but if you opt for the à la carte you get to see what the kitchen can really do, with dishes like linguine with Hokkaido sea urchin and bottarga, or slow-cooked black cod with tripe and white polenta. For dessert, few see past the signature tiramisu.

混入了日本风味以传统手法和新鲜食材制作的意大利菜风味正宗、味道可口。周一至周五午市时段会提供三道菜的Business Set Lunch，当然，有空档慢慢品尝美食的，可以选择单点菜单上的菜式。面质幼滑的香蒜海胆意大利面条(Linguine Pasta 'Aglioe Olio' ai Ricci di Mare)和厨师推介的甜品提拉米苏是不错的选择。

TEL. 6690 7564
One Fullerton, #02-06,
1 Fullerton Road
浮尔顿路1号浮尔顿一号 #02-06
www.forlino.com

■ PRICE 价钱
Lunch 午膳
set 套餐 $ 38-88
à la carte 点菜 $ 80-150
Dinner 晚膳
set 套餐 $ 128-138
à la carte 点菜 $ 80-150

■ OPENING HOURS 营业时间
Lunch 午膳 12:00-14:30 (L.O.)
Dinner 晚膳 16:30-22:30 (L.O.)

ITALIAN 意大利菜

MAP 地图 18/C-1

Garibaldi

Ossobuco, costoletta alla Milanese and tiramisu are some of the signature dishes here at one of the city's best known Italian restaurants. The affable owner, though, wants everyone to be able to find their favourite dish which is why he offers such a large, all-encompassing menu. The impressive wine list, featuring over 7000 labels, is another feature for which this cosy and contemporary-styled restaurant is celebrated.

店东兼主厨年轻时曾于多个欧亚国家跟随多位意大利名厨工作的背景，造就了此家本地最有名的意大利餐馆。这儿选用的食材，大部分来自意大利。藏红花牛肘烩饭(Ossobuco)、米兰炸猪排(Costoletta alla Milanese)及提拉米苏是其名菜。店东任职调酒师的妻子帮忙挑选的酒单，涵盖逾七千款意大利和法国名酿。

TEL. 6837 1468
36 Purvis Street, #01-02
巴米士街 36号 #01-02
www.garibaldi.com.sg

■ PRICE 价钱
Lunch 午膳
set 套餐 $39
à la carte 点菜 $70-240
Dinner 晚膳
set 套餐 $188
à la carte 点菜 $70-240

■ OPENING HOURS 营业时间
Lunch 午膳 12:00-14:30 (L.O.)
Dinner 晚膳 18:30-22:30 (L.O.)

CANTONESE 粤菜　　　　　　　　　　　　　　　MAP 地图　11/A-1

Geylang Claypot Rice
芽籠瓦煲飯

The location and speciality are both there in the name. This modestly decorated place with its big round tables and plastic chairs is all about rice cooked over charcoal – accompanied by sausage, salted fish, chicken or cured meat. There are other Cantonese dishes to choose from the illuminated menu on the wall; the bean curd 'prawn ball' is good. Call in advance to reserve a table and to ensure your rice will be ready for you when you arrive.

餐厅位于芽笼保留区，两旁全是两层高的殖民地时期建筑，临街一面保留着昔日面貌。招牌菜是以炭火炮制的粤式瓦锅煲仔饭，腊肠、润肠、咸鱼、鸡、腊肉等材料集于一锅。此外还供应广式小菜、蒸海鲜，以自制豆腐煮成的豆腐虾球也不错。需致电预约，店方会因应人数和到达时间准备好煲仔饭。

TEL. 6744 4574
639 Lorong 33, Geylang
芽笼 33 巷 639 号

■ PRICE 价钱
Lunch 午膳
à la carte 点菜 $ 20-40
Dinner 晚膳
à la carte 点菜 $ 20-40

■ OPENING HOURS 营业时间
Lunch 午膳　11:30-14:30 (L.O.)
Dinner 晚膳　17:00-23:30 (L.O.)

■ ANNUAL AND WEEKLY CLOSING 休息日期
Closed Monday 周一休息

93

STEAKHOUSE 扒房

MAP 地图 6/B-2

Gordon Grill

Those with fond memories of European-style grill rooms will like Gordon Grill. A feature of Goodwood Park hotel for over 50 years, the restaurant is famed for its meat trolley service which is wheeled over to each table. Along with the meat and plentiful supplies of seafood from the grill, you can expect French-inspired classic dishes. It's a good choice for a quiet business lunch, a romantic dinner for hotel guests or weekend family outings.

餐厅自1963年开业以来一直供应各式扒房菜式，主厨Gan Swee Lai更为餐牌添了欧陆风味，如烤法式田螺、龙虾汤、牛面颊肉伴红酒汁、苹果馅饼等。特别的是手推车会被推到餐厅每个角落，让食客目睹切割、量重等过程。适合商务午餐、烛光晚餐及周末家庭乐。毗邻的酒吧是进餐前后把酒谈心的好地方。

TEL. 6730 1744
Goodwood Park Hotel, 22 Scotts Road
史各士路 22号良木园酒店
www.goodwoodparkhotel.com

■ PRICE 价钱
Lunch 午膳
set 套餐 $ 58-68
à la carte 点菜 $ 80-120
Dinner 晚膳
set 套餐 $ 128
à la carte 点菜 $ 80-120

■ OPENING HOURS 营业时间
Lunch 午膳 12:00-14:30 (L.O.)
Dinner 晚膳 19:00-22:30 (L.O.)

FRENCH 法国菜　　　　　　　　　　　　　　MAP 地图　18/C-1

Gunther's

🍽10　

The owner-chef worked in some well-known restaurants in his native Belgium before coming to Singapore. He may describe his cooking as "simple, honest and down-to-earth" but typical dishes include angel hair pasta with Oscietra caviar, roast rack of black pig, and fine apple tart. Many regulars wait until they've seen the tray of the day's special ingredients before ordering, however. The two dining rooms are enlivened by some colourful art.

不显眼的外观，一不小心便会错过这家瑟缩于小街一角的餐馆!厨师烹调的宗旨一如店子的外观：简单、平实。黑椒帕尔马干酪烤洋葱、鱼子酱凉拌天使面、兰姆酒葡萄冰淇淋等都能在这儿吃到。食客多在观看每日精选食材后才点菜。逾四百款佳酿的酒单内供应的大部分是来自波尔多和勃艮地的名酿。

TEL. 6338 8955
36 Purvis Street, #01-03
巴米士街 36号 #01-03
www.gunthers.com.sg

■ PRICE 价钱
Lunch 午膳
set 套餐 $ 38
à la carte 点菜 $ 70-230
Dinner 晚膳
set 套餐 $ 250
à la carte 点菜 $ 70-230

■ OPENING HOURS 营业时间
Lunch 午膳　12:00-14:30 (L.O.)
Dinner 晚膳　18:30-22:00 (L.O.)

■ ANNUAL AND WEEKLY CLOSING 休息日期
Closed Saturday lunch and Sunday
周六午膳及周日休息

SUSHI 寿司　　　　　　　　　　　　　MAP 地图　6/B-3

Hashida

A typically discreet entrance and corridor lead into two elegant counter restaurants, one of which seats just six and is ideal for a discreet dinner. There are three menu options for lunch while at dinner only an omakase is offered. For the sushi, fish comes four times a week from Tokyo's Tsukiji Market and twice a week from Hokkaido, with selected white-hulled rice also imported from Japan. The signature dish is monkfish liver with sea eel sauce.

素雅的大门，与带禅味的走廊相映成趣。餐厅分为两大区域，均设简洁舒适的寿司吧，渴望私密空间的可选只有六个座位的区域。午膳有Tsubaki、Ayame和Hiiragi三个餐单供选择，而晚膳只提供Omakase餐单。餐厅坚持每周多次由日本筑地或北海道空运食材而来，作结的柚子或绿茶马卡龙会带来惊喜！

TEL. 6733 2114
Mandarin Gallery, #02-37,
333A Orchard Road
乌节路 333A号文华购物廊 #02-37
www.hashida.com.sg

■ PRICE 价钱
Lunch 午膳
set 套餐 $ 80-250
Dinner 晚膳
set 套餐 $ 300-500

■ OPENING HOURS 营业时间
Lunch 午膳　12:00-15:00 L.O. 13:30
Dinner 晚膳　19:00-22:00 L.O. 20:30

■ ANNUAL AND WEEKLY CLOSING 休息日期
Closed Monday　周一休息

Resorts World Sentosa is home to three world-class attractions, six unique hotels, 10 acclaimed celebrity chef restaurants and an award-winning destination spa.

Expect one-of-a-kind experiences in our hotels

From the breathtaking underwater view in Ocean Suites to the exclusive Beach Villas and high-in-the-sky TreeTop Lofts, our luxury hotel rooms promise a stay that you will remember for a lifetime.

Experience the epitome of luxury spa and wellness at award-winning ESPA

A 100,000 sq ft oasis of tranquility, ESPA at Resorts World Sentosa offers a wide range of luxurious treatments in private beach villas and garden spa suites that are immaculately designed for total relaxation.

WINNER OF
2015 WORLD LUXURY SPA AWARDS
Best Luxury Wellness Spa - Country Winner
Best Luxury Destination Spa - Country Winner

COUNTRY WINNER
2015 WELLNESS TRAVEL AWARDS
BEST SPA IN SINGAPORE

Find out more about Resorts World Sentosa Singapore on rwsentosa.com or call +65 6577 8888

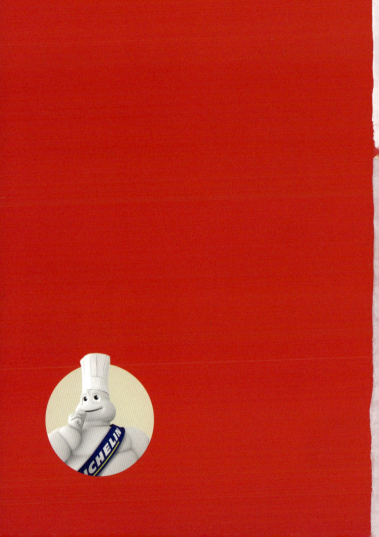

MALAYSIAN 马来西亚菜　　　　　　　　　　　　　　MAP 地图　8/D-3

Hjh Maimunah (Jalan Pisang)

In a narrow street behind Masjid Sultan mosque is a simple Malaysian restaurant that's always busy – and it's easy to see why: the ingredients are fresh, the food is delicious and the prices are affordable. Around 70% of dishes are Malaysian and 30% Indonesian; it's mostly self-service and the dishes to go for include Sundanese grilled chicken, beef rendang, lemak siput and tahu telur. The upstairs room is slightly more comfortable.

用料新鲜、风味正宗、味道浓郁可口、价钱相宜，是这家位于苏丹回教堂背后狭长街道上的马来西亚菜馆客常满的原因。餐馆供应的菜式七成属于马来西亚、三成是印尼美食。圣丹斯烤鸡、椰浆蜗牛、烤鱼、冷当牛肉等，单看名字已令人馋涎欲滴。食客需自行在食物柜台前选购食物。

TEL. 6291 3132
11&15 Jalan Pisang
惹兰比山 11&15号

■ PRICE 价钱
à la carte 点菜 $ 10-15

■ OPENING HOURS 营业时间
07:00-19:00 (L.O.)

97

An important business lunch? The symbol ⇔ indicates restaurants with private rooms.

需要一个合适的地点享用商务午餐？可从注有这个 ⇔ 图标的餐厅中选一家有私人厢房且合你心意的餐馆。

Read 'How to use this guide' for an explanation of our symbols, classifications and abbreviations.

请仔细阅读"如何使用餐厅／酒店指南"，当中的图标、分类等简介助你掌握使用本指南的诀窍，作出智慧选择。

CANTONESE 粤菜　　　　　　　　　　　　　　　　MAP 地图　6/A-2

Hua Ting
華廳

Orchard Hotel's Cantonese restaurant is smart, comfortable and classically decorated. It is also run with great professionalism by a friendly team who are willing to offer advice. The cuisine comes with a contemporary flourish, with signature dishes like scallops with winter melon, and superior bird's nest with egg white; on the dim sum menu look out for baked chicken tartlets with mango. There's a 'smart casual' dress code – and it is enforced!

要进入这家位处酒店内的高级粤菜厅，千万别穿短裤或拖鞋，餐厅经理会将衣冠不整的人拒诸门外。餐厅装潢典雅，职员态度友善，来自香港的主厨锺立辉师傅为广东菜添上不少创意，这里的点心尤其出色，特别推荐上素蒸粉果和招牌香芒鸡挞。

TEL. 6739 6666
Orchard Hotel, Level 1,
442 Orchard Road
乌节路 442号乌节大酒店 Level 1
www.orchardhotel.com.sg

■ PRICE 价钱
Lunch 午膳
set 套餐 $ 78-98
à la carte 点菜 $ 40-200
Dinner 晚膳
set 套餐 $ 78-98
à la carte 点菜 $ 40-200

■ OPENING HOURS 营业时间
Lunch 午膳　11:30-14:30 (L.O.)
Dinner 晚膳　18:30-22:30 (L.O.)

INNOVATIVE 创新菜

Iggy's

MAP 地图 6A/2

It may be inside the Hilton, but this diminutive restaurant is run entirely independently. Ingredients come from as far away as France, Italy and Japan and there's a strong Asian element to the contemporary cuisine – the kitchen makes use of modern cooking techniques and dishes are vibrant and full of colour. It has just 8 tables and 8 seats at the dessert counter which, along with subdued lighting, make it ideal for a romantic dinner.

这里提供带亚洲风味的时尚菜式，每道都美艳如图画，色彩斑斓，别树一帜，将创意和优质食材完美地融合在餐桌上，午膳和晚膳均提供三款套餐，其中一款为素食者而设。客人可透过ipad浏览酒单，选择多达六百款。全店只有八张餐桌，建议预先订座。

TEL. 6732 2234
Hilton Hotel, Level 3,
581 Orchard Road
乌节路 581号希尔顿酒店 Level 3
www.iggys.com.sg

■ PRICE 价钱
Lunch 午膳
set 套餐 $ 85-150
Dinner 晚膳
set 套餐 $ 195-275
à la carte 点菜 $ 155-240

■ OPENING HOURS 营业时间
Lunch 午膳 12:00-13:30 (L.O.)
Dinner 晚膳 19:00-21:30 (L.O.)

■ ANNUAL AND WEEKLY CLOSING 休息日期
Closed Wednesday and Sunday
周三及周日休息

ITALIAN 意大利菜

MAP 地图 6/A-2

Il Cielo

The name means 'The Sky' and this intimate Italian is perched on the top floor of the Hilton, right beside the pool. The cuisine comes with a dash of creativity and uses the best natural and organic ingredients. At lunch you'll find a good value set menu while at dinner the luxurious nature of the produce is clearly apparent. Signature dishes include burratina with basil cream and olives, Hokkaido scallops with pineapple, and roasted Tuscan fish.

厨师将创意和时尚融入意大利菜肴中，选用的食材大多是有机的时令农产品。不妨试试北海道带子佐烤黄梨、带子饼干及鱼子酱、意大利乳酪蛋糕。这里亦提供以砖炉烤制的薄饼和手造意大利面。午膳还提供价格相宜的便当套餐。在酒店顶层池畔边品尝美食，边呷一口意大利或法国佳酿，乃人生一大享受。

TEL. 6730 3395
Hilton Hotel, Level 24,
581 Orchard Road
乌节路 581号希尔顿酒店 Level 24
www.hilton.com

■ PRICE 价钱
Lunch 午膳
set 套餐 $ 35
à la carte 点菜 $ 65-135
Dinner 晚膳
à la carte 点菜 $ 65-135

■ OPENING HOURS 营业时间
Lunch 午膳 12:00-14:30 (L.O.)
Dinner 晚膳 19:00-22:30 (L.O.)

■ ANNUAL AND WEEKLY CLOSING 休息日期
Closed Weekend lunch 周末午膳休息

CANTONESE 粤菜 MAP 地图 16/C-1

Imperial Treasure Cantonese Cuisine (Great World City)
御寶軒(世界城)

The fish tanks and wine cellar at the entrance set the tone for this well-dressed Cantonese restaurant, with its wood panelling and splashes of red. It offers a comprehensive selection of Cantonese dishes, with set menus for 2 to 10 people. Look out for the braised fish maw with goose web. Dim sum, prepared by the restaurant's Hong Kong chefs, is available daily. It is part of the Imperial Treasure Group, which has over 20 restaurants.

隶属御宝饮食集团旗下，经过入口的水族箱和酒柜，迎面的是以红色为主调的用餐区，红色吊灯、深木色陈设为餐厅添上了中国韵味。这儿提供各式受欢迎的广东菜肴，从经典的咕噜肉至令人垂涎的花胶焖鹅掌，包罗万有，更少不了由香港厨师主理的广式点心。亦设二至十人套餐。

TEL. 6732 2232
Great World City, #02-05A/6,
1 Kim Seng Promenade
金声河畔道1号世界城 #02-05A/6

SPECIALITIES TO PRE-ORDER 预订食物
Baked salty chicken 盐焗鸡 /Crispy chicken stuffed with glutinous rice 糯米炸子鸡 /Lamb shoulder 羊肩

■ PRICE 价钱
Lunch 午膳
à la carte 点菜 $ 40-100
Dinner 晚膳
à la carte 点菜 $ 40-100

■ OPENING HOURS 营业时间
Lunch 午膳 11:30-14:30 (L.O.)
Saturday lunch 周六午膳 11:00-14:30 (L.O.)
Sunday lunch 周日午膳 10:30-14:30 (L.O.)
Dinner 晚膳 18:00-22:30 (L.O.)

SHANGHAINESE 沪菜　　　　　　　　　　　　　　　　MAP 地图　6/B-3

Imperial Treasure Shanghai Cuisine
御園

 🅿 🍽15 ☎

Ask for one of the intimate cocoon-like booths when making a reservation at this Shanghainese restaurant, which is in amongst the various boutiques on the 4th floor of Ngee Ann City. The most popular dishes are the pork ribs, salted duck, and braised bean curd. The restaurant is also unusual in that it serves dim sum at dinner as well as lunch – look out for steamed pork and chive dumpling and the pan-fried pork bun.

不论在普通座位或隐秘的厢座，都能轻松、惬意地享用店内的上海菜肴。最受欢迎的菜式有糖醋里脊肉、南京盐香鸭和家常豆腐。有别于本地大部分中式餐厅，这里晚膳时段也供应点心，肉汁淋漓的猪肉韭菜水饺、外层香脆的鲜肉锅贴和生煎包都值得一试。若对上海菜感到陌生，专业的服务员会助你一把。

TEL. 6836 6909
Ngee Ann City, #04-22,
391A Orchard Road
乌节路 391号義安城 #04-22
www.imperialtreasure.com

■ PRICE 价钱
Lunch 午膳
set 套餐 $ 50-108
à la carte 点菜 $ 35-140
Dinner 晚膳
set 套餐 $ 50-108
à la carte 点菜 $ 35-140

■ OPENING HOURS 营业时间
Lunch 午膳　11:00-15:00 L.O. 14:45
Dinner 晚膳　18:00-23:00 L.O. 22:30

103

CANTONESE 粤菜　　　　　　　　　　　　　　　　　　　MAP 地图　6/B-3

Imperial Treasure Super Peking Duck (Paragon)
御寶至尊烤鴨店（百利宮）

 　　　　　　　　　　　　　　　　　　　　　14

Specialising in Peking duck, this restaurant is considered the jewel in the crown of the Imperial Treasure group. It's divided into three rooms, with the main one largely kept for bigger parties. After roasting, the whole duck is presented and sliced at the table with a fair degree of ceremony. The skin is crisp and the meat succulent and flavoursome. Don't ignore other dishes like double-boiled fish maw soup. It's very busy so booking is a must.

所属集团旗下餐厅中的珍宝，京式烤鸭店享负盛名。食客大多为了那皮薄香脆、肉质鲜美的烤鸭而来，厨师会即席将完整的鸭片成薄片，隆重得像宗教仪式!其他菜式如鲨鱼骨炖花胶汤、卤水法国鹅肝豆腐等同样滋味。极繁忙时，用作等候区的香槟吧附近会加设座位，建议订座。套餐只供六人或以上享用。

TEL. 6732 7838
Paragon Shopping Centre, #05-42/45,
290 Orchard Road
乌节路 290号百利宫 #05-42/45
www.imperialtreasure.com

SPECIALITIES TO PRE-ORDER 预订食物
Crispy chicken stuffed with glutinous rice 糯米炸子鸡 /Baked salted chicken 盐焗鸡 /Charcoal grilled lamb 炭烧羊扒 /Beijing style roasted duck 京式烤鸭 /Roasted suckling pig 南乳去骨猪

■ PRICE 价钱
Lunch 午膳
à la carte 点菜 $ 40-200
Dinner 晚膳
à la carte 点菜 $ 40-200

■ OPENING HOURS 营业时间
Lunch 午膳　11:30-15:00 L.O. 14:45
Dinner 晚膳　18:00-23:00 L.O. 22:00

TEOCHEW 潮州菜   MAP 地图 6/B-3

Imperial Treasure Teochew Cuisine
御寶閣

Providing sanctuary from the busy pace outside is this elegantly dressed Teochew restaurant. It offers various traditional Teochew dishes, including some dishes which are not so easy to find these days, like pan-fried taro with prawns or steamed cold mud crabs. For some dishes, you have the option of ordering a smaller portion. If you're a couple, ask for one of the booths for a more intimate dining experience.

卸宝集团首家餐厅，2004年开业，是本地少数高级潮州菜馆之一。位于人流络绎不绝的大商场内，地方不大、布置倒是颇雅致。餐厅供应的传统潮州菜选择丰富，个别菜式如惹味香脆的鲜虾芋头烙及每日限量供应的鲜滑冻黄膏蟹，并不常见。此外，大部分菜式都有大、小份量供应，让食客点菜时更有弹性。

TEL. 6736 2118
Ngee Ann City, #04-20A/21,
391 Orchard Road
乌節路 391号義安城 #04-20A/21
www.imperialtreasure.com

■ PRICE 价钱
Lunch 午膳
à la carte 点菜 $ 30-40
Dinner 晚膳
à la carte 点菜 $ 60-70

■ OPENING HOURS 营业时间
Lunch 午膳 11:30-14:45 (L.O.)
Dinner 晚膳 18:00-22:00 (L.O.)

■ ANNUAL AND WEEKLY CLOSING 休息日期
Closed 2 days Lunar New Year
农历新年 2 天休息

PERANAKAN 娘惹菜　　　　　　　　　　　　　　MAP 地图　6/B-2

Indocafe

Dark wood furniture and antiques add to the elegant colonial feel of this restaurant which lodges within a bungalow and also goes by the name of the 'The White House'. The menu is dominated by Penang-style Peranakan cuisine and, while the dishes look quite simple, their preparation involves the subtle blending of many spices and ingredients. The signature dishes include Rendang, Assam Laksa, and Kueh Pie Tee (pastry with turnips, prawns and crab).

黑、白色殖民风的平房，内里的木地板、深木家具、藤椅和众多的土生华人古董形成强烈的风格。餐厅供应的菜肴结合了马来和华菜的风味，卖相简朴，每一口都交织着多种调料、香料的复杂味道，扑鼻香气深藏层次，小金杯(Kueh Pie Tee)、巴东牛肉(Rendang Sapi)和亚参叻沙(Assam Laksa)都值得一试。

TEL. 6733 2656
35 Scotts Road
史各士路35号
www.thehouseofindocafe.com

■ PRICE 价钱
Lunch 午膳
set 套餐 $49
à la carte 点菜 $45-60
Dinner 晚膳
set 套餐 $59
à la carte 点菜 $45-60

■ OPENING HOURS 营业时间
Lunch 午膳　12:00-15:00 L.O. 14:30
Dinner 晚膳　18:00-22:30 L.O. 22:00

FRENCH CONTEMPORARY 时尚法国菜   MAP 地图 18/C-1

Jaan

As this restaurant is located on the 70th floor of one of South-East Asia's tallest hotels, it's a given that the views won't disappoint. However, it is to the kitchen's credit that the gazes of most customers remain largely on their plates because the contemporary French cuisine merits their full attention. The menu is driven by the ingredients, which are sourced from around the world, and the dishes display evidence of both skill and focus.

时尚简约的设计,带有后现代主义的吊灯和天花配合柔和的灯光、柔软的地毯、淡雅的餐桌布置,餐馆虽小感觉却很舒适;落地琉璃窗让市内景色尽收眼帘,绷紧的神经霎时放松下来!新派的法国菜,菜单以时令和本土食材作主导,为食客提供搜罗自世界各地的新鲜材料,加上厨师精湛的烹调技术,品质与味道俱佳。

TEL. 6837 3322
Swissôtel The Stamford,
Equinox Complex, Level 70,
2 Stamford Road
史丹福路 2号史丹福瑞士酒店 Level 70
www.jaan.com.sg

■ PRICE 价钱
Lunch 午膳
set 套餐 $ 78-158
Dinner 晚膳
set 套餐 $ 198-288

■ OPENING HOURS 营业时间
Lunch 午膳 12:00-14:00 (L.O.)
Dinner 晚膳 18:00-21:30 (L.O.)

■ ANNUAL AND WEEKLY CLOSING 休息日期
Closed Sunday 周日休息

CHINESE 中国菜   MAP 地图   18/C-2

Jade
玉楼

Resplendent in silks, enriched by lacquered woods and engulfed by natural light, this elegant and sophisticated Chinese restaurant is just the sort of place you'd expect to find in the historic Fullerton hotel. Tables allow for much privacy by being large and well spaced and this adds to the restaurant's popularity with those with entertaining to do. The menu blends the classics with the more modern and the care taken by the kitchen is obvious.

高高的天花、米白色调带有纽纹雕花边的墙身、白纱加丝绒窗帘、铺上白餐桌布的圆桌和设计时尚的中式靠背餐椅，展现出现代与传统溶合为一的时尚典雅之美。看似不经意放在墙角的小株绿树，为餐馆平添一分自然之味。高水准的食物令人流年忘返!不论你无肉不欢或清心茹素，清炖冬瓜竹笙汤都能满足你。

TEL. 6733 8388
The Fullerton Hotel,
1 Fullerton Square
浮尔顿广场1号富丽敦酒店
www.fullertonhotel.com

■ PRICE 价钱
Lunch 午膳
set 套餐 $ 58-128
à la carte 点菜 $ 70-140
Dinner 晚膳
set 套餐 $ 58-128
à la carte 点菜 $ 80-180

■ OPENING HOURS 营业时间
Lunch 午膳 11:30-14:30 (L.O.)
Dinner 晚膳 18:30-22:30 (L.O.)

CANTONESE 粤菜　　　　　　　　　　　　　　　　　MAP 地图　6/A-2

Jade Palace
金湖

　　　　　　　　　　　　　　　　　48

Booking is advisable at this conveniently located Cantonese seafood restaurant as it's a favourite of many. In terms of decoration and menu content, it has a pronounced Hong Kong feel. The vast fish tank by the entrance includes plenty of menu items – with crabs and prawns just as popular as the seafood. Along with 12 claypot dishes, there are other Cantonese specialities available too, like stir-fries, soups, and dried seafood dishes.

这家港式海鲜酒家位于乌节路一个商场内，厨师和经理也来自香港，装潢和餐单内容亦渗着浓浓香港味。入口处鱼缸内新鲜的鱼、虾和蟹是最热点的食物，餐单也包罗一系列传统广东小菜，如煲仔菜、小炒、汤品、海味等等，午饭时段当然少不了广东点心。餐厅颇得食客欢心，建议预先订座。

TEL. 6732 6628
Forum The Shopping Mall, #B1-13,
583 Orchard Road
乌节路 583号福临购物中心 #B1-13

■ PRICE 价钱
Lunch 午膳
à la carte 点菜 $ 40-50
Dinner 晚膳
à la carte 点菜 $ 70-80

■ OPENING HOURS 营业时间
Lunch 午膳　11:00-14:30 (L.O.)
Dinner 晚膳　18:00-22:00 (L.O.)

109

The symbol 🍇 denotes a particularly interesting wine list.

🍇 这个图标表示该餐厅提供一系列优质餐酒。

Enjoy good food without spending a fortune! Look out for the Bib Gourmand symbol 😋 to find restaurants offering good food at great prices!

要省钱又想品尝美食,便要留心注有 😋 必比登图标的食店,此类店子提供的是价钱实惠且素质高的美食。

CANTONESE 粤菜

Jiang-Nan Chun
江南春

MAP 地图 6/A-3

Climb the elegant marble staircase at the Four Seasons and you're rewarded with this good-looking Cantonese restaurant. The last refurbishment ensured it kept its warm feel, with the heavy leather seats making it a very comfortable spot. The chef brings some modern touches to the Cantonese food, especially in the presentation of the dishes. As you'd expect from a hotel such as this, the service is exceptionally helpful and well-coordinated.

从四季酒店一楼楼层的大理石楷梯拾级而上即可到达。餐厅刚完成翻新，保持原有的亚洲风情，装饰雅致温暖，厚厚的皮革座椅予人舒适之感。服务水平与酒店同出一辙。餐单以广东菜肴为主，厨师在摆盘时注入了现代元素，令菜式呈现新颖时尚的卖相。

TEL. 6831 7250
Four Seasons Hotel,
190 Orchard Boulevard
乌节林荫道190号四季酒店
www.fourseasons.com/singapore

■ PRICE 价钱
Lunch 午膳
set 套餐 $ 78-188
à la carte 点菜 $ 80-300
Dinner 晚膳
set 套餐 $ 138-258
à la carte 点菜 $ 80-300

■ OPENING HOURS 营业时间
Lunch 午膳 11:30-14:00 (L.O.)
Dinner 晚膳 18:00-22:00 (L.O.)

FRENCH CONTEMPORARY 时尚法国菜

MAP 地图　1/B-1

Joël Robuchon

As one would expect from celebrated French chef Joël Robuchon, only the finest available ingredients are used in the preparation of dishes such as bonito broth with poached lobster and roast guinea fowl with foie gras. Vegetarians have a special 8 course tasting menu and the hugely impressive wine list contains more than 1,000 labels. The sumptuous dining room is inspired by art deco; the indoor winter garden room is particularly attractive.

华丽闪烁的水晶吊灯、名贵沙发与餐桌、具品味的设计，予人幽雅、舒适的感觉。高汤龙虾、黑松露马铃薯、烤凤梨搭提香草冰淇淋全是这儿的著名菜式。然而，为了切合时令，菜单会因应季节的转换而有所调整。细心的主厨还特地为素食人士设计了由八道素菜组成的尝味套餐。餐酒单上提供逾千款餐酒。

TEL. 6577 7888
Hotel Michael, Level 1,
Resorts World Sentosa,
8 Sentosa Gateway
圣淘沙桥门8号名胜世界
迈克尔酒店 Level 1
www.joel-robuchon.com

■ PRICE 价钱
Lunch 午膳
set 套餐 $ 138-428
Dinner 晚膳
set 套餐 $ 138-428

■ OPENING HOURS 营业时间
Saturday lunch 周六午膳　12:00 - 14.30 (L.O.)
Dinner 晚膳　18:00 – 22:30 (L.O.)

■ ANNUAL AND WEEKLY CLOSING 休息日期
Closed Sunday and Monday 周日及周一休息

SINGAPOREAN 新加坡菜　　　　　　　　　MAP 地图　16/D-3

Ka Soh
家嫂

The location is a little unusual but then there's nothing like being surrounded by hospital buildings to remind you of the importance of a good diet. Order the famous speciality here of milky white fish soup with noodles – made by cooking fresh snakehead fish and fish bones for over 4 hours – and you'll feel instantly invigorated. The fried shrimp paste chicken is also worth trying. Ka Soh also has branches in Malaysia and Indonesia.

餐厅位于一幢两层高建筑内，同址有医生会所，四周则是医院建筑群。大厨是土生华人，炮制具本地色彩的潮、粤菜式，其中鱼汤米线不能错过，汤底以鲜鱼骨、生鱼熬制四小时，乳白鲜甜。虾酱鸡也十分惹味。鲜鱼可以选择以粤式、潮式或娘惹方式烹煮。餐厅在马来西亚和印尼都有分店。

TEL. 6473 6686
2 College Road
学院路 2号
www.ka-soh.com

■ PRICE 价钱
Lunch 午膳
à la carte 点菜　$ 20-30
Dinner 晚膳
à la carte 点菜　$ 20-30

■ OPENING HOURS 营业时间
Lunch 午膳　11:30-14:30 (L.O.)
Dinner 晚膳　17:30-21:30 (L.O.)

SINGAPOREAN 新加坡菜　　　　　　　　　　MAP 地图　13/B-2

Keng Eng Kee
瓊榮記

This popular Zi Char restaurant may not be the most conveniently placed but it does some great dishes, like stir-fried ginger onion crab, coffee pork ribs and claypot duck with sea cucumber. The setting and environment are not unlike a hawker centre, although there is a smaller inside area that's air-conditioned. It provides mostly Hainanese cuisine, along with some Cantonese dishes – the stir-fries are particularly delicious.

这主营煮炒菜式的餐厅靠近工业区，就在亚历山大村美食中心后面，虽然地点不算方便，但其姜葱炒蟹、咖啡骨和海参鸡仍吸引不少本地人专程前往品尝。餐单尚包括广东菜，如镬气小炒、煲仔菜和炒粉面等。餐厅环境简单随意，设有半露天位置和面积较小的冷气餐室，订座时可申明座位偏好。

TEL. 6272 1038
Blk 124, Bukit Merah Lane 1, #01-136
红山 1 巷 124 座 #01-136
www.kek.com.sg

■ PRICE 价钱
Lunch 午膳
à la carte 点菜　$ 20-40
Dinner 晚膳
à la carte 点菜　$ 20-40

■ OPENING HOURS 营业时间
Lunch 午膳　12:00-14:30 (L.O.)
Dinner 晚膳　17:00-22:00 (L.O.)

JAPANESE 日本菜   MAP 地图 6/B-2

Ki-sho
葵匠

  14

Home for this charming sushi restaurant is a colonial house, which it shares with Buona Terra – part of the same restaurant group. There are three private dining rooms but if you want to watch the chef in action ask for the counter. The freshest seafood from Hokkaido is used to prepare sushi and sashimi as well as signature dishes like sea urchin with dashi jelly and caviar. There is also a sake bar available for those wishing to learn about sake.

这家位于殖民建筑内的店子，只有十四个座位依附着简约明亮的寿司柜台，食客能欣赏日籍厨师准备食物的手艺，并尝到来自北海道最鲜美的鱼生。店内尚设有三间私人厢房和Kakure清酒吧，供客人品尝和研习清酒知识。酒单选择除法国和意大利红酒外，更有逾八十款从日本进口的清酒可供佐膳。

TEL. 6733 5251
29 Scotts Road
史各士路 29号
www.scotts29.com

■ PRICE 价钱
Lunch 午膳
set 套餐 $ 150-450
Dinner 晚膳
 set 套餐 $ 300-450

■ OPENING HOURS 营业时间
Lunch 午膳 12:00-14:00 (L.O.)
Dinner 晚膳 18:30-22:30 L.O. 21:30

■ ANNUAL AND WEEKLY CLOSING 休息日期
Closed Saturday lunch and Sunday
周六午膳及周日休息

SINGAPOREAN 新加坡菜

MAP 地图 17/A-3

Kok Sen
国成球记

There's always a queue outside this simple coffee shop – join it and hope those already inside are quick eaters. The Wong family have been serving classic Zi Char dishes like prawn paste chicken or bitter gourd pork ribs at various addresses for nearly 50 years – hopefully the 3rd generation of the family will keep things going here for many more years to come. It's run with impressive efficiency, the food is tasty and the prices are friendly.

这里的煮炒菜式十分驰名，店外总有长长的人龙，你只能期待店内的食客快点吃完。东主以家族方式经营餐馆接近半世纪，曾先后迁至不同地址，在现址的是第三代。店内布置简单，食物价格相宜且非常滋味。初次光临的食客可按霓虹招牌上的图片点菜，若茫无头绪不妨试试受欢迎的虾酱鸡和凉瓜排骨。

TEL. 6223 2005
30-32 Keong Saik Road
恭锡路 30-32号

■ PRICE 价钱
Lunch 午膳
à la carte 点菜 $ 15-25
Dinner 晚膳
à la carte 点菜 $ 15-25

■ OPENING HOURS 营业时间
Lunch 午膳 12:00-14:30 (L.O.)
Dinner 晚膳 17:00-23:00 (L.O.)

■ ANNUAL AND WEEKLY CLOSING 休息日期
Closed alternate Mondays 周一不定期休息

INNOVATIVE 创新菜　　　　　　　　　　　　　MAP 地图　18/C-2

Labyrinth

If you want a modern take on Singaporean cuisine, this is your place. Flavours are bold yet authentic – this is innovation without sacrificing tradition – and the presentation is highly artistic. The contemporary dining room, with its local artwork, makes you feel as though you're in on something secret, while the small bar is a great spot for a breezy cocktail and a chance to chat to the keen, well-informed staff about what awaits you.

以创新方式演译的食物，从外观上看易令人生出疑惑，不知所吃为何物，然而品尝一下，风味却传统可口，让你禁不住再三回味。而大厨从祖母身上得到启发、与传统挂不上钩的创意菜凤梨炒饭绝对不是常见的凤梨炒饭:意式蛋黄酱、凤梨雪芭、葡萄干、腰果及米通，食材间的味道与份量调配得刚好，这道菜颇有特色。

TEL. 6223 4098
Esplanade Mall, #02-23,
Marina Bay promenade,
8 Raffles Avenue
莱佛士道 8号滨海艺术中心购物坊 #02-23
www.labyrinth.com.sg

■ PRICE 价钱
Lunch 午膳
set 套餐 $ 58-73
Dinner 晚膳
set 套餐 $ 168

■ OPENING HOURS 营业时间
Lunch 午膳　12:00-14:30 (L.O.)
Dinner 晚膳　18:30-22:30 (L.O.)
Weekends Dinner 周末晚膳
18:00-22:30 (L.O.)

■ ANNUAL AND WEEKLY CLOSING 休息日期
Closed Public Holiday lunch and
Monday 公众假期午膳及周一休息

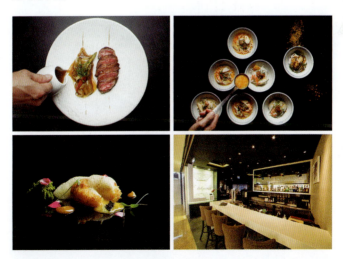

117

INDIAN 印度菜   MAP 地图 8/C-2

Lagnaa

 15

It's up the stairs and off with the shoes to eat at low-set tables in this popular Indian restaurant in the middle of Little India – although there are some regular tables on the ground floor if you prefer. The chef-owner serves dishes from all parts of the country, but you do get to decide yourself on the level of spiciness. Those who like their food particularly fiery can join the Chilli Challenge on full moon nights.

位于印度商店和庙宇林立的小印度区，餐厅有两层，通过木楼梯步上上层餐室，要先脱鞋，狭长的空间布置简洁，罕有地设矮圆桌让客人席地而座，特别且讨人欢心。这里供应南、北印度美食，全是即点即煮，且可选择菜式的辛辣程度。每逢月圆之夜更会举行有趣的Chilli Challenge，测试自己的耐辣程度。

TEL. 6296 1215
6 Upper Dickson Road
狄生路上段 6号
www.lagnaa.com

■ PRICE 价钱
Lunch 午膳
set 套餐 $ 20-25
à la carte 点菜 $ 30-50
Dinner 晚膳
à la carte 点菜 $ 30-50

■ OPENING HOURS 营业时间
11:30-22:00 (L.O.)

FRENCH CONTEMPORARY 时尚法国菜

MAP 地图 1/B-1

L'Atelier de Joël Robuchon

Sharing the same entrance as his restaurant is Joël Robuchon's Atelier. The black and white décor will be familiar to anyone who's tried his other branches around the world. The food is both simple and sophisticated, thanks to a kitchen which treats the ingredients with the utmost respect. All the classics are here: langoustine with basil pistou, caviar on sea bream ceviche, and bone marrow on toast. The set menus represent decent value for money.

与品牌旗下所有餐馆如出一辙的红黑配装潢、柜台式餐桌加开放式厨房，伴随窗边的高脚餐桌与踏脚椅，感觉舒适。这儿的晚饭套餐非常吸引，高品质的烹调水准与食材，实在物超所值!当然，你可以选择单点菜式，还可以因应个人食量或喜好选择分量大小。炸萝勒青酱小龙虾、鱼子酱鲷鱼是此店名菜。

TEL. 6577 7888
Hotel Michael, Level 1,
Resorts World Sentosa,
8 Sentosa Gateway
圣淘沙桥门 8号名胜世界 Level 1
www.rwsentosa.com

■ PRICE 价钱
Lunch 午膳
set 套餐 $ 68-210
à la carte 点菜 $ 170-210

Dinner 晚膳
set 套餐 $ 68-210
à la carte 点菜 $ 170-210

■ OPENING HOURS 营业时间
Sunday Lunch 周日午膳 12:00 -14:30 (L.O.)
Dinner 晚膳 17:30-22:30 (L.O.)

■ ANNUAL AND WEEKLY CLOSING 休息日期
Closed Tuesday and Wednesday
周二及周三休息

CANTONESE 粤菜　　　　　　　　　　　　　　　　　MAP 地图　17/B-1

Lei Garden
利苑

Unlike the other restaurants in the group, this one comes with a more European feel to its decoration, in keeping with the colonial style of the building which hosts it. What isn't different from the other branches is the menu content – so expect authentic Cantonese dishes prepared with care and good quality dim sum at lunch. It's certainly worth ordering the roasted meats and the double-boiled soups in advance.

此店的室内设计有别于集团一贯的中国风，为了与所在的殖民地建筑物互相融合，布置装潢均充满欧陆气息。然而，餐单上的菜式却与集团其他分店没什分别，食物的味道是一贯的正宗，建议预订粤式烧味和炖汤。午市点心同样吸引。

TEL. 6339 3822
#01-24 Chijmes, 30 Victoria Street
维多利亚街 30 号 #01-24 Chijmes

■ PRICE 价钱
Lunch 午膳
à la carte 点菜 $ 30-90
Dinner 晚膳
à la carte 点菜 $ 30-90

■ OPENING HOURS 营业时间
Lunch 午膳　11:30-14:00 (L.O.)
Dinner 晚膳　18:00-22:00 (L.O.)

■ ANNUAL AND WEEKLY CLOSING 休息日期
Closed 3 days Lunar New Year
农历新年 3 天休息

120

Dreams Get Closer
With Platinum

From the big dreams which set your heart racing, to the small ones that put a smile onto the face of a young child, Platinum makes them all possible.

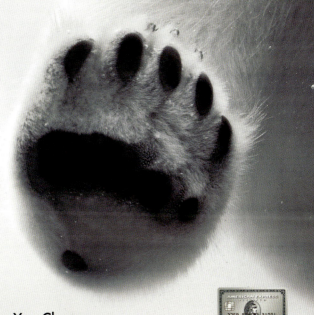

Bringing You Closer

By invitation only. Call 6298 2635 or
e-mail us at PlatCard@aexp.com to express your interest.

FRENCH 法国菜 　　　　　　　　　　　　　　　　MAP 地图　6/B-2

Les Amis

Thanks to continual reinvestment, Les Amis is as good looking today as it was when it opened in 1994. This singularly sophisticated and world renowned restaurant is spread over two storeys and run with impeccable attention to detail. The set menus offer classical French cuisine with the occasional Asian influence; signature dishes include caviar on angel hair pasta, and lobster rouelle. The stunning wine list is one of the best in Asia.

满目的艺术品和画作、华丽的天鹅绒墙壁、天花上垂落的水晶吊灯，加上专业优雅的服务，营造了惬意浪漫的环境。法籍主厨曾于法国和香港工作，擅于展示时令食材的天然风味，且巧妙地将法国传统和日式风格融合于菜式上，招牌菜包括鱼子酱天使面及暖龙虾慕丝卷。餐酒选择广，在亚洲餐厅难得一见。

TEL. 6733 2225
Shawn Centre, #01-16, 1 Scotts Road
史各士路 1 号邵氏中心 #01-16
www.lesamis.com.sg

■ PRICE 价钱
Lunch 午膳
set 套餐 $ 55-145
Dinner 晚膳
set 套餐 $ 170-285

■ OPENING HOURS 营业时间
Lunch 午膳　12:00-14:00 (L.O.)
Dinner 晚膳　19:00-21:30 (L.O.)

121

FRENCH CONTEMPORARY 时尚法国菜   MAP 地图 17/B-1

Lewin Terrace

In an appealingly leafy spot in Fort Canning Park you'll find this attractive colonial-style bungalow, built in 1908 for the eponymous Mr Lewin, the then chief of the Central Fire Station. Its cool white interior is a good spot for lunch, while the pleasant veranda is a better choice at night. The menus offer Japanese ingredients and precision, blended with both classic and modern French cuisine. This results in colourful dishes with delicate flavours.

位于绿树成荫的福康宁公园内,建于1908年,此小平房充满殖民时代气息。由富经验的日籍大厨设计与烹调,选用日本食材,结合细腻的法国烹调技术和日本创意元素制作的小菜,虽有个别不常见的食材配搭,但色彩鲜艳、味道独特可口。午市的梅套餐和晚市的赏味套餐最能让你体验法日相融的独特风味。

TEL. 6338 4868
21 Lewin Terrace, Fort Canning Park
福康宁公园 Lewin Terrace
www.lewinterrace.com.sg

■ PRICE 价钱
Lunch 午膳
set 套餐 $ 38-58
à la carte 点菜 $ 68-121
Dinner 晚膳
set 套餐 $ 108-168
à la carte 点菜 $ 68-121

■ OPENING HOURS 营业时间
Lunch 午膳   12:00-14:00 (L.O.)
Dinner 晚膳 18:30-21:30 (L.O.)

CANTONESE 粤菜

MAP 地图 6/B-2

Li Bai
李白

Impeccable service and opulent surroundings are not the only attributes of the Cantonese restaurant on the lower lobby level of the Sheraton Towers hotel – the food is good too. The emphasis is on authentic, fresh flavours and the menu, which is not overly long, is complemented at lunch by an appealing selection of dim sum. Signature dishes include deep-fried Hong Kong silver fish with salt and pepper, and poached fresh prawn with black fungus.

华丽的室内布置、无可挑剔的服务，令这中菜厅尽显气派。这里提供传统美味的广东菜肴，来自香港的总厨钟光明师傅注重食材素质，并竭尽所能突显材料的鲜美。餐单虽称不上包罗万象，但点心选择不容错过。如要到喜来登酒店用膳，这里是不二之选，招牌菜包括椒盐银鱼和云耳胜瓜浸鲜虾。

TEL. 6839 5623
Sheraton Hotel, Lower Lobby Level,
39 Scotts Road
史各士路 39号喜来登酒店大堂楼层
www.sheratonsingapore.com

SPECIALITIES TO PRE-ORDER 预订食物
Double-boiled winter melon with shrimp, chicken, duck, bamboo, conpoy and crabmeat 八宝冬瓜盅 / Mini bird's nest budha jumps over the wall 迷你燕窝佛跳墙 / Baked fortune chicken 富贵鸡

■ PRICE 价钱
Lunch 午膳
set 套餐 $ 48-148
à la carte 点菜 $ 40-200
Dinner 晚膳
set 套餐 $ 48-148
à la carte 点菜 $ 40-200

■ OPENING HOURS 营业时间
Lunch 午膳 11:30-15:00 L.O. 14:30
Dinner 晚膳 18:30-23:00 L.O. 22:30

STEAKHOUSE 扒房

MAP 地图　18/C-1

Long Bar Steakhouse

Adjacent to the renowned Long Bar is this steakhouse, which opened in 2000 and comes with a large open kitchen. The Mauritian head chef merges the boldness and vitality of his culture with the traditions and precision of classic French cuisine. Expect grilled prime cuts of Australian and US beef cooked to your liking, along with assorted high quality seafood and shellfish, all accompanied by an extensive selection of Old and New World wines.

餐厅于2000年开业，毗邻世界驰名的Long Bar。餐厅内的大型开放式厨房让食客尽览烹调过程。来自毛里求斯的主厨将其文化的充沛生机与法式厨艺的细致完美融合，提供各式大分量的澳式和美式牛肉、海鲜和冷热开胃菜。酒单网罗新旧世界级葡萄酒。

TEL. 6412 1816
Raffles Hotel, 1 Beach Road
美芝路1号莱佛士酒店

■ PRICE 价钱
Lunch 午膳
à la carte 点菜 $ 110-230
Dinner 晚膳
à la carte 点菜 $ 110-230

■ OPENING HOURS 营业时间
18:00-22:30 (L.O.)

■ ANNUAL AND WEEKLY CLOSING 休息日期
Closed Tuesday and Wednesday
周二及周三休息

THAI 泰国菜

MAP 地图　18/D-2

Long Chim

David Thompson is the man who brought royal Thai cuisine to a wider public with his restaurant Nahm, but here at his Singaporean outpost it is Thai 'street' food that he celebrates. It's a young, vibrant spot with the busy open kitchen adding to the bustle, noise and atmosphere; the cocktails are good and the street art all part of the charm. Along with favourites like chicken green curry are dishes like grilled eggplant with dried prawns.

深棕色的木天花、木地板、木椅子餐桌，昏黄的灯光，回廊上的涂鸦及开放式厨房，装潢时尚且富情调，气氛欢闹活泼，令人心情也随之愉快起来！以供应正宗泰国面食和小吃为主。青咖喱鸡的鸡块鲜嫩多汁、油分充足，十分美味。烤茄子鸡蛋沙拉，上桌时茄子余温仍在，质厚肉滑，煞是可口。这儿的鸡尾酒素质也不错。

TEL. 6688 7299
The Shoppes at Marina Bay Sands,
Atrium 2, #02-02, 10 Bayfront Avenue
贝弗兰道10号金沙酒店
金沙购物中心中庭 #02-02
www.longchim.com.sg

■ PRICE 价钱
Lunch 午膳
set 套餐 $ 88
à la carte 点菜 $ 90-180
Dinner 晚膳
set 套餐 $ 88
à la carte 点菜 $ 90-180

■ OPENING HOURS 营业时间
Lunch 午膳　11:30-14:30 (L.O.)
Dinner 晚膳　17:30-23:00 (L.O.)

125

STEAKHOUSE 扒房   MAP 地图   17/B-3

Luke's (Gemmill Lane)

There may be a branch in Orchard Road but this is their true home. Kick off with a cocktail at the attractive marble-topped bar before getting comfortable in the clubby, classically decorated restaurant with its leather seats and wood panelling. Crisp linen on the table and efficient staff complete the picture. The oysters, lobster and steaks are imported from the USA – with such good ingredients and accurate cooking it's hard to fault the end result.

大理石面酒吧台、长皮椅、木板墙、百叶窗、明亮的桌布及制服,是典型的俱乐部式扒房。蟹肉饼、牛肉他他、龙虾、生蚝……食材全由美国进口。优质的食材,虽经长时间运送,但品质不光没受影响,在厨师精湛的厨艺下更是美味可口。优秀的烹调功夫,要论本地最优秀扒房,这间餐馆便是其一。

TEL. 8125 5256
22 Gemmill Lane
仁美巷 22号
www.lukes.com.sg

■ PRICE 价钱
Lunch 午膳
à la carte 点菜 $ 85-180
Dinner 晚膳
à la carte 点菜 $ 85-180

■ OPENING HOURS 营业时间
Lunch 午膳 12:00-15:00 (L.O.)
Dinner 晚膳 18:00-23:45 (L.O.)

■ ANNUAL AND WEEKLY CLOSING 休息日期
Closed Sunday 周日休息

CANTONESE 粤菜　　　　　　　　　　　　　　MAP 地图　17/A-3

Majestic
大華

🍴🍴　　　　　　　　　　　　　　　　🍽 30　📞

As it's located within the boutique New Majestic hotel it's no surprise this Cantonese restaurant is contemporary in both its look and cuisine. The kitchen uses modern techniques and some unusual combinations to add its own twists but, that being said, it's experienced enough to respect the culinary traditions of this historic cuisine. Specialities include braised lobster in a milk and lime sauce, and oven baked sea-perch in a champagne sauce.

时尚的设计，配衬少許中式布置，从餐馆的装潢能窥见這兒供應的菜式特点：以传统食材结合现代烹调及創意配搭，令经典的粤菜透着些微新鲜感。青柠牛奶煨龙虾、香槟焗鲈鱼是这儿的名菜。欲品尝厨师巧手精制、传统却口味新鲜的小菜，由四道菜组合而成的午市套餐可谓不二之选。

TEL. 6511 4718
New Majestic Hotel,
31-37 Bukit Pasoh Road
武吉巴梳路 31-37号新大華酒店
www.restaurantmajestic.com

■ PRICE 价钱
Lunch 午膳
set 套餐 $ 38
à la carte 点菜 $ 50-120
Dinner 晚膳
set 套餐 $ 68
à la carte 点菜 $ 50-120

■ OPENING HOURS 营业时间
Lunch 午膳　11:45-14:15 (L.O.)
Dinner 晚膳　18:00-21:45 (L.O.)

■ ANNUAL AND WEEKLY CLOSING 休息日期
Closed Monday　周一休息

CANTONESE 粤菜

MAP 地图 18/D-2

Majestic Bay
冠華

Among the things to discover in Gardens by the Bay is this Cantonese restaurant just below the popular Flower Dome, which is a great place for families and groups. The fish tanks that welcome you to this large, bright restaurant tell you that seafood is where the kitchen's expertise lies, whether that's their chilli crab or the fun, theatrically flambéed 'Kopi' crab with its notes of coffee. Try too the stewed Mee Sua with baby abalone.

位处观光景点滨海湾花园内，在花穹温室(Flower Dome)下。餐厅接待处水族箱内游来游去的活鱼仿佛在迎接食客，用膳区极为宽敞，落地大窗令餐厅坐拥海湾迷人景致。这里提供粤菜，鲍鱼粒焖面线、潮式粥水蒸白豆腐都值得一试，招牌菜还有咖啡蟹，服务员会在浇有咖啡酒的碟上点火，画面妙趣横生。

TEL. 6604 6604
Flower Dome, #01-10,
Gardens by The Bay,
18 Marina Gardens Drive
滨海花园通道18号滨海湾花园花穹 #01-10
www.majesticbay.sg

■ PRICE 价钱
Lunch 午膳
à la carte 点菜 $ 60-110
Dinner 晚膳
à la carte 点菜 $ 60-160

■ OPENING HOURS 营业时间
Lunch 午膳 11:30-14:30 (L.O.)
Dinner 晚膳 17:45-21:45 (L.O.)

CANTONESE 粤菜 MAP 地图 8/C-3

Man Fu Yuan
满福苑

A comfortable space, professional service and a fairly priced menu combine to make this Cantonese restaurant, within the InterContinental hotel, a good choice. The kitchen brigade has remained unchanged for a long time and is celebrated for a number of its dishes: double-boiled black chicken soup with fish maw and conch; tea-smoked duck; and roasted suckling pig, for which two day's notice is required – the seafood is also always a popular choice.

厨房团队由经验丰富的香港主厨领导。花胶海螺炖鸡汤、樟茶鸭、烧乳猪及海鲜都是这儿无人不晓的名菜。装潢方面，以木地板、米色墙身、中式摆设及柔和的灯光作布置，感觉舒适自然。价钱相宜，侍应的服务态度也专业，是一间不错的粤菜馆。

TEL. 6338 7600
Intercontinental Hotel, Level 2,
80 Middle Road
密驼路 80号洲际酒店 Level 2
www.intercontinental.com/singapore

SPECIALITIES TO PRE-ORDER 预订食物
Roasted suckling pig (2 days in advance) 烧乳猪 (2 天前)

■ PRICE 价钱
Lunch 午膳
set 套餐 $ 48-78
à la carte 点菜 $ 50-100
Dinner 晚膳
set 套餐 $ 88-138
à la carte 点菜 $ 50-100

■ OPENING HOURS 营业时间
Lunch 午膳 11:45-14:30 (L.O.)
Dinner 晚膳 18:00-22:00 (L.O.)

SEAFOOD 海鲜   MAP 地图   2/A-1

Mellben Seafood (Ang Mo Kio)
龍海鮮螃蟹王(宏茂桥)

It may not be in the most convenient location but that doesn't deter the crowds from descending on this open-air space. Nearly everyone is here for one thing: crab. The chef has 15 different ways to cook them, from black pepper crab to creamy butter crab and that, of course, includes the classic chilli crab. There's also live seafood available, along with Zi Char dishes – and the claypot bee hoon soup is delicious.

这里颇受本地人欢迎。晚市设开放式餐室，虽无空调但轻松随意。墙上挂满名人食客签名的螃蟹，鲜艳别致。招牌菜是螃蟹，有多达十五种烹煮方式，除经典的辣椒蟹、黑胡椒蟹和牛油蟹外，不妨试试砂煲螃蟹米粉汤，非常鲜美。也供应每天到货的海鲜和各式本地煮炒菜式。星期六、日及假期不设订座。

TEL. 6285 6762
Blk 232, Ang Mo Kio Avenue 3, #01-1222
宏茂桥道 3号 232座 #01-1222

■ PRICE 价钱
Dinner 晚膳
à la carte 点菜 $ 40-60

■ OPENING HOURS 营业时间
17:00-22:00 (L.O.)

INTERNATIONAL 国际菜 MAP 地图 18/C-1

Melt Café

The buffet has always been a popular concept in the city but not just any buffet will do. Plenty of hotel guests, business types and locals clearly know that the Mandarin Oriental have got theirs right and it's certainly a great spot – you'll find everything from fragrant Indian food to a meaty shepherd's pie or roast zucchini with pesto. At dinner get ready for the live BBQ station; you'll find the vast dessert buffet overwhelmingly appealing too.

偌大的用餐区四周尽是不同国界的美食：香气满溢的印度菜、肉香淋漓的牧羊派、令人垂涎欲滴的烧烤美食……想尝尝法式鹅肝酱?请同时取一片有嚼头的法式长棍面包配合。完结前别忘了逛一逛琳琅满目的甜品区。这里服务周到，难怪食客中除了酒店住客，亦不乏本地人和上班一族。

TEL. 6885 3500
Mandarin Oriental Hotel,
5 Raffles Avenue, Marina Square
莱佛士道5号滨海广场文华东方酒店
www.mandarinoriental.com

■ PRICE 价钱
Lunch 午膳
set 套餐 $68-108
Dinner 晚膳
set 套餐 $68-108

■ OPENING HOURS 营业时间
Lunch 午膳 12:00-14:30 (L.O.)
Sunday Brunch 周日早午餐
12:00-15:00 (L.O.)
Dinner 晚膳 18:30-21:30 (L.O.)

INNOVATIVE 创新菜

MAP 地图   17/A-3

Meta

Sit at the black marble-topped counter to watch the chefs go about their business at this modern, innovative restaurant. The energetic Korean chef is a protégé of Tetsuya Wakuda and his cooking infuses European dishes with strong Korean and Asian influences. Dishes are refined, inventive and make good use of seasonal ingredients; the seafood is largely imported from various Asian countries while the meat comes mostly from Australia.

装潢现代简洁,大部分空间划分为开放式厨房,沿着厨房是黑色大理石铺成的餐桌,顾客边坐在高椅上用餐,边观赏厨房内的烹调细节,倒也趣味盎然。这里只供应厨师套餐,韩国主厨以现代欧陆烹调方法作基础,渗入韩国元素,并选用来自韩国、亚洲和澳洲的时令食材,惊喜处处。

TEL. 6513 0898
9 Keong Saik Road
恭锡路 9号
www.metarestaurant.sg

■ PRICE 价钱
Lunch 午膳
set 套餐 $ 58
Dinner 晚膳
set 套餐 $ 118-150

■ OPENING HOURS 营业时间
Lunch 午膳 12:00-14:00 (L.O.)
Dinner 晚膳 18:00-23:00 (L.O.)

■ ANNUAL AND WEEKLY CLOSING 休息日期
Closed Sunday 周日休息

INTERNATIONAL 国际菜 MAP 地图 6/B-2

Mezza9

When you know you want to eat but aren't sure what you want to eat, there's always Mezza9 at the Grand Hyatt. This restaurant offers nine different 'dining experiences' from Thai to Japanese, grills to seafood – you can sit anywhere you like and order from any of the show kitchens. If you still can't decide then start with a drink – the restaurant also offers the largest selection of martinis in town. Sunday brunch is a veritable institution.

在这家供应国际菜式的餐厅，你能享受到目不暇给的环宇美食，九大开放式厨房提供中西佳肴、烧烤美食、海鲜、泰菜、寿司、甜点和美酒，尽情满足贪吃的味蕾。其中酒吧的马天尼选择于新加坡称冠。星期日的早午合餐供应香槟，门庭若市，即使全场有四百个座位亦座无虚席，建议预先订座。

TEL. 6738 1234
Mezzanine Level, Grand Hyatt Hotel,
10 Scotts Road
史各士路 10 号君悦酒店
www.singapore.grand.hyattrestaurants.com

■ PRICE 价钱
Lunch 午膳
set 套餐 $ 36-64
à la carte 点菜 $ 55-235
Dinner 晚膳
set 套餐 $ 79-99
à la carte 点菜 $ 55-235

■ OPENING HOURS 营业时间
Lunch 午膳 12:00-15:00 L.O. 14:45
Dinner 晚膳 18:00-23:00 L.O. 22:45

JAPANESE 日本菜

MAP 地图　18/C-1

Mikuni

If entertaining for business or pleasure, you can't go wrong at this well-rounded Japanese restaurant – look out for the gently floating noren. The thick tablecloths and plush carpeting keep all conversations to a low murmur. The menu offers a host of choices, from the sushi counter to dishes hot off the robatayaki grill or teppanyaki items. You could go for the 'Grand Tasting Tour' menu with dishes cooked in various ways.

若非入口处闪烁着蓝色霓虹灯，很容易会与这隐藏于食肆中的日式餐厅擦身而过。餐厅以黑色为主调，气氛典雅，毛绒地毯将嘈杂声都化为喁喁细语。餐单选择丰富，从热腾腾的炉端烧、铁板烧以至寿司都应有尽有。欲品尝主厨多变的烹调手艺，可点选Grand Tasting Tour Menu。适合公务或私人聚会。

TEL. 6339 7777
80 Bras Basah Road
勿拉士峇沙路 80号

■ PRICE 价钱
Lunch 午膳
set 套餐 $ 65-120
à la carte 点菜 $ 73-120
Dinner 晚膳
set 套餐 $ 168
à la carte 点菜 $ 104-200

■ OPENING HOURS 营业时间
Lunch 午膳　12:00-14:30 (L.O.)
Dinner 晚膳　18:30-22:30 (L.O.)

CHINESE 中国菜　　　　　　　　　　　　　MAP 地图　6/B-2

Min Jiang
岷江川菜馆

The graceful and immaculately kept Min Jiang has been a celebrated part of Goodwood Park hotel since 1982. It's named after the Min River in Sichuan province and serves dishes from this region, along with Cantonese specialities. Highlights include crispy chicken, sautéed prawns with dried red chilli, hairy crab in season, and hot and sour soup. The restaurant is also well known for its very popular dim sum, served from trolleys at lunchtime.

这里能尝到各式受欢迎的川菜、粤菜和沪菜，招牌菜包括金牌吊烧鸡、宫保虾球、酸辣汤及一系列健康素菜和大闸蟹，午膳时间随点心车出现的广式点心亦不容错过。餐厅以木地板衬托色调柔和的典雅家具，洋溢着现代东方韵味。爱于户外用餐之士可选择池畔旁的用餐区。设有私人厢房，适合商务午餐。

TEL. 6730 1704
Goodwood Park Hotel, 22 Scotts Road
史各士路 22号良木园酒店
www.goodwoodparkhotel.com

■ PRICE 价钱
Lunch 午膳
set 套餐 $ 38-58
à la carte 点菜 $ 40-230
Dinner 晚膳
set 套餐 $ 78-128
à la carte 点菜 $ 40-230

■ OPENING HOURS 营业时间
Lunch 午膳　11:30-14:30 (L.O.)
Dinner 晚膳　18:30-22:30 (L.O.)

JAPANESE 日本菜　　　　　　　　　　　　　　　MAP 地图　6/A-2

Nadaman
滩万日本料理

Nadaman is a long-established Japanese group and their restaurant in Singapore is hosted by the Shangri-La hotel. You can choose to sit in the neatly laid out restaurant, at the sushi counter or at one of the teppanyaki tables for a more interactive experience. The restaurant is known for kaiseki-ryori – traditional, multi-course cuisine – which is the best way to experience the skills of the chefs and the quality of the ingredients.

隶属著名的滩万集团，亚洲区的食客对她也许不会感到陌生。餐厅设有寿司柜台、具现代气息的主要用餐区、能和厨师互动的铁板烧区和私人榻榻米厢房共四个区域。这里以传统怀石料理闻名，虽价格高昂，却保证尝到厨师的高超技艺，食材也是顶级的。午膳套餐或自由点菜是较经济的选择。

TEL. 6213 4571
Shangri-La Hotel, Lobby Level,
22 Orange Grove Road
柑林路22号香格里拉酒店大堂楼层
www.shangri-la.com

■ PRICE 价钱
Lunch 午膳
set 套餐 $ 40-80
à la carte 点菜 $ 60-160
Dinner 晚膳
set 套餐 $ 100-185
à la carte 点菜 $ 60-160

■ OPENING HOURS 营业时间
Lunch 午膳　12:00-14:30 L.O. 14:15
Dinner 晚膳　18:30-22:30 L.O. 22:15

136

NOODLES 面食   MAP 地图 17/B-2

Nam Seng Noodles
南生

Queues stretch down the street at lunchtime, thanks to the reputation of the Leongs, who have run a noodle shop in the city since 1958 – they moved here from Stamford Road a few years ago. Madam Leong, or 'Ah Mah' as she is called, can still be found behind the counter, taking your order and preparing your tray. They offer just six classic Cantonese dishes but they are known particularly for wanton mee, fried rice and venison hor fun.

1958年开业，数年前搬至现址，是狮城有名的面店，由第三代传人掌舵，其祖母、八十高龄的梁老太至今仍然坐镇柜台后方打点一切。餐牌只供应六款经典广东食物，当中以云吞面、炒饭和鹿肉河粉最受食客爱戴。每天午饭时间，长长的排队人龙延伸到街上，为能安心吃上一顿，紧记先占一席位才下单啊！

TEL. 6438 5669
25 China Street
中国街 25 号

■ PRICE 价钱
Lunch 午膳
à la carte 点菜 $ 4-10
Dinner 晚膳
à la carte 点菜 $ 4-10

■ OPENING HOURS 营业时间
08:00-20:00 (L.O.)

■ ANNUAL AND WEEKLY CLOSING 休息日期
Closed Saturday dinner and Sunday
周六晚膳及周日休息

The best way to immerse yourself in local life is by trying street food 🚐. To find great food and local specialities, check out our selection of hawker centres and street food vendors.

品尝道地的街头小吃是了解一个地方生活文化的最佳渠道，让经我们精挑细选的熟食小贩中心及街头小吃推介 🚐 作你的向导，带你品尝最道地经典的小吃，满足你的口腹之欲吧！

Symbols shown in red indicate particularly charming establishments 🏠 XxX.

红色图标 🏠 XxX 表示酒店和餐馆在同级别舒适程度的酒店和餐馆中较优秀。

SINGAPOREAN 新加坡菜 MAP 地图 17/B-1

National Kitchen

Art and sculptures are not the only treasures to be found in the National Gallery – on the third floor you'll find the celebrated National Kitchen by Violet Oon, who is Singapore's own national treasure and one of its most greatest ambassadors. The handsome dark-panelled dining room is an appropriate backdrop to the cooking which, through its spicing, contrasting textures and enticing aromas, memorably showcases Singapore's unique culinary history.

格调高雅的餐厅，墙壁挂满手抄食谱、装裱过的相片和怀旧而富艺术感的瓷砖。由新加坡美食界标志性人物Violet Oon主理，提供传统的新加坡美馔。餐厅坚持亲自调配所有香料、酱料和咖哩，且每天新鲜研磨，难怪每一口食物都完美交织出复杂的香气、质感和层次，令人一试难忘！

TEL. 9834 9935
National Gallery Singapore, #02-01,
1 St. Andrew's Road
圣安德烈路1号国家美术馆 #02-01

■ PRICE 价钱
Lunch 午膳
à la carte 点菜 $ 68-92
Dinner 晚膳
à la carte 点菜 $ 78-142

■ OPENING HOURS 营业时间
Lunch 午膳 11:00-14:30 (L.O.)
Dinner 晚膳 18:00-21:30 (L.O.)

SINGAPOREAN 新加坡菜　　　　　　　　　　　　MAP 地图　2/A-2

New Ubin

As you stand surrounded by auto repair shops, your first thought will be to question whether you've got the right address. Your second will be to wonder whether you've travelled back in time, such is the appearance of the place. But look closer and you'll see a small lounge, a fish tank and a sizeable wine cellar. On offer are mostly Zi Char dishes and seafood, like butter crab, but don't ignore the charcoal-grilled American rib-eye.

餐厅选址叫人生疑，四周满是汽车维修房，其所处的平房以帆布围绕，内里装潢简朴，放满圆桌和塑胶椅，却不搭调地设了鱼池、小酒吧和藏酒量过百的酒柜。不过，包罗万有的餐单才是主角，除了提供地道的海鲜和煮炒菜式，尚包括必点菜炭烤美国肉眼扒。餐厅气氛轻松，适合各式聚餐，且欢迎自携餐酒。

TEL. 6466 9558
Blk 27,
Sin Ming Industrial Estate Sector A
新明工业村 A区 27座

■ PRICE 价钱
Lunch 午膳
à la carte 点菜　$ 10-30
Dinner 晚膳
à la carte 点菜　$ 40-80

■ OPENING HOURS 营业时间
Lunch 午膳　11:30-14:00 (L.O.)
Dinner 晚膳　17:30-22:15 (L.O.)

■ ANNUAL AND WEEKLY CLOSING 休息日期
Closed 2 days Lunar year and Monday lunch 农历新年 2 天及周一午膳休息

FRENCH 法国菜

Nicolas

The eponymous French chef has been quietly going about his business in this comfy and intimate little restaurant for some years now. Choose the Tasting menu to best experience his cooking skills, which are ruddered by classical French techniques and rely on top quality ingredients, like langoustines from New Zealand and pigeon from Brittany. If you want a light lunch he's also involved in Comptoir Soori, the wine bar next door but one.

名称源自法籍东主兼主厨，餐厅已扎根狮城九年。店内有二十个座位和厨房旁的主厨餐桌，餐厅气氛亲密而舒适，厨师执着于选用最佳食材，故不难看到来自纽西兰的小龙虾或法国西北部的鸽子。上乘的材料加上正宗不花巧的烹调方法，成就了经典可口的法国菜肴。Tasting Menu充分展现主厨的烹饪造艺。

TEL. 6224 2404
10 Teck Lim Road
德霖路10号
www.restaurantnicolas.com

■ PRICE 价钱
Lunch 午膳
set 套餐 $ 42-68
Dinner 晚膳
set 套餐 $ 78-98

■ OPENING HOURS 营业时间
Lunch 午膳 12:00-13:30 (L.O.)
Dinner 晚膳 18:30-21:30 (L.O.)

■ ANNUAL AND WEEKLY CLOSING 休息日期
Closed Saturday lunch, Sunday and Monday 周末午膳、周日及周一休息

AMERICAN CONTEMPORARY 时尚美国菜　　　MAP 地图　1/B-1

Ocean

How often do you get the opportunity to eat while watching hundreds of fish swim by? This collaboration between S.E.A. Aquarium and the American celebrity chef Cat Cora is one of the most extraordinary restaurants around. The contemporary Californian cuisine boasts specialities like smoked eel on sunchoke jelly; ikura and shave fennel salad; lobster dumpling; with Mont Blanc for dessert. The set lunch menu offers the best value.

位于S.E.A.海洋馆下层，壮丽的海洋之境，令你目不暇给。位置较隐蔽，可从海洋馆直接进入餐馆，或致电餐馆，让侍应出来为你引路。来自美国的名厨创作多款时尚加州菜，龙虾饺子炸丸子、低温真空慢煮三文鱼等是这儿的著名菜式。财政不充裕却想在如此扣人心弦的环境中享用佳肴，可考虑午市套餐。

TEL. 6577 6688
S.E.A. Aquarium, Level B1M,
8 Sentosa Gateway
圣淘沙桥门8号名胜世界
S.E.A.海洋馆 B1M
www.rwsentosa.com

■ PRICE 价钱
Lunch 午膳
set 套餐 $55
Dinner 晚膳
set 套餐 $98-168
à la carte 点菜 $80-170

■ OPENING HOURS 营业时间
Lunch 午膳　11:30-14:15 (L.O.)
Dinner 晚膳　18:00-22:00 (L.O.)

FRENCH CONTEMPORARY 时尚法国菜

MAP 地图 17/B-2

Odette

     12

What was once the registration room of the Supreme Court is now a very beautiful and sophisticated dining room. But the reason everyone has fought for a table is Julien Royer's cooking. His dazzling culinary creations guarantee an intriguing meal, where the superlative ingredients are cleverly juxtaposed and there's a finesse and elegance to every dish. The glass doors into the kitchen give glimpses of the alchemy within.

当食客置身这高雅的餐厅，透过琉璃观摩厨师们在厨房奋力工作时，难以想像餐厅前身是高等法院的登记处。奉上餐桌的食物同样叫人惊叹，厨师Julien Royer配搭食材的巧思使每道菜都挂满复杂的味道，加上令人拍案叫绝的摆盘设计，带来引人入胜的用餐体验，一分一毫都物超所值，令人想一试再试。

TEL. 6385 0498
National Gallery Singapore, #01-04,
1 St. Andrew's Road
圣安德烈路1号国家美术馆 #01-04
www.odetterestaurant.com

■ PRICE 价钱
Lunch 午膳
set 套餐 $ 88-128
Dinner 晚膳
set 套餐 $ 208-268

■ OPENING HOURS 营业时间
Lunch 午膳 12:00-14:00 (L.O.)
Dinner 晚膳 19:00-21:30 (L.O.)

■ ANNUAL AND WEEKLY CLOSING 休息日期
Closed Sunday and Monday lunch
周日及周一午膳休息

EUROPEAN CONTEMPORARY 时尚欧陆菜　　　MAP 地图　16/C-3

Open Door Policy

In the heart of Tiong Bahru is an appropriately cool restaurant, under the management of Ryan Clift. The menu specialises in contemporary European bistro cuisine and signature dishes include crab cakes with pea salad, homemade pasta, braised beef cheek with black truffle mash and 8-spice apple crumble. The long, narrow room is a blend of the rustic, the contemporary and the funky. The lunch menu is a steal and Tuesday is BYO.

木地板、金属天花、绿色墙身搭红色砖墙，这家四周环绕着书店、时装店、艺廊的餐馆展现出乡村和时尚风味。食物走的是时尚欧陆小馆菜式，法式蛋黄酱蟹饼豌豆沙拉、巧克力开心果梳乎厘是此店名菜。餐馆还有供应自然发酵的餐酒。每逢周二，食客都可自携餐酒用膳。午市套餐附送餐酒一杯，可谓经济实惠。

TEL. 6221 9307
19 Yong Siak Street
永锡街19号
www.odpsingapore.com

■ **PRICE** 价钱
Lunch 午膳
set 套餐 $ 35
à la carte 点菜 $ 62-75
Dinner 晚膳
set 套餐 $ 62
à la carte 点菜 $ 62-75

■ **OPENING HOURS** 营业时间
Lunch 午膳　12:00-14:30 (L.O.)
Brunch Saturday and Sunday 周末早午合餐
11:00-15:00 (L.O.)
Dinner 晚膳　18:00-22:00 (L.O.)

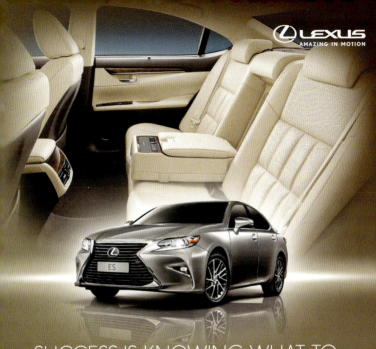

SUCCESS IS KNOWING WHAT TO REFINE OVER TIME, WHILE STAYING TRUE TO YOURSELF.

THE LEXUS ES. THE ESSENCE OF LUXURY.

As your equal, the Lexus ES takes the art of refinement to new levels. All made possible with 12 Lexus master craftsmen – or Takumi – who possess the level of skill and precision that makes every Lexus ES a masterpiece of refinement and luxury. Experience it all with rear seat controls, air-conditioned seats, front passenger shoulder switch and blind spot monitor – just a few of the indulgences a refined individual like you can enjoy. With the Lexus ES, success speaks for itself.

◊ Fuel consumption: 5.5 - 8.0L/100km

◊ CO_2 emissions: 130 - 188g/km

Available in 2.5-litre ES 250 and ES Hybrid models.
Call 66-31-1388 or visit the Lexus Boutique at 33 Leng Kee Road. **Lexus.com.sg**

CLASSIC
— FINE FOODS —

PARTNER OF PASSIONATE CHEFS

7a Chin Bee Drive 619858 SINGAPORE
Ph: +65 6501 5555 – Fax: +65 6501 5556
Email: info@classic.com.sg

INTERNATIONAL 国际菜

Open Farm Community

MAP 地图 5/B-3

It's all about nature and locally sourced, seasonal ingredients at this single-storey glasshouse, which is surrounded by a beautiful garden where many of the herbs and plants for the kitchen come from. The restaurant is bright and colourful and the kitchen, under the guidance of Ryan Clift of Tippling Club, uses influences and flavours from around the world. Come in a group – the place is always full of life and there's usually plenty of noise.

餐厅于2015年夏天开业，坐落于绿意盎然的花园，自然光透过琉璃外墙透入室内，明亮缤纷的环境、开放式厨房和别具风格的桌椅，营造了舒适的用餐环境。食客可坐于室外大阳伞下酌饮一番。提供的环宇美食均选用本地或马来西亚的时令农作物，或花园里的香草植物。气氛友善但较嘈杂，适合聚餐。

TEL. 6471 0306
130E Minden Road
民登路 130E号
www.openfarmcommunity.com

■ PRICE 价钱
Lunch 午膳
à la carte 点菜 $ 55-75
Dinner 晚膳
à la carte 点菜 $ 55-75

■ OPENING HOURS 营业时间
Lunch 午膳　12:00-16:30 (L.O.)
Dinner 晚膳　18:00-22:00 (L.O.)

AUSTRALIAN CONTEMPORARY 时尚澳洲菜

MAP 地图   1/A-1

Osia
澳西亚

"Every dish has a story to tell" is how the young chef, under the direction of Scott Webster, describes his cuisine. The creative dishes use prime produce from Australia and Asia and the chefs in their open kitchen take centre stage in the light, modern dining room. Start with ceviche before moving on to main courses like sea perch with soy milk curd, grilled Grainge Black Angus beef, or Byron Bay Berkshire pork chops cooked in the stone hearth oven.

油封挪威Fjord trout兰姆酒果冻、味噌鲈鱼、牛肝菌红酒煮安格斯牛排、Valrhona巧克力黑胡椒冰淇淋……年轻的新加坡厨师说，每道菜式都是一个故事。这儿的用料选材非常严谨，食材全经过澳洲主厨悉心挑选，主要来自澳洲和环太平洋地区。餐酒单内供应的酒品约有二百款包含新、旧世界品种的葡萄酒。

TEL. 6577 6560
Resorts World Sentosa, Level 2,
8 Sentosa Gateway
圣淘沙桥门8号名胜世界梦之湖沿石级上
www.rwsentosa.com

■ PRICE 价钱
Lunch 午膳
set 套餐 $ 45-135
Dinner 晚膳
set 套餐 $ 85-135
à la carte 点菜 $ 80-150

■ OPENING HOURS 营业时间
Lunch 午膳 12:00-14:30 (L.O.)
Dinner 晚膳 18:00-22:00 (L.O.)

■ ANNUAL AND WEEKLY CLOSING 休息日期
Closed Wednesday 周三休息

ITALIAN 意大利菜　　　　　　　　　　　　MAP 地图　17/B-3

Otto

Authentic and recognisable dishes from across Italy draw plenty of customers to this well-regarded, well-established and comfortable Italian restaurant that's proven a good fit with the CBD. The various pasta dishes are not to be missed, as are the ossobuco and suckling pig; a truffle menu is offered in season and the lunch menu is great value. To accompany it all is a well-chosen wine list sourced entirely from Italy.

位处中央商业区,时尚具气派的装潢,邀约合作伙伴到此聚餐也不失礼。然而,公事其次,品尝美食才是重点。意国厨师烹调的经典意大利菜风味正宗,炖小牛肘、烤乳猪、卡帕奇奥牛肉等不可不试。在特定的季节里,会推出一些特别餐单如松露菜式。美酒配佳肴,这儿供应的红酒全部从意大利进口,品质俱佳。

TEL. 6227 6819
32 Maxwell Road
麦士威路 32 号
www.ottoristorante.com.sg

■ PRICE 价钱
Lunch 午膳
set 套餐　$ 38-138
à la carte 点菜　$ 71-120
Dinner 晚膳
set 套餐　$ 138
à la carte 点菜　$ 71-120

■ OPENING HOURS 营业时间
Lunch 午膳　12:00-14:30 (L.O.)
Dinner 晚膳　18:30-22:30 (L.O.)

■ ANNUAL AND WEEKLY CLOSING 休息日期
Closed Saturday lunch and Sunday
周六午膳及周日休息

SEAFOOD 海鲜   MAP 地图 18/C-2

Palm Beach Seafood
棕榈滩海鲜

Food, theatre and Singaporean hospitality combine to make this longstanding restaurant a favourite with many. Tables of families come for the great views, alfresco dining options and fish fresh out of the aquariums – and, of course, for the gloriously messy Chilli Crab. There are over 100 items on the menu – you can choose the mode of cooking for your chosen fish and be sure to have your greens because they will also be a highlight.

欣赏窗外壮美的景色前，你可先到鱼池挑选喜欢的生猛海鲜，并选定喜爱的烹调法，然后才回到座位静待即选即烹的海产菜式上场。这是一家历史悠久、受大众欢迎的餐厅，餐单有多达百项选择，招牌菜有辣椒蟹，亦供应时蔬、饭面和甜品。其中潮洲蒸鱼和松菇芦笋都值得一试。

TEL. 6336 8118
One Fullerton, #01-09,
1 Fullerton Road
浮尔顿路 1 号浮尔顿一号 #01-09
www.palmbeachseafood.com

■ PRICE 价钱
Lunch 午膳
à la carte 点菜 $ 80-160
Dinner 晚膳
à la carte 点菜 $ 100-250

■ OPENING HOURS 营业时间
Lunch 午膳 12:00-14:30 (L.O.)
Dinner 晚膳 17:30-23:00 (L.O.)

148

CANTONESE 粤菜　　　　　　　　　　　　　　MAP 地图　18/C-1

Peach Blossoms
鸿桃轩

The location on the 5th floor of a busy, unremarkable hotel may not be its greatest selling point but this is a sophisticated and comfortable Cantonese restaurant worth seeking out. The set menus offer the best option for enjoying their authentic cuisine – do try their terrific double-boiled soups like sea whelk with dendrobium herb, or almond with fish maw. To accompany the food is an equally appealing menu of teas.

这位处酒店内的餐厅颇得食客欢心，餐单上是选择丰富的经典广东菜肴，其中杏汁炖花胶汤、石斛花菇炖海螺等炖汤都值得一试。若令人垂涎的食物未够吸引，花样繁多的茶饮选择可会叫你动心？以狮峰龙井或田七花茶搭配一桌子美肴，绝对是赏心乐事。服务细心有礼。不同价格的套餐适合各式聚会。

TEL. 6845 1118
Marina Mandarin Hotel, Level 5,
6 Raffles Boulevard, Marina Square
莱佛士林荫道6号滨海广场
滨华大酒店 Level 5
www.meritushotels.com/marina-mandarin-singapore/

■ PRICE 价钱
Lunch 午膳
à la carte 点菜 $ 75-100
Dinner 晚膳
à la carte 点菜 $ 88-122

■ OPENING HOURS 营业时间
Lunch 午膳　12:00-14:30 (L.O.)
Dinner 晚膳　18:30-22:30 (L.O.)

149

Don't confuse the rating ✗ with the Stars ✲! The first defines comfort and service, while Stars are awarded for the best cuisine.

千万别混淆了餐具 ✗ 和星星 ✲ 图标！餐具图标表示该餐厅的舒适程度和服务素质，而星星图标代表的是食物素质和味道非常出色而获授予米其林星级的餐馆。

An important business lunch? The symbol ⇔ indicates restaurants with private rooms.

需要一个合适的地点享用商务午餐？可从注有这个 ⇔ 图标的餐厅中选一家有私人厢房且合你心意的餐馆。

CANTONESE 粤菜

MAP 地图 19/A-2

Peony Jade (Keppel)
玉河畔（吉宝）

You don't need to be a member of Keppel Club to visit its Cantonese restaurant. In a large room with beams, dark wood panelling and hanging red lanterns, you'll find food that's full of flavour, carefully prepared and reasonably priced. On the dim sum lunch menu, the hot and sour meat dumplings and pan-fried radish cake with preserved meat are a must. On the main menu try the deep-fried prawns with creamy egg yolk along with some Sichuan dishes.

香软奶皇流沙包、京川饺子、腊味煎萝葡糕、鲜虾腐皮卷、脆皮明虾角、京都排骨……全是光听名字便会令你口角垂涎的经典粤式美食，也是主厨的拿手菜。木梁天花、红红的灯笼、绘有国画的中式屏风和红木中式家俱摆设，带有浓浓中国风的设计，让你不论在味觉还是视觉上都能饱尝传统的味道。

TEL. 6276 9138
Keppel Club, M level,
10 Bukit Chermin Road
武吉慈明路 10号 Keppel Club M Level
www.peonyjade.com

■ PRICE 价钱
Lunch 午膳
set 套餐 $ 39
à la carte 点菜 $ 40-100
Dinner 晚膳
set 套餐 $ 68
à la carte 点菜 $ 40-100

■ OPENING HOURS 营业时间
Lunch 午膳　11:00-14:30 (L.O.)
Dinner 晚膳　18:00-22:30 (L.O.)

INDIAN 印度菜　　　　　　　　　　　　　MAP 地图　18/D-2

Punjab Grill

Getting noticed when you're located on the food court level of the Marina Bay Sands isn't easy but this smart Indian restaurant has managed to build up quite a following. Its gleaming glass and metal décor and the polished service have certainly helped but it is the North West specialities that have really cemented its reputation. The kitchen's talent is evident even in the everyday dishes like their wonderfully flavoursome sarson da saag.

餐厅内的装饰闪闪生光，装有不同颜色香料的琉璃瓶放满四周，穿着丝质印度服饰的服务员来回穿梭，形成高尚的用餐环境。这里供应的北印度菜式同出一辙地精彩，尤其推介sarson da saag(以芥菜和香料制成的素菜咖哩)。餐厅陈列的酒不光是最引人注目的布置，也是不错的佐餐选择。

TEL. 6688 7395
The Shoppes at Marina Bay Sands,
South Podium, #B1-01 A,
2 Bay Front Avenue
贝弗兰道2号滨海湾金沙购物商城 #B1-01A
www.punjabgrill.com.sg

■ PRICE 价钱
Lunch 午膳
set 套餐 $ 45-98
à la carte 点菜 $ 80-120
Dinner 晚膳
set 套餐 $ 45-98
à la carte 点菜 $ 80-120

■ OPENING HOURS 营业时间
Lunch 午膳　11:30-14:45 (L.O.)
Dinner 晚膳　18:30-22:30 (L.O.)

FUJIAN 福建菜　　　　　　　　　　　　　　MAP 地图　8/D-2

Putien (Kitchener Road)
莆田 (吉真那路)

　　　　　　　　　　　　　　　🍴20　🍽

Putian people are known for putting their guests before themselves – and service is certainly friendlier here than in many similarly simple restaurants. Opened in 2000, this was the first branch of this small chain which has another 8 or so shops in Singapore. Dishes may not always resemble their pictures on the menu but are fresh and tasty. Signature dishes include seaweed with mini shrimps, braised pig intestine and stewed yellow croaker.

大概因为店东来自福建莆田、此店对待客人的态度也一如莆田人的待客之道：以客为先并将最好的献上。这里提供的菜式是混合了中国各地风味的福建菜。虾苗拌紫菜、九转粉肠、百秒黄花鱼、药膳竹筒虾全是此店名菜、品味俱佳、是不得不尝的菜式。这家开业于2000年的餐馆，是集团的第一家店子。

TEL. 6295 6358
127-129 Kitchener Road
吉真那路 127-129号
www.putien.com

■ PRICE 价钱
Lunch 午膳
set 套餐 $ 20
à la carte 点菜 $ 26-50
Dinner 晚膳
à la carte 点菜 $ 26-50

■ OPENING HOURS 营业时间
Lunch 午膳　11:30-14:30 (L.O.)
Dinner 晚膳　17:30-22:00 (L.O.)

FRENCH CONTEMPORARY 时尚法国菜

MAP 地图 18/C-1

Raffles Grill

XXXX

In 1899 the entire ground floor of the main hotel building was given over to dining; in 1923 a section was set aside as a Grill Room. A meal here offers a beguiling reminder of why Raffles is such a famous name and the immaculately kept period furnishings add to the appeal, as do the views through the French windows out to the Palm Court. The cuisine is largely French with the subtle addition of some light Asian touches.

餐厅于1899年时属于莱佛士酒店主餐厅的一部分，到了1923年才被划出成为Raffles Grill烧烤餐厅。它保存了闪闪生辉的水晶吊灯和年代家具，偌大的法式窗户让餐厅透进明亮的自然光。这里提供的时尚法国菜揉合了亚洲元素，葡萄酒选择琳琅满目。

TEL. 6412 1816
Raffles Hotel, 1 Beach Road
美芝路1号莱佛士酒店

■ PRICE 价钱
Lunch 午膳
set 套餐 $ 48-58
à la carte 点菜 $ 150-200
Dinner 晚膳
set 套餐 $ 228
à la carte 点菜 $ 150-200

■ OPENING HOURS 营业时间
Lunch 午膳 12:00-14:00 (L.O.)
Dinner 晚膳 19:00-22:00 (L.O.)

■ ANNUAL AND WEEKLY CLOSING 休息日期
Closed Saturday lunch, Sunday, Monday and Public Holidays
周六午膳、周日、周一及公众假期休息

INDIAN 印度菜　　　　　　　　　　　　　　MAP 地图　18/C-1

Rang Mahal

✗✗✗　　　　　　　　　　　　　　　　　♿ 🚗 🍽 12

If you want plush without the fuss, consider this Indian restaurant on Level 3 of the Pan Pacific hotel – the double-height dining room is tastefully furnished, comfortable and contemporary. At lunch go with the flow by joining the dozens of business people here for the impressively bounteous buffet; dinner is the time to investigate the à la carte menu. The kitchen displays a respectful knowledge of the vast repertoire of Pan-Indian cuisine.

餐厅以一条暗暗的走廊和下方透光的印度神像迎接食客，用餐区环境奢华时尚。每天的午膳时间，络绎不绝的上班族会在这里出现，为的是餐厅所供应的印度式自助餐，孟加拉咖哩鱼(Bengali fish curry)、印式羊肉香饭(lamb biryani)等源源不绝地上场，爱吃印度菜的你，可会蠢蠢欲动？

TEL. 6333 1788
Pan Pacific Hotel, Level 3,
7 Raffles Boulevard
莱佛士林荫道 7号泛太平洋大酒店 Level 3
www.rangmahal.com.sg

■ PRICE 价钱
Lunch 午膳
set 套餐 $ 58-78
à la carte 点菜 $ 80-150
Dinner 晚膳
à la carte 点菜 $ 80-250

■ OPENING HOURS 营业时间
Lunch 午膳　12:00-14:30 (L.O.)
Dinner 晚膳　18:30-22:30 (L.O.)

155

FRENCH 法国菜

MAP 地图　17/A-3

Rhubarb

XXX　　　　　　　　　　　　　　　　　　⇔14 ☏¶

Tranquil Duxton Hill is the setting for this smart French restaurant opened by two alumni of Au Petit Salut. Backed by their former employer, they have created an intimate spot with just seven tables and an open kitchen. The sophisticated cooking is deeply rooted in French classical cuisine but subtly and intelligently updated without recourse to gimmicks. To accompany the food is a thoughtfully compiled, predominantly French wine list.

因着大厨Paul Longworth对经典法国菜的热爱，也凭藉他的丰富经验和烹饪天赋，这儿供应的高级精致法国菜味道正宗、忠于传统之馀，还有点不经意的现代风味。细腻的烹调功夫让食物味道的平衡与对比拿捏得恰到好处。葡萄大黄玫瑰乳鸽是此店名菜。悉心挑选过的法国红酒单内全是有名的法国佳酿。

TEL. 8127 5001
3 Duxton Hill
达士敦山 3 号
www.rhubarb.sg

■ PRICE 价钱
Lunch 午膳
set 套餐 $ 42
à la carte 点菜 $ 65-104
Dinner 晚膳
set 套餐 $ 138
à la carte 点菜 $ 65-104

■ OPENING HOURS 营业时间
Lunch 午膳　11:45-14:15 (L.O.)
Dinner 晚膳　18:30-22:00 (L.O.)

■ ANNUAL AND WEEKLY CLOSING 休息日期
Closed Saturday lunch and Sunday
周末午膳及周日休息

SINGAPOREAN 新加坡菜 MAP 地图 12/D-3

Roland
東皇

P 200

In 1956 Mdm Cher Yam Tian created her famous chilli crab and, together with her husband Lim Choon Ngee, opened a small restaurant along the Kallang River. Now occupying a vast space atop a multi-storey carpark in Katong (with a hard-to-find entrance) and run by the second and third generations, chilli crab rightly remains the bestseller. Other dishes to look out for are black sauce prawn, crispy baby squid and pomfret done in two ways.

要数新加坡美食,一定少不了辣椒螃蟹。这道由1956年面世以来一直为人乐道的菜式,原来是原创者(东主祖母)徐炎珍女士为了满足对食物要求特高的丈夫而创作的,谁想到后来竟成了家喻户晓的美食!除了这道有名的辣椒螃蟹,此店其他必吃的特色菜还包括黑酱油虾及双宝花枝油条。

TEL. 6440 8205
Marine Parade, Block 89, #06-750
马林百列中心大牌 89座停车场 #06-750
www.rolandrestaurant.com.sg

■ PRICE 价钱
Lunch 午膳
à la carte 点菜 $ 40-80
Dinner 晚膳
à la carte 点菜 $ 40-80

■ OPENING HOURS 营业时间
Lunch 午膳 11:30-14:00 (L.O.)
Dinner 晚膳 18:00-22:00 (L.O.)

INDIAN 印度菜　　　　　　　　　　　　　　　　MAP 地图　17/B-2

Saha

　　　　　　　　　　　P ⌂12 ◯

Regional Indian cuisine gets a modern makeover. Not only does the kitchen use some untypical ingredients and the occasional unfamiliar flavour combination, it also mixes up methods of preparation, from the traditional to the latest technique. The presentation of the dishes is decidedly contemporary and this modern outlook extends to the look of the room. The hospitable waitresses provide keen and helpful service.

有别于一般印度餐厅，这里的装潢富现代感，以丝绒长沙发、设计时尚的吊灯及大琉璃储酒柜作装饰，予人新鲜感。餐单供应的菜式以北印度菜为主，亦有南印度菜式，均按传统方法烹调，间或选用国际化食材，卖相摩登，令人耳目一新。不懂如何点菜？好客的侍应将乐于给予协助和建议。店内设有私人厢房。

TEL. 6223 7321
National Gallery Singapore, #01-03,
1 Saint Andrew's Road
圣安德烈路1号国家美术馆 #01-03

■ PRICE 价钱
Lunch 午膳
set 套餐 $ 38-48
à la carte 点菜 $ 50-80
Dinner 晚膳
set 套餐 $ 98-168
à la carte 点菜 $ 50-80

■ OPENING HOURS 营业时间
Lunch 午膳　12:00-14:30 (L.O.)
Dinner 晚膳　18:00-22:30 (L.O.)

■ ANNUAL AND WEEKLY CLOSING 休息日期
Closed Sunday dinner and Monday
周日晚膳及周一休息

FRENCH CONTEMPORARY 时尚法国菜

MAP 地图 18/C-2

Saint Pierre

Not only did chef-owner Emmanuel Stroobant move his well-known restaurant to these premises in 2016, he also reduced the number of tables so that he could be sure to check each and every plate as it leaves his kitchen. His accomplished, contemporary cuisine comes with pronounced Asian elements, with much of his produce sourced from Japan. Alongside 'Earth' is an imaginative 'Nature' menu for vegetarians; he also offers a menu for children.

刚于本年初乔迁至现址的店子，座位数目比旧店小，却实是主厨兼东主刻意而为，好让他从厨房走到店面出巡时，能逐一检视每位食客碟子上的菜肴。时尚且有水准的美馔混入了亚洲烹调元素、选用日本食材炮制而成。以素食为主的食客，可选择Nature菜单，此外，还有专为小童而设的菜单。

TEL. 6438 0887
One Fullerton, #02-02B,
1 Fullerton Road
浮尔顿路1号浮尔顿一号 #02-02B
www.saintpierre.com.sg

■ PRICE 价钱
Lunch 午膳
set 套餐 $ 85-100
Dinner 晚膳
set 套餐 $ 158-188

■ OPENING HOURS 营业时间
Lunch 午膳　11:30-14:00 (L.O.)
Dinner 晚膳　18:30-21:30 (L.O.)

■ ANNUAL AND WEEKLY CLOSING 休息日期
Closed Saturday lunch, Monday lunch and Sunday 周六、周一午膳及周日休息

INDIAN 印度菜　　　　　　　　　　　　　　　　MAP 地图　18/C-1

Shahi Maharani

Panels, paintings, sculptures and assorted ornaments help lend an appealingly authentic feel to this Indian restaurant in Raffles City. The menu covers all parts of India and includes dishes inspired by traditional street snacks as well as more sophisticated choices influenced by the kitchens of the maharajas. The best dishes are specialities from the more northerly parts of the country and these include dishes cooked in the tandoor.

这印度餐厅位于地铁站上的商场内，位置极佳。餐厅四周放满充满印度色彩的石雕、木饰和挂画，晚上更可观赏现场传统印度音乐表演，气氛浓厚。餐单以北印度美食为主，选择丰富，不花巧的卖相下是依传统方法烹调而成的美味，其中即场烤制的Tandoor菜式颇受欢迎，令人吮指回味。

TEL. 6235 8840
Raffles City Shopping Centre, #03-21B,
252 North Bridge Road
桥北路252号莱佛士城购物中心 #03-21B
www.shahimaharani.com

■ PRICE 价钱
Lunch 午膳
set 套餐 $ 25-36
à la carte 点菜 $ 30-60
Dinner 晚膳
à la carte 点菜 $ 30-60

■ OPENING HOURS 营业时间
Lunch 午膳 12:00-14:30 (L.O.)
Dinner 晚膳 18:30-22:30 (L.O.)

CANTONESE 粤菜　　　　　　　　　　　　　　　　　MAP 地图　6/A-2

Shang Palace
香宫

The delicate floral theme at this comfortable and graceful Cantonese restaurant within the Shangri-La hotel is designed to add to the impression that you're 'dining in a Chinese garden'. Cantonese cuisine is the mainstay of the menu but there are also Shanghainese and Sichuan influences and presentation comes with some innovative twists. Dishes to look out for include Imperial Beggar's chicken, crispy yellow croaker and stewed lobster noodle.

获誉为狮城最高级食府之一，餐厅以花卉和中式庭园为装潢主题，散发浓浓的东方韵味。主厨将上海和四川元素揉合到粤菜中，卖相令人感到耳目一新。推介菜式有雪花玉佩、金枕头富贵鸡、金棒子外婆东坡肉、姜葱龙虾焖生面和各式点心等等。服务周到，餐酒选择丰富，甚至包括中国的黄酒和烈酒。

TEL. 6213 4473
Shangri-La Hotel, Lobby Level,
22 Orange Grove Road
柑林路 22号香格里拉酒店大堂楼层
www.shangri-la.com

SPECIALITIES TO PRE-ORDER 预订食物
Master Chef roasted lamb shoulder, pickle 功夫明炉烧羊肩 /Imperial beggar's chicken 金枕头富贵鸡

■ PRICE 价钱
Lunch 午膳
set 套餐 $ 48-138
à la carte 点菜 $ 40-250
Dinner 晚膳
set 套餐 $ 68-138
à la carte 点菜 $ 40-250

■ OPENING HOURS 营业时间
Lunch 午膳　12:00-14:30 (L.O.)
Dinner 晚膳　18:00-22:30 (L.O.)

SUSHI 寿司

MAP 地图 18/C-1

Shinji (Beach Road)

Shinji Kanesaka's first restaurant outside Japan occupies a discreet corner of Raffles hotel – so discreet that it may take you a couple of attempts to find the door. This suitably serene space provides a fitting backdrop to his traditional Edomae-style sushi – the counter, carved from a single piece of hinoki, is a thing of beauty. The three set menus at lunch provide an affordable opportunity to try the excellent sushi prepared by his team.

合理的价格是吸引食客蜂拥而至的一大原因，尝过一遍后，寿司的素质就会成为再度光临的理由。餐厅以传统的江户风格设计，环境宁静舒适，熟练的厨师在原木切割而成的寿司柜台后为你准备食物。推介午膳的雪/月/花套餐，各包括汤品、甜品和九至十五件寿司。无论选哪一个，都能尝到最甜美的鲜鱼。

TEL. 6338 6131
Raffles Hotel, #02-20, 1 Beach Road
美芝路1号莱佛士大酒店 #02-20
www.shinjibykanesaka.com

■ PRICE 价钱
Lunch 午膳
à la carte 点菜 $ 75-200
Dinner 晚膳
à la carte 点菜 $ 100-500

■ OPENING HOURS 营业时间
Lunch 午膳 12:30-14:30 (L.O.)
Dinner 晚膳 18:00-22:30 (L.O.)

■ ANNUAL AND WEEKLY CLOSING 休息日期
Closed Sunday 周日休息

SUSHI 寿司　　　　　　　　　　　　　　　　MAP 地图　6/A-2

Shinji (Tanglin Road)

The second restaurant under the aegis of celebrated Japanese chef Shinji Kanesaka is here on the lobby level of the St-Regis hotel. The entrance is typically discreet and leads into an intimate space with seating at the hinoki cypress counter for 18. Three set menus are offered – for a memorable experience the omakase is the best choice. The ingredients are as fresh as can be, with fish flown in from Tokyo's Tsukiji market.

全店装潢雅致朴素，只得十八个座位，食客可观摩厨师的精湛厨艺，食材由东京筑地市场新鲜运到。午膳和晚膳分别设三款套餐，只想吃寿司的话不妨点选有十五件寿司的江户前(Edomae)套餐，否则建议试试Omakase套餐，会带来难以忘怀的味觉体验。

TEL. 6884 8239
The St. Regis Hotel, Lobby Level,
29 Tanglin Road
东陵路29号瑞吉酒店大堂楼层
www.shinjibykanesaka.com

■ PRICE 价钱
Lunch 午膳
set 套餐 $ 125-250
Dinner 晚膳
set 套餐 $ 220-450

■ OPENING HOURS 营业时间
Lunch 午膳　12:00-15:00 L.O.14:00
Dinner 晚膳　18:00-22:30 L.O.21:30

■ ANNUAL AND WEEKLY CLOSING 休息日期
Closed Sunday 周日休息

163

The symbol 🍇 denotes a particularly interesting wine list.

🍇 这个图标表示该餐厅提供一系列优质餐酒。

The best way to immerse yourself in local life is by trying street food 🍜. To find great food and local specialities, check out our selection of hawker centres and street food vendors.

认识一个地方和体验当地文化的最佳渠道是品尝道地的街头小吃，跟着我们的熟食小贩中心及街头小吃推介 🍜 去寻找最经典、最受欢迎的美点吧！

SUSHI 寿司　　　　　　　　　　　　　　　　　　　MAP 地图　18/D-1

Shiraishi
白石

　　　　　　　　　　　　　　　　　　6

Concealed in the shadows of the Ritz-Carlton hotel is this serene sushi restaurant with a counter so soft it feels like velvet. The eponymous chef is chatty yet intense in his demeanour as he prepares the Edomae-style sushi, using fish flown in from Tokyo's Tsukiji Market. There are a number of menu options but it's best to leave yourself in his hands with the omakase, where equal care and attention goes into every ingredient.

餐厅藏身于丽思卡尔顿美年酒店内，位置隐蔽，但值得花时间寻找。热情而健谈的主厨Shiraishi Shinji在金黄色的长木桌后招待食客，这里提供的是传统江户前寿司，每件鱼生都经严格挑选，切割得恰到好处，连主菜外的味噌汤或前菜素质都叫人喜不自胜。有多种套餐选择，但建议交由厨师发办(Omakase)。

TEL. 6338 3788
The Ritz-Carlton, Millenia, #03-01/02,
7 Raffles Avenue
莱佛士道7号丽思卡尔顿美年酒店
#03-01/02
www.shiraishi.sg

■ PRICE 价钱
Lunch 午膳
set 套餐 $ 40-150
à la carte 点菜 $ 60-200
Dinner 晚膳
set 套餐 $ 40-150
à la carte 点菜 $ 100-400

■ OPENING HOURS 营业时间
Lunch 午膳　12:00-14:00 (L.O.)
Dinner 晚膳　18:00-22:00 (L.O.)

165

CHINESE 中国菜　　　　　　　　　　　　　　MAP 地图　6/B-3

Shisen Hanten
四川飯店

The Mandarin Orchard hotel plays host to the first overseas branch of this Sichuan restaurant group from Japan. Crystal chandeliers and high ceilings add a certain grandeur to a room which is perched on the 35th floor – ask for a window table for the city views. The Sichuan specialities include steamed fish with diced hot red peppers and stewed beef in hot pepper sauce – but it is Chen's Mapo doufu which is not to be missed.

为日本四川饭店在国外首间分店。餐厅位于酒店较高楼层，主餐室高耸的天花和水晶吊灯别具气派，两边窗户可饱览城市景色。菜式以川菜为主，如水煮菜式和剁椒蒸鲈鱼等，招牌菜陈麻婆豆腐绝不能错过，此外也提供受欢迎的中国菜如北京烤鸭和广式烧味。设四间私人厢房，建议预订主餐室两边靠窗位置。

TEL. 6831 6262
Mandarin Orchard Hotel,
Orchard Wing Level 35,
333 Orchard Road
乌节路 333号文华大酒店 Level 35
www.shisenhanten.com.sg

■ PRICE 价钱
Lunch 午膳
set 套餐 $ 42
à la carte 点菜 $ 50-100
Dinner 晚膳
à la carte 点菜 $ 50-100

■ OPENING HOURS 营业时间
Lunch 午膳　12:00-14:30 (L.O.)
Dinner 晚膳　18:00-21:30 (L.O.)

INDIAN 印度菜 MAP 地图 8/C-3

Shish Mahal

Don't be put off by the disconcertingly long menu at this modestly decorated Indian restaurant near the impressive Lasalle College of the Arts building, because the food is carefully prepared and full of flavour. Try the North Indian dishes like Mahal Ka butter chicken and the biryanis, or explore the Nepalese specialities such as momo. Vegetarians will also find they have much to savour, with dishes like reshmi saag paneer and gobi matar.

邻近拉萨尔艺术学院，这间装潢简朴的店子，供应的却是道地味美的北印度和泥泊尔美食。从食物的搭配和可口程度，可见厨师对每道菜花了不少心思。Mahal ka奶油鸡(butter chicken)、鸡肉蒸饺子(chicken steamed momo)及素菜系的reshimi saag paneer是不错的选择。想欣赏街道上的景色，可选择露台上的座位。

TEL. 6837 3480
180 Albert Street
亚巴街180号
www.shishmahal.com.sg

■ PRICE 价钱
Lunch 午膳
set 套餐 $ 12
à la carte 点菜 $ 28-50
Dinner 晚膳
à la carte 点菜 $ 28-50

■ OPENING HOURS 营业时间
11:30-23:00 (L.O.)

167

SUSHI 寿司

MAP 地图 18/C-2

Shoukouwa
小康和

A couple of appetisers, four cooked dishes, terrific sashimi and around 13 pieces of wonderful sushi – not only will you leave feeling wholly satisfied and fulfilled, you'll also be fully aware that the ingredients you've just enjoyed were of the highest quality possible. The counter sits just 8 people and you're treated to an expertly balanced seasonal omakase, with fish flown in from Tokyo's Tsukiji market on a daily basis.

精巧细小的店子,设计简约,只有一张寿司柜台。台前设有八个座位,台后是厨师大展身手的舞台。店内使用的食材全是每天从日本筑地鱼市场空运而来,素质高兼非常新鲜。造诣精湛的厨师专注而细心地处理食材,为食客奉上质优味美且最时令的Omakase套餐,高素质的烹调和食材,实在物有所值。

TEL. 6423 9939
One Fullerton, #02-02B,
1 Fullerton Road
浮尔顿路 1号浮尔顿一号 #02-02B
www.shoukouwa.com.sg

■ **PRICE** 价钱
Lunch 午膳
set 套餐 $ 150
Dinner 晚膳
set 套餐 $ 380

■ **OPENING HOURS** 营业时间
Lunch 午膳 12:00-14:30 (L.O.)
Dinner 晚膳 18:00-21:30 (L.O.)

■ **ANNUAL AND WEEKLY CLOSING** 休息日期
Closed Monday 周一休息

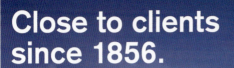

SEAFOOD 海鲜

MAP 地图 16/D-2

Sin Hoi Sai (Tiong Bahru)
新海山(中峇鲁)

Located in a residential area and with over 30 years of history is this well-known seafood restaurant. On offer is live seafood only, from fish to shellfish – customers choose what they want from the tank. Don't miss the famous local choices of chilli crab and black pepper crab; the local Zi Char dishes are also good. You can sit inside or outside – the latter is the more atmospheric and relaxing area.

这家饭馆拥有约三十年历史，位于住宅区内、在两栋楼房的地面层，室内室外均设有桌椅，室外的用餐区气氛较轻松自在。食物方面，此店以鲜活海鲜炮制的菜式驰名，食客可直接从水缸中挑选喜欢的海鲜。当然，别错过本地名菜辣椒蟹和黑胡椒蟹。还有道地的煮炒小菜供应。

TEL. 6223 0810
Blk 55, #01-59, Tiong Bahru Road
中巴鲁路 55座 #01-59

■ PRICE 价钱
Lunch 午膳
à la carte 点菜 $30-60
Dinner 晚膳
à la carte 点菜 $30-60

■ OPENING HOURS 营业时间
11:00-04:00 (L.O.)

169

INNOVATIVE 创新菜

MAP 地图 18/D-2

Sky on 57

Uninterrupted views, a chance to linger late into the night, and delicious fusion cuisine makes the 57th floor of the Marina Bay Sands hotel the place to be. Lunch is always busy, thanks to the number of quick and easy menu options offered. Dinner is a more languid affair – start with a delicious Malaka Mojito before trying specialities like roasted crackling suckling pig or mushroom cappuccino – and don't leave without having the Gula Java macaron.

在这用膳有众多叫人惊喜之处，例如可从高空俯瞰城市的迷人景致，又或令人宾至如归的服务。菜式创新且混合亚洲和西洋元素，设早餐、午餐、下午茶和晚餐时段，午膳提供便捷的商务午餐，经常坐无虚席，建议订座。晚膳餐单的选择较多，例如驰名的脆皮烤乳猪和蘑菇汤，不要错过番石榴马卡龙。

TEL. 6688 8888
Marina Bay Sands Hotel, Tower 1, Level 57,
10 Bayfront Avenue
贝弗兰道10号金沙酒店一号塔 Level 57
www.marinabaysands.com

■ PRICE 价钱
Lunch 午膳
set 套餐 $ 55-98
à la carte 点菜 $ 90-155

Dinner 晚膳
set 套餐 $ 250
à la carte 点菜 $ 90-280

■ OPENING HOURS 营业时间
Lunch 午膳　12:00-14:30 (L.O.)
Weekend lunch 周末午膳　12:15-14:30 (L.O.)
Dinner 晚膳　18:00-22:30 (L.O.)

SINGAPOREAN 新加坡菜　　　　　　　　　　　MAP 地图　17/B-2

Song Fa Bak Kut Teh (New Bridge Road)
松發肉骨茶（新桥路）

Much has changed since Mr Yeo started selling bak kut teh from his pushcart in Johor Road back in the late '60s – nowadays it's the second generation of the family who are running the show. They are still selling their celebrated pork ribs and peppery broth but are now doing so from 5 shops – and this one, the simplest, seems to be the best. Queue, order, pay, and then tuck into your soup – when you've finished they'll top it up for you.

创办人杨先生曾是街头小贩，从1969年起，伴他走过数十载、让他养活妻儿的，是一辆木头车和一碗香喷喷热腾腾的肉骨茶。从木头车到店铺，松發肉骨茶也是我们的共同回忆，现由杨氏长子继承，卖的仍是为人熟悉的肉骨茶和同样美味的鱼汤。店内常常座无虚席，欲寻找回忆中的味道，便要乖乖排队候座。

TEL. 6533 6128
11 New Bridge Road, #01-01
新桥路 11号 #01-01
www.songfa.com.sg

■ PRICE 价钱
à la carte 点菜 $ 10-20

■ OPENING HOURS 营业时间
09:00-21:15 (L.O.)

■ ANNUAL AND WEEKLY CLOSING 休息日期
Closed Monday 周一休息

PAN FUSION 混合菜

MAP 地图 18/D-2

Spago

They may call their cooking Californian in deference to where Wolfgang Puck made his name but that really translates as fusion, with dishes mixing together European, Asian and American influences with clever tweaks and twists. This well-lit restaurant, next to the famous swimming pool on the top of Marina Bay Sands, has a warm, comfortable atmosphere and great views through the French windows of the sea or the city.

位处滨海湾金沙酒店顶层、著名的无边际泳池旁，有两条电梯可前往。设有两个用膳区，木制壁板令餐厅气氛添了几分暖和，大琉璃窗让市内的迷人景致尽收眼底。餐厅由美国星级名厨Wolfgang Puck主理，提供渗入亚洲和欧洲元素的加州菜，食材选料新鲜，并可配搭来自世界各地的佳酿。

TEL. 6688 9955
Marina Bay Sands Hotel, Tower 2 Level 57,
10 Bayfront Avenue
贝弗兰道10号金沙酒店二号塔楼57层
www.marinabaysands.com

■ PRICE 价钱
Lunch 午膳
set 套餐 ＄55-95
à la carte 点菜 ＄98-156
Dinner 晚膳
à la carte 点菜 ＄120-200

■ OPENING HOURS 营业时间
Lunch 午膳　12:00-14:30 (L.O.)
Dinner 晚膳　18:00-22:00 (L.O.)

PERANAKAN 娘惹菜   MAP 地图   17/B-3

Straits Chinese

🍽 30

The owner's family opened Singapore's first Nyonya restaurant in 1953 – this branch has been in the CBD since 2011. Ornaments and wooden furniture lend a Chinese aesthetic. The versatile menu features dishes made with local produce and lots of spices and herbs, all prepared using traditional Chinese cooking methods. Dishes to try include Ayam Buah Keluak (chicken with local nuts) and Ikan Assam Nanas Pedas (sweet and sour fish).

店东家族是本地娘惹餐馆的始祖,其餐厅早于1953年开业。这家位于CBD内的餐厅于2011年营业,内有大量中式木家具和摆设,洋溢着浓浓的东方色彩。菜单选择丰富,厨师以本地食材和大量香料,结合中国技艺煮出传统娘惹风味,味道丰富且具特色。推介以坚果和鸡肉煮成的Ayam Buah Keluak和酸甜开胃的Ikan Assam Nanas Pedas。

TEL. 6225 8683
Keck Seng Tower #B1-01,
133 Cecil Street
丝丝街133号激成大厦 #B1-01
www.straitschinese.com

■ PRICE 价钱
Lunch 午膳
set 套餐 $ 12
à la carte 点菜 $ 25-35
Dinner 晚膳
à la carte 点菜 $ 25-35

■ OPENING HOURS 营业时间
Lunch 午膳   11:30-14:30 (L.O.)
Dinner 晚膳   18:00-21:30 (L.O.)

173

CANTONESE 粤菜

MAP 地图　6/A-3

Summer Palace
夏宫

A sense of calm and serenity pervades this authentic Cantonese restaurant, located within the Regent Singapore hotel, thanks largely to the personable and professional service. The signature dishes include braised baby abalone soup with dried seafood, sautéed fillet of soon hock with seasonal vegetables, and scrambled eggs with caviar and crabmeat. If you've never tried crocodile before, look out for dishes like wok-fried crocodile with asparagus.

这中菜厅的装潢带浓浓中国色彩，金黄、大红等色调尽显富丽堂皇，宽敞的布置予食客宁静而舒适的用膳空间。这里由中国厨师主理，供应味道丰饶多姿的粤菜，包括蒜香百花骨、三翠笋壳球、西柠杏香鸡等等，砂锅鳄鱼掌和酱爆鳄鱼肉更不容错过。

TEL. 67253288
Regent-Four Seasons Hotel, Level 3,
1 Cuscaden Road
卡斯加登路 1号丽晶酒店 Level 3
www.regenthotels.com

SPECIALITIES TO PRE-ORDER 预订食物
Beggar chicken 富贵鸡 /Winter melon soup 冬瓜盅

■ PRICE 价钱
Lunch 午膳
set 套餐 $ 48-178
à la carte 点菜 $ 40-250
Dinner 晚膳
set 套餐 $ 84-178
à la carte 点菜 $ 40-250

■ OPENING HOURS 营业时间
Lunch 午膳　12:00-14:30 (L.O.)
Dinner 晚膳　18:30-22:30 (L.O.)

174

CANTONESE 粤菜　　　　　　　　　　　　　　MAP 地图　18/D-1

Summer Pavillion
夏苑

　　　　　　　　　　　　　　&. 🛁 🍽30 🍇

Start with a cool drink in the Chihuly lounge before you're ushered into this sumptuous dining room which proves the ideal environment in which to enjoy the high quality Cantonese cooking. The polished service and stunning porcelain merit a mention, as does the wonderfully fluid choreography of the tea service. Look out for the roasted duck and the double-boiled sea whelk soup and fish maw which is presented in a whole coconut.

翻新后重开的夏苑，点心异常出色，作为配角的中国茶以典雅多样的瓷质茶具盛载，赏心悦目，每喝一口舌尖都沐浴在如丝般润滑的美茶中，服务员适时添茶，值得一赞。点心以外，椰皇花胶响螺炖鸡汤、北京片皮鸭、大红片皮乳猪或自制参巴酱同样值得一试。不论你以乌龙茶或杨枝甘露作结，都是难忘的体验。

TEL. 6434 5286
The Ritz-Carlton, Millenia, Level 3,
7 Raffles Ave
莱佛士道 7 号
丽思卡尔顿美年酒店 Level 3
www.ritzcarlton.com

■ PRICE 价钱
Lunch 午膳
à la carte 点菜 $ 100-400
Dinner 晚膳
à la carte 点菜 $ 100-400

■ OPENING HOURS 营业时间
Lunch 午膳　11:30-14:15 (L.O.)
Dinner 晚膳　17:30-22:15 (L.O.)

175

SUSHI 寿司　　　　　　　　　　　　　　　　　MAP 地图 6/B-2

Sushi Ichi
鮨一

The silky smooth and tactile counter was fashioned from a 300 year old cypress and the wooden ornaments on the wall were handmade by a celebrated carpenter in Nara. This is about traditional Edomae sushi using seasonal seafood and vegetables all imported from Japan. The rice is cooked with either red or white vinegar according to the accompanying ingredient. As well as the 14 seats at the counter, there is a smaller room for private parties.

餐厅处处尽显细致——长十余尺的餐柜枱以超过三百年的柏木所造，墙上木饰出自奈良名匠手笔，餐单只供应传统寿司套餐，寿司饭按食材分别用红醋或白醋制作，时令海产、蔬菜皆由日本运到，酱汁亦由日本本店调制，以保持味道一致。推介厨师套餐Omakase。主餐室只有十四个座位，小餐室则适合私人聚会。

TEL. 6235 5514
Marriott Tang Plaza Hotel, #01-04,
320 Orchard Road
乌节路320号万豪董厦酒店 #01-04
www.ginza-sushiichi.jp

■ PRICE 价钱
Lunch 午膳
set 套餐 $ 70-390
Dinner 晚膳
set 套餐 $ 220-390

■ OPENING HOURS 营业时间
Lunch 午膳　12:00-14:00 (L.O.)
Dinner 晚膳　18:00-21:30 (L.O.)

■ ANNUAL AND WEEKLY CLOSING 休息日期
Closed Monday 周一休息

SUSHI 寿司　　　　　　　　　　　　　　　　MAP 地图　17/A-3

Sushi Mitsuya

　　　　　　　　　🍽16 🚇 ☎

'Mitsuya' translates as 'three arrows' and refers to the three partners who own this conventional sushi restaurant. The chef comes with plenty of experience in Japan and Hong Kong and a seat at the counter is the place to sit as he is an engaging man happy to explain and demonstrate his skills and knowledge. There are four menus to choose from: 'Shoju', with its various dishes before the sushi, is the one that best shows off those abilities.

店名Mitsuya意即三枝箭，喻意三位合作伙伴团结强大。曾于日本、香港工作的主厨富经验且乐于分享，邻近厨师台的座位是不二之选，亦设两间小厢房。四款套餐中以海味和珠玉最受欢迎，松寿则能充分展现主厨技艺，他擅长将不同食材和个人风格揉合，同时不忘满足食客需要。想喝清酒？店员将乐于协助。

TEL. 6438 2608
60 Tras Street
道拉实街 60号
www.sushimitsuya.com

■ PRICE 价钱
Lunch 午膳
set 套餐 $ 50-180
Dinner 晚膳
set 套餐 $ 100-300

■ OPENING HOURS 营业时间
Lunch 午膳　12:00-14:00 (L.O.)
Dinner 晚膳　18:00-21:00 (L.O.)

■ ANNUAL AND WEEKLY CLOSING 休息日期
Closed Sunday 周日休息

Enjoy good food without spending a fortune! Look out for the Bib Gourmand symbol 😊 to find restaurants offering good food at great prices!

要省钱又想品尝美食，便要留心注有 😊 必比登图标的食店，此类店子提供的是价钱实惠且素质高的美食。

Symbols shown in red indicate particularly charming establishments 🏠 XxX.

红色图标 🏠 XxX 表示酒店和餐馆在同级别舒适程度的酒店和餐馆中较优秀。

JAPANESE CONTEMPORARY 时尚日本菜　　　　　　　　MAP 地图　1/A-1

Syun
春

One should never judge restaurants by their façades but it's hard not to have one's expectations raised by the sight of the sweet little garden at the entrance to this discreet and warmly run Japanese restaurant. The contemporary cuisine comes with lots of modern twists, with dishes like sea urchin rolled in Wagyu beef, and grilled cod with yuzu miso sauce and dried millet powder. Equal thought has gone into the sake list.

进入由黑白石头组成的仿日本花园入口后，是这家布置柔和温暖的日本食店。两位经验丰富的日本师傅合力制作的菜式，融合了富创造力的时尚风味和传统味道，选用的材料亦非常新鲜。和牛海胆卷、西京味噌鳕鱼和寿司盖饭是这儿的名菜。清酒单还包含了厨师推介的生酛酒系列，颇为特别。

TEL. 6577 6867
Resorts World Sentosa, Festive Walk,
8 Sentosa Gateway
圣淘沙桥门8号名胜世界节庆大道
www.rwsentosa.com

■ PRICE 价钱
Lunch 午膳
set 套餐 $ 28-68
Dinner 晚膳
set 套餐 $ 98-168
à la carte 点菜 $ 60-160

■ OPENING HOURS 营业时间
Lunch 午膳　12:00-14:30 (L.O.)
Dinner 晚膳　18:00-22:30 (L.O.)

■ ANNUAL AND WEEKLY CLOSING 休息日期
Closed Monday 周一休息

INDONESIAN 印尼菜　　　　　　　　　　　　　MAP 地图　6/A-2

Tambuah Mas (Tanglin)

🍴　　　　　　　　　　　　　　　　　　🍽24　📞🍴

Founded in 1981, Tambuah Mas specialises in Indonesian home-style cuisine from Padang, Sulawesi, and Java. The look has remained largely unchanged over the years but no one is here for the décor – they come for dishes like sop buntut (spicy oxtail soup), rendang lembu (braised beef) and nasi goreng istimewa (fried rice with prawns, chicken satay and fried egg). The menu is not overlong and the dishes are full of flavour and nicely balanced.

餐厅于1981年开业，吸引食客的并非多年来不变的木餐桌和绿色藤椅，而是餐厅所炮制的印尼巴东菜。菜单选择不算丰富，以巴东经典菜式为主，用料简单但每一道都富含味道，酱汁多加入椰汁以中和辣味。招牌菜有牛尾汤、仁当咖哩和印尼炒饭。十人以上可点选套餐。

TEL. 6733 3333
Tanglin Shopping Centre, #04-10/13,
19 Tanglin Road
东陵路19号东陵购物中心 #04-10/13
www.tambuahmas.com.sg

■ **PRICE** 价钱
à la carte 点菜 $ 18-31

■ **OPENING HOURS** 营业时间
11:00-22:00 (L.O.)

CONTEMPORARY 时尚菜　　　　　　　　　　　　MAP 地图　1/A-1

Tangerine
天滋林

You don't need to be an ESPA customer to enjoy this 'spa restaurant'. Unsurprisingly, its look and feel are very relaxing, thanks to the dark wood and large windows looking out onto nature. The food is all about freshness with few calories and is a blend of East and West; creative dishes include Thai-inspired sous-vide pork, Asian-style sea bass and salsa and 'guilt-free' chocolate mousse. The set menus are reasonably priced and it's open all day.

店子虽在水疗中心内，但也招待非使用水疗中心的顾客。由泰国和本地厨师创作的菜式，不论是选料、配搭和创意上都充满新鲜感。真空低温泰式猪肉(Thai-inspired sous-vide pork)、萨尔萨辣酱沙拉(Asian style seabass and salsa)等是著名菜式。餐牌上印有fit for life、de-stress等标示，提醒食客每道菜的功效。

TEL. 6577 6688
ESPA, Resort Worlds Sentosa,
8 Sentosa Gateway
圣淘沙桥门 8号名胜世界 ESPA
www.rwsentosa.com

■ PRICE 价钱
Lunch 午膳
set 套餐 ＄36-68
à la carte 点菜 ＄50-75
Dinner 晚膳
set 套餐 ＄36-68
à la carte 点菜 ＄50-75

■ OPENING HOURS 营业时间
11:30-21:15 (L.O.)

■ ANNUAL AND WEEKLY CLOSING 休息日期
Closed Monday 周一休息

ITALIAN 意大利菜

MAP 地图　17/A-3

Terra

The food is Italian so don't get confused by the 'Tokyo-Italian' strapline – it refers to the two countries' shared respect for seasonal ingredients. To fully experience the considerable skills of Tokyo-born chef-owner Seita Nakahara it's best to have his 'omakase' menu which may include his homemade bottarga with Hokkaido sea urchin and spaghetti, or roasted scallops with vegetables. The dining room is equally pleasing on the eye.

餐厅口号Tokyo-Italian令人对其菜式产生疑窦，其实是曾在意国工作的年青主厨Seita Nakahara 希望将两地对食材的敬重融合在菜式上，食材均来自日本和意大利，采购不到时会自制。多种元素构成满是惊喜的Omakase餐单，如海胆金枪鱼子手造意大利面，烹调方法简朴却溢满滋味。午间套餐物有所值。

TEL. 6221 5159
54 Tras Street
道拉实街 54号
www.terraseita.com

■ PRICE 价钱
Lunch 午膳
set 套餐 $ 42-58
Dinner 晚膳
set 套餐 $ 128-208

■ OPENING HOURS 营业时间
Lunch 午膳　12:00-14:00 (L.O.)
Dinner 晚膳　18:30-22:00 (L.O.)

■ ANNUAL AND WEEKLY CLOSING 休息日期
Closed Saturday lunch and Sunday
周末午膳及周日休息

SINGAPOREAN 新加坡菜   MAP 地图 18/C-2

The Clifford Pier

Live music, great views, terrific cocktails and a wonderful setting - it's hard to beat this most glamorous of spots. The food honours the hawkers who once lined the pier and who made Singapore such a great food city, so expect traditional fare like spicy chilli clam bowl and prawn laksa. There's also plenty on offer for those not wanting to venture too far outside their comfort zones, with dishes like crispy chicken and salmon tandoori.

餐馆设于码头之上，港湾景色一览无遗，除了食客外还吸引无数游人到此停驻，气氛亦因此而变得热闹。高高的拱型天花、时尚中带点古典味的吊灯，令原已偌大的餐馆空间更为广阔。独泊在一隅的黄包车，提醒食客这儿供应的是传统新加坡美食。辣椒花蛤、龙虾叻沙等风味独到。

TEL. 6597 5266
The Fullerton Bay Hotel,
80 Collyer Quay
哥烈码头 80 号富丽敦海湾酒店
www.fullertonbayhotel.com

■ PRICE 价钱
Lunch 午膳
set 套餐 $ 48-65
à la carte 点菜 $ 67-115
Dinner 晚膳
à la carte 点菜 $ 88-125

■ OPENING HOURS 营业时间
Lunch 午膳 12:00-14:30 (L.O.)
Weekends & Public Holidays
周末及公众假期早午合餐   11:30-14:30 (L.O.)
Dinner 晚膳 18:30-22:00 (L.O.)

INNOVATIVE 创新菜　　　　　　　　　　　　MAP 地图　17/B-2

The Kitchen at Bacchanalia

What is it about an understated glass façade that so often hints at something special inside? The idea here is that there are no barriers between you and the chefs – and with an open kitchen on both sides there's no danger of that. The two chefs worked at the Fat Duck in the UK so are experienced in modern techniques although, instead of theatrics, they often rework classic dishes to deliver the expected flavours in stimulating and original ways.

朴实无华的外观与室内布置、殷勤热情的招待，一如其供应的食物—没有花巧精致的外表，味道与创意的配搭却令人喜出望外。精于现代烹调技巧的厨师，将来自世界各地的食材精心组合，务求在味道、质感和配搭上带给食客新刺激。以全新处理方式制作的经典菜式，在原来味道的基础上更添了点刺激与新鲜感。

TEL. 6509 1453
39 Hong Kong Street
香港街 39号
www.bacchanalia.asia

■ PRICE 价钱
Lunch 午膳
set 套餐 $ 48-150
Dinner 晚膳
set 套餐 $ 65-150

■ OPENING HOURS 营业时间
Lunch 午膳　12:00-14:30 (L.O.)
Dinner 晚膳　18:00-22:30 (L.O.)

■ ANNUAL AND WEEKLY CLOSING 休息日期
Closed Monday and Tuesday lunch, and Sunday 周二午膳、周一及周日休息

ITALIAN 意大利菜　　　　　　　　　　　　　　MAP 地图　18/C-2

The Lighthouse

Great views, warm service and Italian food – for those looking for a romantic meal this is as close to a sure thing as you can get. Be sure to start with a drink on the rooftop to take in the dramatic vista before moving inside to enjoy the familiar Italian fare. The menu pays much attention to the southern coastal regions; the cooking eschews ostentation and instead focuses on what is needed to make a particular dish delicious.

甫步出电梯，映入眼廉的是亲切友善的笑容，若天公造美不妨在入席前到顶层酒吧浅尝一杯，景色醉人。餐厅供应的是质朴传统的意大利风味，在主厨 Sandro Falbo严密的监督下，菜色水准无庸置疑。服务员知识丰富，大量地道的意大利食材、迷人的景致，加起来就是一餐叫人满足的意式盛宴。

TEL. 6877 8140
The Fullerton Hotel, Level 8,
1 Fullerton Square
浮尔顿路 1号富丽敦酒店 Level 8
www.rwsentosa.com

■ PRICE 价钱
Lunch 午膳
à la carte 点菜　$ 68-118
Dinner 晚膳
à la carte 点菜　$ 78-158

■ OPENING HOURS 营业时间
Lunch　午膳　12:00-14:30 (L.O.)
Dinner　晚膳　18:00-22:30 (L.O.)

■ ANNUAL AND WEEKLY CLOSING 休息日期
Closed Weekends lunch 周末午膳休息

INDIAN 印度菜　　　　　　　　　　　　　　　　　　　MAP 地图　6/B-2

The Song of India

　　　　　　　 12

The less-than-convenient location is quickly forgotten when you climb the few steps of this period bungalow and get your first glimpse of the restaurant. The stylish interior and regularly changing Indian artwork add to the appealingly sophisticated feel. The menu features delicacies from across India and the kitchen uses both traditional methods of preparation and more modern cooking styles to create an impressive array of dishes.

餐厅位于一幢殖民时期独立大宅内，踏上梯级，推开大门，你会被餐室内雍容华贵的布置和墙上的精美挂画所迷住。印度各地的美食都可在这所高级印度餐厅的餐单内找到，主厨将现代元素融合到印度传统烹调上，务求给客人不一样的味觉体验。地点不太便利，但环境和食物都令人感到不枉此行。

TEL. 6836 0055
33 Scotts Road
史各士路33号
www.thesongofindia.com

■ PRICE 价钱
Lunch 午膳
set 套餐 $ 30-40
à la carte 点菜 $ 55-125
Dinner 晚膳
set 套餐 $ 49-129
à la carte 点菜 $ 55-125

■ OPENING HOURS 营业时间
Lunch 午膳　12:00-14:30 (L.O.)
Dinner 晚膳　18:00-22:30 (L.O.)

SINGAPOREAN 新加坡菜　　　　　　　　　　　MAP 地图　12/D-2

328 Katong Laksa (Joo Chiat)
328加東叻沙（如切路）

Look out for the colourful façade on busy East Coast Road if you want to try one of the best laksas in town. Nasi lemak and otah are on offer too but really it's all about laksa and the only decision to make is whether you want large or small –don't even think about asking for the recipe because it's a family secret. The 'wall of fame' advertises its many famous clients.

获誉为最美味叻沙之一，此店的叻沙果然不赖！秘制汤汁处理得非常好，香料、鱼肉、鱼饼和椰浆间浓郁的味道发挥和平衡得恰到好处。除了叻沙，还供应椰浆饭和乌打。店子面积虽小，供客人歇脚的只是简单的木桌和胶椅，然而却无损顾客到来品尝叻沙的兴致。贴满一场的名人照片是此店名闻遐迩的明证。

TEL. 9732 8163
51 East Coast Road (Joo Chiat)
东海岸路 51号（如切路）
www.328katonglaksa.com.sg

■ PRICE 价钱
à la carte 点菜 $ 5-10

■ OPENING HOURS 营业时间
10:00-22:00 (L.O.)
Weekends & Public Holidays 周末及公众假期
09:00-22:00 (L.O.)

SEAFOOD 海鲜

MAP 地图　17/B-2

Tian Tian Fisherman's Pier Seafood
天天渔港

Don't be put off by the garish advertising boards – just take a seat on the tidy terrace by the water and enjoy their fresh seafood. The family have been on the quay for over 20 years and Tian Tian is their most recent reinvention. Bamboo clams with garlic, salt and pepper king prawns, and sea bass Hong Kong style are among the popular choices. You can also pick from the live seafood tanks and choose your preferred cooking method.

东主家族在驳船码头经营逾二十载，与相邻的姊妹店相比，这儿的装潢摆设较富现代感，所在地段更优越。香蒜蒸竹蛏、避风塘大虾和港式蒸海鲈也值得一试；也可以从外面自购海产，请厨房炮制成你喜爱的风味。不要让俗艳的广告板破坏了雅兴，在新加坡河岸享受鲜活海产菜式绝对是赏心乐事！

TEL. 6534 1771
73-75 Boat Quay
驳船码头 73-75号

■ PRICE 价钱
Lunch 午膳
à la carte 点菜 $60-110
Dinner 晚膳
à la carte 点菜 $60-110

■ OPENING HOURS 营业时间
11:30-00:00 (L.O.)

DIM SUM 点心　　　　　　　　　　　　　　　MAP 地图　7/B-3

Tim Ho Wan (Plaza Singapura)
添好運 (Plaza Singapura)

　　　　　　　　　　　　　　　　　　　　✦6

Anyone who's been to Hong Kong will know Tim Ho Wan and its celebrated dim sum. It now has a few branches in Singapore but this was the first one to open, in 2013. As with Hong Kong, you can expect to find a queue as it's first-come-first-served, but once seated you're treated to freshly made dim sum made with excellent ingredients. As well as the baked bun with bbq pork, try the vermicelli roll with pig's liver and finish with the egg cake.

这家来自香港的著名食肆于2013年进驻狮城，现已发展至六家分店。邻近地铁站、位处购物商场内的这间店子，是本地首家分店。餐厅不设订位，所以店外不难见到人龙。各式广式点心采用优质新鲜食材制作，价格合理，酥皮焗叉烧包、黄沙猪润肠和香滑马来糕都值得一试。

TEL. 6251 2000
Plaza Singapura, #01-29A,
68 Orchard Road
乌节路 68号 #01-29A
www.timhowan.com

■ PRICE 价钱
à la carte 点菜 $ 15-25

■ OPENING HOURS 营业时间
10:00-22:00 L.O. 21:30

189

INNOVATIVE 创新菜

MAP 地图　17/A-3

Tippling Club

🍽 14

Ryan Clift's discreetly signed flagship restaurant is dominated by a long kitchen counter, which is where most diners choose to sit so that they can engage with the chefs and watch them in action – lunch is a simpler affair so come for dinner to fully appreciate their ability and ambition. They embrace all the latest techniques to produce quite elaborate and exciting dishes with some challenging combinations of flavour and texture.

Ryan Clift麾下餐厅的旗舰店，以精细的烹调技术为立店之本。厨房团队紧贴烹饪潮流，采用最新烹调方式制作菜式，精致与创意兼备，为食客带来味觉与质感的冲击。长长的餐柜台让厨师的烹调过程一览无遗。邻房为环境舒适的酒吧，为客人提供多款实验鸡尾酒，要找一款合你口味的鸡尾酒并不困难。

TEL. 6475 2217
38 Tanjong Pagar Road
丹戎巴葛路 38 号
www.tipplingclub.com

■ PRICE 价钱
Lunch 午膳
set 套餐 $ 60
Dinner 晚膳
set 套餐 $ 160-260

■ OPENING HOURS 营业时间
Lunch 午膳　12:00-14:30 (L.O.)
Dinner 晚膳　18:00-22:00 (L.O.)

■ ANNUAL AND WEEKLY CLOSING 休息日期
Closed Saturday lunch, Sunday and Public Holidays
周六午膳、周日及公众假期休息

JAPANESE 日本菜 MAP 地图 17/A-1

Toritama Shirokane
酉玉白金 FUN.

DINNER 1/20/17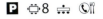

If you're looking for authentic yakitori then this outpost of the Tokyo-based Toritama group is the place to come. The appetite-enhancing aromas hit you as soon as you enter the room. There are 20+ chicken parts to choose from, so the more adventurous eater will find much to excite them. The skewers are grilled over charcoal in the open kitchen in front of the customers, although you're protected from the cooking by a glass shield.

装潢富现代气息，开放式烧烤厨房设在餐厅中央，烤炉与吧座之间有琉璃相间，阻隔了油烟。餐厅提供正宗日式烧鸡串，可选择鸡皮、不同部位的鸡肉、内脏，以至牛、猪等肉食及日本蔬菜，厨师即席以炭火烤制，香气扑鼻，适合亲友聚会。

TEL. 6836 5680
Robertson Walk, #01-02,
11 Unity Street
团结街11号罗拔申廊 #01-02

■ PRICE 价钱
Dinner 晚膳
set 套餐 $27-39
à la carte 点菜 $50-60

■ OPENING HOURS 营业时间
18:00-22:00 (L.O.)

■ ANNUAL AND WEEKLY CLOSING 休息日期
Closed Sunday 周日休息

PERANAKAN 娘惹菜　　　　　　　　　　　　　　MAP 地图　17/B-1

True Blue Cuisine

It's less like walking into a restaurant, more like falling into the warm embrace of a much loved family member. Here it's about nostalgia and paying homage to the food, history and customs of the Peranakans – you'll find all the classic dishes, prepared in an authentic way, and the hard part is narrowing down your choice. The setting really is unique and on the way out it's hard to resist buying a keepsake from the True Blue Shoppe.

创办人兼主厨Benjamin Seck指这儿是活的遗产，餐厅内布置大量怀旧娘惹古董，气氛陈旧，仿如置身某家庭的饭厅之中。作为狮城其中一家历史最长的娘惹餐厅，餐单上是数之不尽的传统菜式，选菜可能会费尽脑力。尝完美味的菜肴，逛逛餐厅外的博物馆和商店，体会浓浓的娘惹风情。

TEL. 6440 0449
47/49 Armenian Street
亚米尼亚街 47/49号
www.truebluecuisine.com

■ PRICE 价钱
Lunch 午膳
set 套餐 $ 32
à la carte 点菜 $ 40-100
Dinner 晚膳
set 套餐 $ 42
à la carte 点菜 $ 40-100

■ OPENING HOURS 营业时间
Lunch 午膳　11:30-14:00 (L.O.)
Dinner 晚膳　18:00-21:00 (L.O.)

DOWNLOAD
THE CHOPE APP

AND MAKE **INSTANT RESERVATIONS** ON THE GO

CHOPE IS THE OFFICIAL RESERVATION SYSTEM
PROVIDER FOR THE MICHELIN GUIDE SINGAPORE

www.chope.co

CHINESE 中国菜

Tunglok Signatures
同樂经典

Good ingredients and authentic flavours make this Chinese restaurant a worthy choice if you're seeking sustenance in The Central shopping mall. It is one of four branches in Singapore and you can choose between Cantonese, Shanghainese and Sichuan dishes. Specialities include charcoal-grilled honey pork shoulder, and crisp fried Sakura chicken. It's a big, busy and keenly run restaurant, with outside tables that provide good views of Clarke Quay.

位处克拉码头地鉄站之上，晚膳时段可选择户外座位，饱览码头的醉人景致。餐厅有四家分店，其餐牌和供应的菜式一样绚烂夺目，在这里可尝到广东菜、上海菜和四川菜。上乘的食材、传统的风味融合厨师的时尚风格，带来讨人欢心的菜式，例如炭烧蜜汁猪肩肉、脆皮樱花鸡等等。服务殷勤友善。

TEL. 6336 6022
The Central, #02-88,
6 Eu Tong Sen Street
余东旋街 6号 The Central#02-88
www.tungloksignatures.com

SPECIALITIES TO PRE-ORDER 预订食物
Barbecued Suckling Pig 烧乳猪

■ PRICE 价钱
Lunch 午膳
à la carte 点菜 $ 42-110
Dinner 晚膳
à la carte 点菜 $ 42-110

■ OPENING HOURS 营业时间
Lunch 午膳 11:30-14:30 (L.O.)
Dinner 晚膳 18:00-22:15 (L.O.)

SEAFOOD 海鲜

MAP 地图 18/C-1

Umi + Vino

Embedded within an 'integrated Japanese Emporium' is this seafood and wine bar, whose menu is similar to the type you'd find in a typical New England-style seafood shack – even the location at Marina Square can seem a little like Boston Harbor! Scallops, oysters, crudo and items cooked a la plancha are offered, to be accompanied by perfectly paired wines. It's worth ordering the pièce de résistance – the seafood platter.

这西餐厅设于日式食店云集的日式综合食品杂货店Emporium Shokuhin内，故显得与别不同。餐厅提供揉合英伦和美国风格的海鲜菜式，生蚝选择极为丰富，带子和其他贝壳类海产亦值得一试。餐单列出适合各类别菜式的餐酒，配搭别出心裁。

TEL. 6812 2175
Marina Square, #01-18,
6 Raffles Boulevard
莱佛士林荫道6号滨海广场 #01-18
www.emoriumshokuhin.com.sg

■ PRICE 价钱
Lunch 午膳
à la carte 点菜 $ 60-158
Dinner 晚膳
à la carte 点菜 $ 70-158

■ OPENING HOURS 营业时间
11:30-22:00 (L.O.)

194

CANTONESE 粤菜

MAP 地图 17/B-1

Wah Lok
華樂

     P   🍽36   📞

A loyal clientele have made this comfortable, classically decorated Cantonese restaurant their own. The chef was born in Guangzhou but really developed his culinary skills and honed his craft in Hong Kong. His Cantonese dishes range from banquet delicacies like abalone and bird's nest soup to seafood dishes such as steamed fish. There are also Guangdong roast meats, claypot dishes and home-style dishes like steamed mined pork with salted fish.

華樂是本地很受欢迎的粤菜馆之一，设于酒店主楼座的二楼，设计富现代感的餐室非特别豪华却讨人欢喜。原籍广州的大厨于香港学艺，餐单提供种类繁多的广东菜，无论是宴席菜式如鲍鱼燕窝，海鲜菜式如蒸海鱼，以至别具风味的煲仔菜、广东烧味和家常菜式，都让你品尝到正宗的粤菜口味。

TEL. 6311 8188
Carlton Hotel, 76 Bras Basah Road
勿拉士峇沙路 76号卡尔登酒店

■ PRICE 价钱
Lunch 午膳
à la carte 点菜 $ 50-120
Dinner 晚膳
à la carte 点菜 $ 50-120

■ OPENING HOURS 营业时间
Lunch 午膳　11:30-14:15 (L.O.)
Dinner 晚膳　18:00-22:15 (L.O.)

An important business lunch? The symbol ⟠ indicates restaurants with private rooms.

需要一个合适的地点享用商务午餐？可从注有这个 ⟠ 图标的餐厅中选一家有私人厢房且合你心意的餐馆。

Read 'How to use this guide' for an explanation of our symbols, classifications and abbreviations.

请仔细阅读"如何使用餐厅/酒店指南"，当中的图标、分类等简介助你掌握使用本指南的诀窍，作出智慧选择。

JAPANESE 日本菜 MAP 地图 18/D-2

Waku Ghin

Gather up all your winnings at the casino – for you will need them – and head to this sophisticated Japanese restaurant courtesy of Tetsuya Wakuda. The doors magically open as if your very approach was anticipated and the cosseted care taken by the staff will leave an indelible impression. Incredible ingredients in detailed and precise compositions will also amaze. End with dessert overlooking the world's largest atrium-covered casino.

无微不致的服务、美味得超乎想像的味道和极致高级的食材，加起来令在此的用餐经验无可比拟。这里有三间用餐室，每间由一位厨师负责，呈献包含十道菜的餐单。然后食客会被引领至主餐室，边远眺新加坡壮美的天际线，边享用甜品。这里是到访滨海湾金沙时的其中一个好去处。

TEL. 6688 8507
The Shoppes at Marina Bay Sands,
L2-01, Atrium2,
10 Bayfront Avenue
贝弗兰道10号金沙酒店金沙购物商城
中庭楼层 2 L2-01
www.marinabaysands.com

■ PRICE 价钱
Dinner 晚膳
set 套餐 $ 450-600

■ OPENING HOURS 营业时间
Dinner 晚膳　17:30-19:30
　　　　　　　20:00-22:00

AUSTRALIAN CONTEMPORARY 时尚澳洲菜 MAP 地图 17/B-1

Whitegrass

Contemporary Australian cuisine has found a home here in this chic space enhanced by some imaginative murals. The chef-owner imports much produce from his home country and that includes some less familiar ingredients. He offers 5 or 8 course tasting menus and his dishes are artful constructions with subtle Japanese influences; these are explained in detail at the table by the charming and willing service team.

餐室装潢十分型格时尚，本地艺术家的壁画及别致的花草装饰，为其添了点生气，令人好感顿增。这儿只供应指定套餐，菜式全是大厨以独特的澳洲和本地食材，加上带点和风的个人风格炮制而成，感觉颇新颖。热情好客的侍应生会为食客详述每道菜式的原由。还有供应素菜餐单供素食人士享用。

TEL. 6837 0402
#01-26/27 Chijmes, 30 Victoria Street
維多利亞街 30 号 #01-26/27chijmes
www.whitegrass.com.sg

■ PRICE 价钱
Lunch 午膳
set 套餐 $ 48-135
Dinner 晚膳
set 套餐 $ 170-265

■ OPENING HOURS 营业时间
Lunch 午膳 12:00-14:00 (L.O.)
Dinner 晚膳 18:30-21:30 (L.O.)

■ ANNUAL AND WEEKLY CLOSING 休息日期
Closed Tuesday, Wednesday and Saturday lunch, Monday and Sunday
周二、周三及周六午膳，周一及周日休息

VEGETARIAN 素菜

MAP 地图 17/A-3

Whole Earth
環界

"Vegetarian cuisine for non-vegetarians" is how Phyllis and Wood describe their longstanding Thai and Peranakan restaurant. They wanted diners to feel they were eating meat even though they weren't and this they achieve through an understanding of textures and flavours and the clever use of bean curd and tofu. With dishes like Tom Yam soup and classic Assam Pedas, the food is full of flavour as well as being good for you – and it's great value too.

给无肉不欢者的素食，是店主和经理对餐馆的形容。为了让味道较清淡的豆腐和豆类制品变得惹味可口，餐厅选用泰国和娘惹菜的烹调方法炮制风格独特的健康素菜，如泰式的南泰东炎汤味道浓烈鲜明、经典娘惹菜阿参鱼，质感与肉类无异，啖啖素鱼肉，非常滋味。

TEL. 6323 3308
76 Peck Seah Street
柏城街 76号
www.wholeearth.com.sg

■ PRICE 价钱
Lunch 午膳
à la carte 点菜 $ 30-45
Dinner 晚膳
à la carte 点菜 $ 30-45

■ OPENING HOURS 营业时间
Lunch 午膳　11:30-14:30 (L.O.)
Dinner 晚膳　17:30-21:15 (L.O.)

199

INNOVATIVE 创新菜 　　　　　　　　　　　　　　MAP 地图　7/B-3

Wild Rocket

  18

After spending a few years as a lawyer the owner-chef decided to follow his dream and open a restaurant. The result is this bright, modern room on a hill with a charming Japanese aesthetic. He describes his cooking as 'Mod Sin': this means he takes traditional Singaporean dishes and adds his own innovative touches and modern accents, whether they be Thai, Japanese or Italian. Go for the omakase menu to best experience his cooking.

原是律师的店东兼主厨因着对烹饪的热诚而开设这餐厅，时尚的室内设计和周遭环境相当融和，落地大琉璃透入自然光，同时令窗外景色一览无遗。店东形容菜式为现代新加坡(Mod Sin)派系，将新加坡传统食物跟泰、日或意大利美食混合创新而成。厨师套餐以时令食材炮制，值得一试。

TEL. 6339 9448
Hangout Hotel, 10A Upper Wilkie Road
威基路上段 10A
www.wildrocket.com.sg

■ PRICE 价钱
Lunch 午膳
set 套餐 ＄35-45
à la carte 点菜 ＄65-75
Dinner 晚膳
set 套餐 ＄75-160
à la carte 点菜 ＄65-75

■ OPENING HOURS 营业时间
Lunch 午膳　12:00-14:30 (L.O.)
Dinner 晚膳　18:30-21:30 (L.O.)

■ ANNUAL AND WEEKLY CLOSING 休息日期
Closed Sunday 周日休息

CANTONESE 粤菜　　　　　　　　　　　　　　MAP 地图　6/A-2

Yan Ting
宴庭

As the name translates as 'Imperial Court' it's no real surprise that this is a very comfortable room that's ideal for impressing visitors and friends. The extensive Cantonese menu focuses on traditional dishes, with specialities like braised supreme sea cucumber with corn broth; prawn and pumpkin soup; and braised oxtail in a clay pot. The weekend dim sum is popular, as are the small alcoves for those wanting a more intimate experience.

和煦的色调、时尚典雅的布置和宽敞的扶手椅,都令这餐厅成为浪漫晚餐和商务午餐的上佳之选。这里提供经典的广东菜肴,餐单选择丰富,驰名菜式包括小米扣辽参、金粟烧汁煎带子、南瓜浓汤烩虾球、头抽煎羊肚菌鸡脯和红酒烩牛尾煲。而周末才供应的点心早午合餐亦享负盛名。

TEL. 6506 6887
The St. Regis Hotel, Level 1U,
29 Tanglin Road
东陵路 29号瑞吉酒店 Level 1-U
www.yantingrestaurant.com

SPECIALITIES TO PRE-ORDER 预订食物
Buddha jumps over the wall 佛 跳 墙 /
Salted baked chicken 盐焗鸡 /Hangzhou
beggars chicken 杭州叫化鸡

■ PRICE 价钱
Lunch 午膳
set 套餐 $98-168
à la carte 点菜 $40-240
Dinner 晚膳
set 套餐 $98-168
à la carte 点菜 $40-240

■ OPENING HOURS 营业时间
Lunch 午膳　12:00-15:00 L.O. 14:30
Dinner 晚膳　18:30-22:30 L.O. 22:00

THAI 泰国菜

MAP 地图 18/C-1

Yhingthai Palace
銀泰

Founded in the '90s by a couple passionate about Thai cuisine, this restaurant is spread over three colourful rooms decorated with Thai artefacts. Added authenticity comes courtesy of the helpful waitresses in their delightful traditional dress. The Thai and Thai-Chinese dishes are prepared with obvious care, with choices like deep-fried pomfret with mango sauce. Prices are reasonable, both for this neighbourhood and for the quality of the food.

女店东曾于泰国工作多年，夫妇二人对泰国菜均情有独锺。此店供应正宗和混合了中式口味的泰国菜。鲜芒果沙拉、芒果汁拌炸鲳鱼、青咖喱鸡是此店名菜。泰式艺术摆设及穿着传统泰式服装的女服务员在店内穿梭往来，将菜式奉送到客人面前，满有泰国风情。具素质的食物和相宜的价钱，是不错的选择。

TEL. 6337 1161
36 Purvis Street, #01-04
巴米士街 36号 #01-04
www.yhingthai.com.sg

■ PRICE 价钱
Lunch 午膳
à la carte 点菜 ＄38-50
Dinner 晚膳
à la carte 点菜 ＄38-50

■ OPENING HOURS 营业时间
Lunch 午膳　11:30-13:45 (L.O.)
Dinner 晚膳　18:00-21:45 (L.O.)

202

ITALIAN 意大利菜   MAP 地图 17/B-2

Zafferano

This authentic Italian gem occupies a sizeable space on the 43rd floor of the Ocean Financial Centre and provides wonderful views to go with your Brunello. But it's not just the terrace that draws the crowds – the kitchen shows passion and flair in all it does. Stand-outs include creamy burrata pomodorini with Cutrera olive oil and the various pasta dishes, like paccheri with Canadian lobster claw and luscious tomato sauce.

这家意大利餐厅置身四十楼层以上，坐拥广阔迷人景致。菜式以传统、正宗方法炮制，滋味无穷，如经典的水牛乳酪罗勒番茄沙拉，材料和调味配搭恰到好处，尝罢仿佛置身意大利之中。服务虽仍有改善之处，但为着无可挑剔的美食，值得再度登门造访。酒单提供多款Biondi Santi佳酿。

TEL. 6509 1488
Ocean Financial Centre, Level 43,
10 Collyer Quay
哥烈码头 10号海洋金融中心 Level 43
www.zafferano.sg

■ PRICE 价钱
Lunch 午膳
set 套餐 $ 118
à la carte 点菜 $ 90-150
Dinner 晚膳
à la carte 点菜 $ 90-150

■ OPENING HOURS 营业时间
Lunch 午膳 11:30-14:30 (L.O.)
Dinner 晚膳 17:30-23:30 (L.O.)
Thursday to Saturday 周四至周六
17:30-24:00 (L.O.)

■ ANNUAL AND WEEKLY CLOSING 休息日期
Closed Sunday 周日休息

203

Don't confuse the rating ✗ with the Stars ✿! The first defines comfort and service, while Stars are awarded for the best cuisine.

千万别混淆了餐具 ✗ 和星星 ✿ 图标！餐具图标表示该餐厅的舒适程度和服务素质，而星星图标代表的是食物素质和味道非常出色而获授予米其林星级的餐馆。

Enjoy good food without spending a fortune! Look out for the Bib Gourmand symbol ☺ to find restaurants offering good food at great prices!

要省钱又想品尝美食，便要留心注有 ☺ 必比登图标的食店，此类店子提供的是价钱实惠且素质高的美食。

INDIAN 印度菜　　　　　　　　　　　　　MAP 地图　12/D-2

Zaffron Kitchen (East Coast)

Housed in a modern building on a busy road, this bright, modern Indian bistro comes with metal framed chairs, exposed brick walls, old tiles and an open kitchen. While the look and the technology used are very 21st century – menus are presented on an iPad– the cooking is much more traditional, with dishes from the tandoor being particularly tasty. The restaurant is also family-friendly and comes with a small play area for children.

橘红色的旧式砖墙、状似没修葺的天花、曝露在空气中的水管，予人返璞归真的味道。与其装潢一样，此店提供的传统北印度菜风味正宗。咖喱角(samosa)、坦都烤虾(tandoori jhinga)、香烤鸡块(chicken tikka)等均是北印度的传统菜式，也是此店名菜之一。店子内设有儿童小型玩乐场地，适合有小朋友的家庭。

TEL. 6440 6786
135-137 East Coast Road
东海岸路 135-137号
www.zaffronkitchen.com

■ PRICE 价钱
Lunch 午膳
set 套餐 $15
à la carte 点菜 $23-40
Dinner 晚膳
à la carte 点菜 $23-40

■ OPENING HOURS 营业时间
Lunch 午膳　11:30-14:30 (L.O.)
Dinner 晚膳　17:00-21:30 (L.O.)
Friday & Saturday 周五及周六　17:00-22:30 (L.O.)
Sunday 周日　17:00-22:00 (L.O.)

HAWKER CENTRES AND STREET FOOD
熟食小贩中心和街头小吃

Hawker Centres in alphabetical order
熟食小贩中心-以英文字母顺序排列 —————— 208

Street Food in alphabetical order
街头小吃-以英文字母顺序排列 —————— 238

ABC Brickworks Market & Food Centre
ABC红砖巴刹及熟食中心

Blk 6 Jalan Bukit Merah 惹兰红山大牌6　　　　　Map 地图: 14/C-2

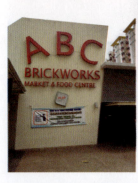

Opened in 1974, near to industrial and residential areas, it has almost 100 stalls and is one of the most popular hawker centres. It was the birthplace of the Archipelago Brewery Company and, in remembrance of the company, was named ABC market.

于1974年开业，ABC三个字是为了纪念其前身----Archipelago Brewery Company----首家本地酿酒厂。中心内的店子不到100家，但食物种类却蛮多元化。因邻近工业和住宅区，使她跻身最受欢迎的小贩中心之列，当然，令人垂涎的美食绝对是主因：一碗香喷喷的香菇肉脞冬粉、一口骚香味浓的羊肉汤，光想已叫人馋涎欲滴。

Lao Jian Cheng
老堅成

Fish ball; minced meat served with noodles; kway teow noodles or dong fen

潮州鱼圆或香菇肉脞，可选配面、粿条或冬粉。

Stall 铺 #01-51

10:00-18:00
$ 3-5

Y. R Ahmad

18 kinds of cooked-to-order roti prata and murtabak; mutton soup

十八款即点即制印度煎饼、馅料煎饼和羊肉汤。

Stall 铺 #01-10

10:00-19:00
$ 2-8

Albert Centre
雅柏中心

270 Queen Street, Bugis 奎因街大牌270

Map 地图: 8/C-3

What makes this centre one of the best? Certainly one of the reasons is the food. Its location in a heritage district and near a famous shopping mall could be another reason why it attracts so many visitors.

风味道地的罗惹、香热惹味的沙爹，阵阵食物香从楼内飘出，实在引人遐思！丰富多样的美食、独具名气的经典小吃店，成就了雅柏中心的卓越地位。地处充满历史感的亚巴街和奎因街交界，邻近多个著名景点如专门售卖便宜货品的武吉士中心，占尽地利之便，不难明白为何她成为最受欢迎的小贩中心之一。

Pondok Makan Indonesia

Offers 6 kinds of dishes; the cooked-to-order mutton satay is worth a try

只供应六款食物，现点现烤的羊肉沙爹值得一试。

Stall 铺 #01-123

08:00-20:30
$ 3-6

Singapore Famous Rojak
新加坡罗惹

Run by the second generation of the family. Local-style salad with a special homemade sauce

由第二代经营，以地瓜、油条等拌以特制酱料和花生制作的罗惹，风味独特。

Stall 铺 #01-45

12:00-20:30
$ 3-5

209

Alexandra Village Food Centre
亞历山大村美食中心

Blk 120 Bukit Merah Lane 红山口巷大牌120

Map 地图: 14/C-2

The centre was re-opened in 2010 after the upgrade from the HUP project. It's always crowded by students, local workers and nearby residents as it's surrounded by car workshops and HDB. Tourists also come here to try famous local dishes like claypot laksa or Shui Jing Pau.

经HUP计划翻新后于2010年12月重开的亚历山大村美食中心，四周不是车房便是公共房屋或设施，尽享地理上的便利。打工一族、上学一族或是附近住宅的街坊在午饭时、下课后或闲暇时都喜欢到这里闲逛或大快朵颐。中心内的名店名食多不胜数：砂煲叻沙、猪尾汤、潮州蒸粿……总有一款对你的口味。

Claypot Laksa
德普路真善美驰名砂煲叻沙

Ask for claypot laksa with blood cockles and you'll find the soup much tastier

可选择在叻沙中加入鲜蜊蚶，味道更鲜美。

Stall 铺 #01-75

08:30-15:30
$ 3-6
Closed Monday 周一休息

Leon Kee Claypot Pork Rib Soup
諒記砂鍋當歸肉骨茶

The pork rib soup cooked with Chinese herbals is the signature dish; it also offers pigtail soup and pork liver

以中药材烹调的肉骨茶是招牌菜，此外亦有供应猪尾汤和猪肝等食物。

Stall 铺 #01-18

08:00-22:00
$ 5-12
Closed Wednesday 周三休

Tiong Bahru Lien Fa Shui Jing Pau
中峇鲁联发水晶包

Teochew dumplings with jicama filling; also dumplings with red bean paste or taro paste after 1pm

除了传统的沙葛馅潮州蒸粿外，下午一点后还供应红豆和芋泥馅的蒸粿。

Stall 铺 #01-10

09:00-15:00
$ 3-6
Closed Sunday and Monday
周日及周一休息

Xiang Jiang Soya Sauce Chicken
香江豉油鸡

Along with the signature soya sauce chicken, it also offers other kinds of noodles like wonton noodles

除了招牌豉油鸡外，还有云吞面类的面食供应。

Stall 铺 #01-77

08:00-14:30
$ 3-18
Closed Tuesday 周二休息

Amoy Street Food Centre
厦门街熟食中心

7 Maxwell Road 麦士威路大牌7　　　　　　　　Map 地图: 17/B-3

Built in 1983, it has been renovated twice since. It's only 5-10 minutes from the MRT station and being near the CBD means that there are queues everywhere at lunchtime.

滋味香浓的卤面、馅丰味佳的肉粽、惹味香辣的咖喱鸡肉卜等驰名小吃,并不是令这栋建于1983年曾先后历两次翻新的熟食中心人流络绎不绝的唯一原因。邻近中央商业区,距丹戎巴葛MRT站约五至十分钟步程,也是吸引在中央商业区工作的行政人员到此享用午餐的原因。价廉味美的食物和便利的地点,难怪如此受欢迎!

A Noodle Story
超好面

The stall has an interesting look and sells local, traditional noodles cooked in an innovative way

以新颖烹调方式制作的本土面食,店面设计同样创新。

Stall 铺 #01-39

11:00-19:00
$ 6-10
Closed Weekends and Public Holidays
周末及公众假期休息

Famous Crispy Curry Puff
驰名香脆咖喱卜

Popular street food - the curry chicken puff and yam paste puff are excellent

很普及的街头小吃,咖喱鸡肉卜和芋泥卜甚是出色。

Stall 铺 #01-21

08:00-17:00
$ 1-2
Closed Sunday and Public Holidays
周日及公众假期休息

212

Hong Kee Beef Noodle
桐記牛肉粿條

Has over 60 years of history. The tasty beef stock is cooked for 24 hours
六十多年老字号，用作汤底的牛肉汤经二十四小时烹调，喝一口即齿颊留香。

Stall 铺 #01-42

11:00-19:00
$ 4-6
Closed Public Holidays
公众假期休息

 ## Hoo Kee Rice Dumpling
和記肉粽

Glutinous rice mixed with salted duck egg york; pork and chestnut wrapped with bamboo leaf
咸蛋黄、猪肉、栗子与糯米混合后，以粽叶包裹蒸煮，传统中国食品。

Stall 铺 #01-18

10:00-14:00
$ 3-4
Closed Sunday and Public Holidays
周日及公众假期休息

 ## Lian He Shao La Fan Mian
聯合燒臘飯•麵

Cantonese roasted duck; chicken and BBQ pork
粤式烧鸭、烧鸡及叉烧。

Stall 铺 #01-20

12:00-20:00
$ 4-8

 ## Yuan Chun Famous Lor Mee
源春馳名鹵麵

Typical local food with strong flavours
味浓色深，很地道正宗的面食。

Stall 铺 #02-79

08:00-15:30
$ 4-6
Closed Monday and Tuesday
周一及周二休息

213

The best way to experience the intrinsic part of local life is to taste the street food there, let's follow our selection of hawker centres and street 🍴 and enjoy the popular snacks.
认识一个地方和体验当地文化的最佳渠道是品尝道地的街头小吃，跟着我们的熟食小贩中心及街头小吃推介 🍴 去寻找最经典、最受欢迎的美点吧！

Read 'How to use this guide' for an explanation of our symbols, classifications and abbreviations.
请仔细阅读"如何使用餐厅/酒店指南"当中的图标、分类等简介助你掌握使用本指南的诀窍，作出智慧的选择。

Ang Mo Kio 724 Food Centre
宏茂桥724座巴刹与熟食中心

Blk 724, Ang Mo Kio Avenue 6 宏茂桥6道大牌724   Map 地图: 2/A-1

Thanks to its convenient location, this centre is always packed. It has 45 stalls offering a range of dishes to satisfy your tastebuds. The minced meat noodles, fried Hokkien prawn mee, Char Kway Teow and Hainanese chicken rice are always worth trying.

交通便利，加上相宜的价格，令这中心经常人头涌涌。虽然只得45家店子，但绝对不会令你的味蕾失望，不妨试试这里的肉脞面、炒福建虾面、炒粿条和海南鸡饭，全都色香味具全，且物超所值，会让你感到不枉此行。

 Hup Hup Minced Meat Noodle
合合香菇肉脞麵

The Teochew minced meat is delicious
潮式肉脞面配上两片炸脆了的云吞皮，口感丰富。

Stall 铺 #01-39

11:00-20:00
$ 3-5

215

Chinatown Complex Market & Food Centre
牛车水

335 Smith Street 史密斯街大牌335　　　　　　　Map 地图: 17/A-3

Built in 1983 and upgraded in 2008 under the HUP project, this is the biggest centre in Singapore, with over 700 stalls, including 226 cooked food stalls, and comes with an authentic Chinese atmosphere.

兴建于1983年并于2008年透过HUP计划翻新过的牛车水，楼高五层，内有逾700家店铺，当中包括226家熟食店，是现时新加坡最大的小贩中心。位处华人聚居地的中心地带，不论楼内楼外都是浓浓的中华文化气息。鸡油面、饺子、云吞……逛着看着，厨具碰撞声和扑鼻而来的灶香令肚子不禁饥肠辘辘。

 Hong Kong Soy Sauce Chicken Rice & Noodle
香港油鸡饭面

Always a queue. Offers Cantonese soy sauce chicken and BBQ pork
店外总看见排队的人龙。售卖粤式油鸡和叉烧。

Stall 铺 #02-126

11:00-20:00
$ 3-14

 **168 CMY Satay**
168春满园沙爹

Cooked to order satay with a tasty sauce
即叫即烤肉串配美味酱汁；斑兰叶包饭团。

Stall 铺 #02-168

10:00-19:00
$ 6-10

216

SAVOUR THE MOMENT.

Nespresso Boutiques:
ION Orchard #01-14
Takashimaya Department Store, B1

Discover more at www.nespresso.com

NESPRESSO.
What else?

The 50s
五十年代

The classic taste of Singapore: kaya toast with a cup of kopi kosong
一客咖椰吐司、一杯黑咖啡,一份不变的星洲经典口味。

Stall 铺 #02-048

07:00-19:00
$ 2-3

Zhong Guo La Mian Xiao Long Bao
中国拉面小笼包

Hand-pulled noodles; dumplings and Xiao Long Bao
供应手拉面、云吞、饺子及小笼包。

Stall 铺 #02-135

11:00-21:00
$ 3-6

85 Redhill Food Centre
红山巷第85座巴刹与熟食中心

Blk 85, Redhill Lane 红山巷85座

Map 地图: 15/A-2

This 44-year-old building houses over 90 stalls, some of which have been in business for decades. Visitors are kept happy with satisfying dishes like aromatic fried carrot cake and mouth-watering braised duck rice. No wonder well-known political faces have been spotted in the queue.

此中心于1972年兴建,当中有超过90家店子,个别已经营数十载,吸引食客一再光临的菜式多不胜数,包括香喷喷的菜头粿、令人难以抗拒的卤鸭饭等等。有评论甚至说全新加坡最佳的海南鸡饭就在此地,难怪连政界名人也曾被发现出现于大楼内的人龙中。

Lor Duck Rice and Noodle
卤鸭饭面

The soy sauce duck is popular and is always sold out by 1pm
卤水鸭颇受欢迎,经常在下午一点前售罄。

Stall 铺 #01-79

09:00-13:00
$ 3

Shi Le Yuan
實叻園

Local snack Kway Chap (soy sauce pork belly; pork skin and egg etc.), with flat rice noodles
地道小吃粿汁如卤水豬腩肉、豬腸、豬皮、蛋和豆腐等配一碗放湯平河粉,頗滋味。

Stall 铺 #01-82

11:00-20:00
$ 3-5

Empress Market
皇后巴刹与熟食中心

Blk 7, Empress Road 皇后路大牌7   Map 地图: 5/A-2

When it opened in 1976 it was known as Farrer Road Market; later, after being renovated, it was renamed Empress Market. It's a small centre, with just 40 cooked food stalls. However, it is still a bustling hawker centre as it is located above the wet market.

这座兴建于1976年的市场曾经翻新，面积细小，店子不多，只有40家，但由于身处新加坡其中一个最负盛名的街市之上，所以各小贩店子前亦人潮不断。顾客不但能找到各式新加坡经典小贩美食，亦有机会试试粤式粥品、云吞面等广东美馔。

 Seng Kee Porridge
成記粥品

Cantonese-style congee and fish soup with rice
粤式粥品和鱼汤饭。

Stall 铺 #01-93

07:00-14:00
$ 3-5

219

Golden Mile Food Centre
黄金熟食中心

505 Beach Road 美芝路大牌505

Map 地图: 9/A-3

Situated below the Army Market, this centre was opened in 1975 to house resettled hawkers from the Jalan Sultan street market and has 111 stalls. You'll find hawkers with over 60 years of history and popular dishes like chilli mee, along with various vegetarian dishes.

于1975年开业，这里是为了安置另一市场的小贩而兴建，故中心内有不少历史悠久的店子。这里共有111家店子，提供地道辣椒面、虾面、叻沙、炒粿条，更能找到各式素食，诸如汉堡、沙爹、乌打、罗惹、素鸡饭等，菜香飘飘，彷若是素食者的天堂。

Chung Cheng
崇正

Typical local food: chilli mee, prawn mee and laksa
供应辣椒面、虾面及叻沙。

Stall 铺 #01-59

08:30-20:00
$ 3-5
Closed Tuesday 周二休息

91 Fried Kway Teow Mee
91翠绿炒粿條麵

The Kway Teow Mee fried with greens is good
锅气十足的炒粿条，因加了炒青菜在粿条上，故名翠绿炒粿条。

Stall 铺 #01-91

11:00-20:00
$ 3-4

The Fishball Story
魚緣

The secret recipe for the non-flour fish ball has been handed down through the family

不含面粉的鲜鱼蛋以家传秘方制作,可醮酱汁和配面条吃。

Stall 铺 #01-85

10:00-17:00
$ 3-5

Wedang

Only serves five dishes; Tahu Goreng and Gado Gado are worth a try; satay is served after 12:30pm

只供应五款食物,炸豆腐和加多加多值得一试；中午12:30后才有沙爹供应。

Stall 铺 #B1-28

11:00-19:00
$ 3-5

Enjoy good food without spending a fortune! Look out for the Bib Gourmand symbol 🙂 to find restaurants offering good food at great prices!

要省钱又想品尝美食,便要留心注有 🙂 必比登图标的食店,此类店子提供的是价钱实惠且素质高的美食。

Don't confuse the rating 🍴 with the Stars ✽! The first defines comfort and service, while Stars are awarded for the best cuisine.

千万别混淆了餐具 🍴 和星星 ✽ 图标!餐具图标表示该餐厅的舒适程度和服务素质,而星星图标代表的是食物素质和味道非常出色而获授予米其林星级的餐馆。

Haig Road Market & Food Centre
海格路巴刹与熟食中心

14 Haig Road 海格路大牌14　　　　　　　　　　Map 地图: 11/B-1

It's no surprise that this centre is congested with customers as it's located between Katong and Geylang, two of the most popular eating areas in Singapore. There is so much to sample, like wanton mee and mee rebus - and no one should miss the famous putu piring.

邻近新加坡著名的食肆集中地，此中心受食客青睐绝非奇事，种类繁多的美食亦是其广受欢迎的一大主因。值得一试的菜式多不胜数——中华菜式如云吞面、粿汁；马来美食如卤面、米暹都令人一试难忘。传统小食putu piring由店员即场制作，软糯可口，味道极具层次，是旅客到此必尝的美食！

Traditional Haig Road Putu Piring

Handmade soft pudding made with rice flour and melted brown sugar, served with shredded coconut
由一班女工即场制作；以米粉和黄糖混合造成的白色小软糕，配以鲜椰丝进食。

Stall 铺 #01-07

10:00-18:00
$ 2-4

223

Hong Lim Market and Food Centre
芳林巴刹与熟食中心

Blk 531A, Upper Cross Street 克罗士街上段大牌531A　　Map 地图: 17/B-2

Built in 1978 and renovated in 2009, this was the first hawker centre in the Chinatown area. The 104 stalls offer Bak Kut Teh, fruit juice Mee Siam, curry chicken noodles, fish head Bee Hoon, etc. Expect long queues during lunch hours.

兴建于1978年，这是牛车水区内第一家小贩中心。它于2009年曾经翻新，现时共有104家店子，游走其中，仿如置身美食大观园：肉骨茶、果汁米暹、咖喱鸡面、鱼头米粉等美食的香气扑鼻而来，难怪在午膳时间总会看见长长的人龙，想吃就得有点耐性了。

Ah Heng Curry Chicken Bee Hoon Mee
亚王咖喱鸡米粉面

Potato and tofu puffs curry soup served with rice noodles; Hainanese chicken; and sliced fish
马铃薯豆卜咖喱汤可配米粉或面，拌以海南鸡及鱼片。

Stall 铺 #02-57/58

11:00-18:00
$4-6

Famous Sungei Road Trishaw Laksa
驰名结霜桥三轮車叻沙

The laksa is famous for its rich flavour. The fruit juice Mee Siam is the signature dish
配料丰富汤底鲜美的叻沙非常受欢迎；首创的果汁米暹也蛮特别。

Stall 铺 #02-66

10:30-18:00
$3-7
Closed Sunday 周日休息

224

Hokkien Street Bak Kut Teh
福建街肉骨茶

The dark coloured Bak Kut Teh has a strong flavour. There's also offers pork knuckle, pork intestine and steamed fish
福建肉骨茶色深而味浓；此外还有供应猪脚、大肠和蒸鱼。

Stall 铺 #01-66

09:00-19:00
$ 5-30

Ji Ji Wonton Noodle
基記麵家

Local wonton and noodle dishes like chicken feet noodle and Ipoh Sar Hor Fun
口味地道的云吞面食如鸡脚面、怡保河粉。

Stall 铺 #02-48/49

09:00-18:00
$ 4-8

Outram Park Fried Kway Teow
歐南園炒粿條麵

The fried kway teow is dark in colour; you can add cockles to the noodles. Always a long queue
炒河粉颜色很深，可加鲜蜊蚶，味道很地道。档口前常见人龙。

Stall 铺 #02-17

06:00-16:00
$ 3-5
Closed Sunday and Public Holidays
周日及公众假期休息

Tai Wah Pork Noodle
大華肉脞麵

Noodles mixed with soup; meat balls; dried fish and pork liver
与汤汁混和的面条再配上肉丸、鱼干及鲜猪肝等，十分滋味。

Stall 铺 #02-16

10:00-20:00
$ 4-6

Maxwell Food Centre
麦士威熟食中心

1 Kadayanallur Street 卡达耶那鲁街大牌1   Map 地图: 17/A-3

This centre began life in 1935 and has become one of the most iconic hawker centres in the city. Most typical dishes can be found here, including Rojak, banana fritter and popiah. Some celebrity chefs such as Gordon Ramsay have been known to visit its stalls.

早于1935年开业的麦士威熟食中心，已成为新加坡最具代表性的小贩中心，林林总总非吃不可的小贩美食尽在其中——香脆味甜的炸香蕉、炸芋头、炸凤梨和薄饼，当然少不了地地道道的罗惹。此中心吸引力无远弗届，甚至引来不少国际名厨到访。

Lim Kee (Orchard) Banana Fritters
林记油炸芎蕉

Apart from the sweet banana fritter, it also offers taro fritters and pineapple fritters
除了香甜味美的炸香蕉外，还有炸芋头和炸凤梨。

Stall 铺 #01-61

11:00-20:00
$ 2-3

Rojak•Popian & Cockle
囉喏•薄餅•鮮蛤

A clean and tidy stall with just three kinds of food. The popiah with egg, vermicelli and bean sprouts is very appealing
整洁的小店只供应三款食物，以包着粉丝、鸡蛋、豆芽、生菜等的薄饼最吸引。

Stall 铺 #01-56

10:00-22:00
$ 3-8

Tian Tian Hainanese Chicken Rice
天天海南雞飯

Don't be surprised to see a long queue at this shop. It specialises in Hainanese Chicken rice – and their chicken is deliciously succulent.
驰名海外的海南鸡饭店。鸡肉非常嫩滑细致。

Stall 铺 #01-10/11

10:30-20:00
$ 4-12

Mei Ling Market & Food Centre
美玲巴刹与熟食中心

159 Mei Chin Road, Queenstown 女皇镇美景路大牌159   Map 地图: 13/B-1

This two-storey building was renovated in 2009 and is now home to 47 stalls. Some of them were once at the Commonwealth Food Centre, which explains why there is such a high concentration of quality hawker stalls in this market.

这市场楼高两层,于2009年透过HUP计划翻新,现有47家店铺,当中不少来自另一小贩中心,故即使场内店子数量不多,叫人惊喜的店铺仍举目皆是。必尝美食包括粤式牛腩面、猪脚面……软硬恰到好处的面条,配上香浓肉汁,光是想想已叫人兴奋不已。

 Lao Jie Fang
老街坊

Cantonese-style braised beef noodle; pork leg noodle and beef tendon noodle are pretty good
粤式牛腩面、猪脚面及牛筋面甚为出色。

Stall 铺 #02-15

08:00-15:00
$ 4-8

 Shi Hui Yuan
實惠園

Thin, smooth Hor Fun and gravy - with chicken, duck or chicken feet toppings
幼滑河粉拌入香浓肉汁,可选配鸡、鸭或凤爪等。

Stall 铺 #02-33

08:00-14:00
$ 3-5
Closed Monday, Tuesday and Friday
周一、周二及周五休息

Newton Food Centre
纽顿熟食中心

500 Clemenceau Avenue North 克里门梭道大牌500　　Map 地图: 7/A-1

Upgraded and reopened in 2006, this is considered by many as the best hawker centre in the city and is popular with both locals and tourists. There are many signature dishes in the centre, such as BBQ seafood and black pepper crab, so it can be challenging getting a seat during busy periods.

中心于2006年7月经过翻新,被誉为全新加坡最佳的小贩中心,深得本地老饕或旅客喜爱,若有幸到访,记得品尝惹味的海鲜烧烤和沙爹、风味独特的福建虾面和印度薄饼,络绎不绝的食客致使场内一席难求。

Alliance Seafood
聯合海鮮燒烤　　　　　　　　　　　　　　

BBQ seafood. Don't miss the chilli crab or the black pepper crab - made using live crabs

烧烤海鲜,以活蟹制作的辣椒炒蟹和黑胡椒蟹绝不可错过。

Stall 铺 #01-27

11:00-22:00
$ 15-40

115 Bukit Merah View Market & Hawker Centre
红山景大牌115

Blk 115 bukit Merah View 红山景大牌115　　　　　Map 地图: 15/B-2

This hawker centre, opened In 1973, comprises 84 cooked food stalls and 167 market produce stalls. Located in the Henderson area and close to office buildings, schools and residential flats, the centre is always flooded with people thanks to its delicious, great value lunch choices.

这幢座落于红山区、建于1973年的小贩中心现有超过150家商店和84家熟食小贩，提供各式各样经济实惠的地道美食。由于四周尽是办公室、学校和住宅，午膳时间总是肩摩毂击。楼内飘来浓浓咖哩香，咖哩迷必能捧着肚子满足而回。

 ### Na Na Curry
南南咖喱

Curry fish; chicken, mutton and curry fish-head in claypots are delicious
咖喱鱼、羊、鸡及砂锅咖喱鱼头很美味。

Stall 铺 #01-48

11:00-20:00
$ 3-10

230

127 Toa Payoh West Market & Food Centre
大巴窑大牌127

Blk 127, Lorong 1 Toa Payoh 大巴窑1巷大牌127　　　　Map 地图: 3/A-1

This small hawker centre consists of only 40 stalls, yet the food on offer is more than satisfying. One must-try item is the handmade Teochew pau - bite-sized and full of amazingly delicious fillings. The very tasty carrot cake is also worth having.

即使这中心只有40家店子，还是值得远道而来。潮式包点是其中一种必尝美食，别看它个子小小，松软的包皮裹着各式诱人馅料，一口大小正好可多尝几款。而菜头粿亦值得一试，裹着蛋浆的菜头粿煎得外脆内软，一试难忘。

Chey Sua Carrot Cake
青山菜頭粿　　　　　　　　　　　　　　　　

The pan-fried cake is popular. They'll deliver the food to your table when there's no queue at the stall

煎萝卜糕非常受欢迎。下单时报上桌子号码，店方会把食物送到你的桌上。

Stall 铺 #02-30

08:00-15:00
$ 2-4

Teochew Handmade Pau
潮洲自制飽點

Lotus seed paste pau; steamed chicken pau; and Shou Tao bao…all handmade

莲蓉包、大鸡包及寿桃包等潮式包点全部人手炮制。

Stall 铺 #02-02

06:00-14:00
$ 2-3
Closed Monday 周一休息

231

People's Park Complex Food Centre
珍珠坊

32 New Market Road 纽马吉路大牌32　　　　　　Map 地图: 17/A-2

This two-level building is a favourite spot with local seniors and is conveniently located outside one of the entrances of Chinatown MRT Station.

随着饺子冒起的热腾腾蒸气、手拉面制作的即场展示、小笼包的丰腴肉香，交织出市场内人头涌涌的热闹画面。珍珠大厦楼高两层，深受本地年长一辈喜爱。对旅客而言，此熟食中心内的食物不光价格相宜，且位处牛车水地铁站出口旁，是大快朵颐的便利之选。

Hong Peng La Mian Xiao Long Bao
洪鹏拉面小笼包

Offers Xiao Long Bao and hand-pulled noodles
小笼包、饺子及即场制作的手工拉面。

Stall 铺 #01-1016B

09:30-21:00
$ 4-5

People's Park Hainanese Chicken Rice
珍珠坊海南鸡饭

Offers Cantonese roast meats, such as pork chop and duck; and, of course, the signature dish – Hainanese chicken rice
各款粤式烧味如脆皮烧肉、叉烧、烧鸭等，当然，还有海南鸡饭 。

Stall 铺 #01-1098

10:00-19:00
$ 6-10

Tekka Centre
竹脚中心

665 Buffalo Road 巴弗罗路大牌665

Map 地图: 8/C-2

This centre, in Little India, was originally named Zhujiao Centre. However, the word was too hard for non-Chinese locals to pronounce so it was renamed Tekka Centre in 2000. As it's a landmark in Little India, expect plenty of Indian fare.

竹脚中心位于小印度,外墙色彩斑斓,内有繁盛的香料市场,印度服饰和商品林罗满目,洋溢着浓浓的印度风情。游走其中,你会找到口碑载道的印度香饭(黄姜饭),颗颗饭粒都渗着咖喱香气,搭配羊肉、鸡肉或鱼,吃得饱足;场内中式美食亦具水准,尤其推荐卤水鹅鸭。

Allauddin's Briyani

The biryani is very famous; you may choose mutton, chicken or fish as a topping

口碑载道的印度香饭,可选配羊肉、鸡肉或鱼等。

Stall 铺 #01-232

10:00-19:00
$ 4-6

Heng Gi Goose and Duck Rice
興記鵝・鴨飯

The soya sauce duck is very popular
这儿的卤水鸭在区内很受欢迎。

Stall 铺 #01-335

08:00-15:00
$ 4-10
Closed Monday 周一休息

233

Tiong Bahru Market
中峇鲁市场

30 Seng Poh Road 成保路大牌30　　　　　Map 地图: 16/C-2

Located in one of the city's oldest residential areas, this market is one of the most popular hawker centres. There are too many great food items to choose from, like Lor mee, porridge and roast chicken. The silky white Chwee kueh, topped with hot diced radish, is very tempting.

座落于新加坡最古老的住宅区，中峇鲁市场一直是本地人最爱的小贩中心，场内驰名美食不能尽录，卤面、鱼粥、烧鸡等等都香气四溢，而水粿由米浆蒸熟而成，佐以煎至咸香的菜脯粒，叫人垂涎欲滴。

Hong Heng Fried Sotong Prawn Mee
鴻興炒蘇東蝦麵　　　　　　　　　　　　　　　

Cooked to order, the noodles stir-fried with sliced fish, squid and prawn and served with homemade chilli sauce is a favourite

即点即炒的油面加米线，配鱼片、鱿鱼、虾及秘制辣酱，带有浓浓虾膏咸香。

Stall 铺 #02-01

11:00-20:00
$ 3-5

Jian Bo Shui Kueh
楗柏水粿

Typical local street food: a white rice cake with preserved vegetables and a secret sauce recipe

雪白的米糕浇上秘制酱汁配以菜脯，很地道的街头小吃。

Stall 铺 #02-05

07:00-21:00
$ 2-4

234

Lor Mee 178
鹵麵178

As well as Lor Mee, you should try the fish nuggets
除了卤面，还可来一客炸鱼片。

Stall 铺 #02-23

11:00-21:00
$ 3-4

 Teochew Fish Porridge
潮洲魚粥

Live-cooked fish soup or seafood soup served with a bowl of rice
即时烹调的鱼汤或海鲜汤配以白饭一碗，很本土的粥品。

Stall 铺 #02-73

08:00-20:00
$ 4-6

 Tiong Bahru Hainanese Boneless Chicken Rice
中峇鲁海南起骨雞飯

Along with the signature Hainanese boneless chicken rice, it offers roasted chicken
除了不容错过的镇店之宝—海南鸡外，还有供应烧鸡。

Stall 铺 #02-82

10:00-21:00
$ 3-24

235

Whampoa Makan Place
黄埔熟食中心
90/91 Whampoa Drive 黄埔通道大牌90/91　　　　Map 地图: 4/C-2

There are 52 stalls housed between two blocks. Stalls in Block 91 mostly offer breakfast food and many close after lunch; stalls in Block 90 are usually open for lunch and dinner or even until midnight. A wide array of good food can be found here.

这市场只有50多家店子，散布于两幢建筑内，其中91号的店以贩售早餐为主，午膳过后便会停业；而90号的店子主营午膳、晚膳，个别甚至营业至午夜。老饕可以在这里消磨一整天，从早餐的烤面包、粥，道地小吃煎蚝饼、豆沙饼，以至令人捧着肚子的鲍鱼面和海南鸡饭，总能满足你的胃口。

 ### Balestier Road Hoover Rojak
豪華羅雜

Local-style salad with fresh ingredients; can be served with preserved duck egg
以新鲜食材炮制的地道风味沙拉，可加皮蛋拌吃。

Stall 铺 #01-06

10:00-15:00
$ 4-6
Closed Tuesday 周二休息

 ### China Whampoa Home Made Noodle
中國黃埔麵粉粿

Abalone mee is the most popular dish
全部面条均为自家制作，最驰名的是鲍鱼面。

Stall 铺 #01-24

07:00-14:00
$ 4-12
Closed Monday 周一休息

Huat Heng Fried Oyster
發興炒蚝煎

Fried baby oysters with eggs cooked to order
即点即炒蚝仔煎。

Stall 铺 #01-26

12:00-20:00
$ 5-8
Closed Monday and Tuesday
周一及周二休息

Liang Zhao Ji
梁照记

Soya duck served with congee; or with soya sauce cooked rice
卤水鸭可配以白粥或用卤汁煮的黑饭。

Stall 铺 #01-07

08:00-17:00
$ 3-38
Closed Monday and Tuesday
周一及周二休息

237

Street Food 街头小吃
Popular places for local dishes
驰名小吃店

Bismillah Biryani

Biryani with fish or meat inside and flavoured with various Indian herbs.
以多种香料烹调的印度香饭像小山般堆在碟上,鱼和肉藏在其中,色香味美。

$ 6-20　　　　　　　11:00-15:00, 17:30-22:00
MAP 地图　8/C-2
50 Dunlop Street
南洛街 50号

Hill Street Tai Hwa Pork Noodle 大華豬肉粿條麵

Using fresh ingredients, the noodles are cooked to order and every bowl comes with its own instantly-made sauce and soup.
材料新鲜,每碗面均是独立烹煮,酱汁也是即时调和,常见人龙。

$ 5-10　　　　　　　09:30-21:00
Closed 1st and 3rd Monday of the month
每月第一及第三个周一休息
MAP 地图　9/A-2
#01-12 Blk 466, Crawford Lane
哥罗福巷 466座 #01-12

Jalan Sultan Prawn Mee 惹蘭蘇丹蝦麵

A famous noodle stall with over 70 years of history; pork rib prawn mee is the most popular dish.
逾七十年历史的街头面档,经常满座,最有名的是汤底鲜甜的排骨虾面。

$ 5-10　　　　　　　08:00-15:30
Closed Tuesday
周二休息
MAP 地图　9/B-2
2 Jalan Ayer, Lorong 1 Geylang
芽笼 1巷惹兰亚逸 2号

JB Ah Meng 新山亞明

Offers Cantonese stir-fries and local dishes like white pepper crab. Always lively after the sun goes down.
供应锅气十足的广东小炒和本地菜式如白胡椒蟹等。入夜后非常热闹。

$ 10-30 18:00-03:00
MAP 地图 10/D-1
2 Lorong 23 Geylang
芽笼 23 巷 2 号

Lor 9 Beef Kway Teow 九巷牛河

Beef Kway Teow is their very popular signature dish. They also offer stir-fried dishes and seafood.
差不多每位客人都会点的牛肉炒河粉是招牌菜，此外，还供应小炒菜式和海鲜。

$ 6-30 11:00-03:00
MAP 地图 10/C-1
237 Lorong 9 Geylang
芽笼 9 巷 237 号

Nasi Lemak Kukus

The flavoursome Nasi Lemak comes with a wide selection of dishes. Beef rendang and paru-paru are very popular.
以传统方法蒸熟的椰浆饭，带有清香；配菜选择丰富。冷当牛肉和烩牛肺最受欢迎。

$ 4-8 12:00-22:30
Closed Sunday
周日休息

MAP 地圖 8/C-3
229 Selegie Road
实利基路 229 号

Sin Huat Eating House 新發

Rice noodles with crab and fish cake are the signature dishes.
螃蟹米粉和鱼饼是招牌菜，原只肉蟹，与葱、蒜、辣椒及米粉同煮，味道鲜美。

$ 20-40 19:00-24:00
MAP 地图 11/A-1
659/661 Lorong 35 Geylang
芽笼 35 巷 659/661 号

HOTELS
酒店

In order of comfort —— 242
以舒适程度分类

In alphabetical order —— 244
以英文字母顺序排列

HOTELS IN ORDER OF COMFORT
酒店 — 以舒适程度分类

Raffles 莱佛士	268
Mandarin Oriental 文华东方	259
The Ritz-Carlton, Millenia 丽思卡尔顿美年	277

Shangri-La 香格里拉	270
Regent-Four Seasons 丽晶	269

The St. Regis 瑞吉	278
Four Seasons 四季	252
The Fullerton 富丽敦	275
The Fullerton Bay 富丽敦海湾	276
Intercontinental 洲际	256

Fairmont 费尔蒙	250
Grand Hyatt 君悦	254
Goodwood Park 良木园	253
Marina Bay Sands 滨海湾金沙	260
Parkroyal on Pickering 皮克林宾乐雅	267
Equarius 逸濠	249
Sheraton 喜来登	271
Hilton 希尔顿	255

W Singapore Sentosa Cove	281

Sofitel So Singapore 索菲特	273
Sofitel Sentosa Resort & Spa 圣淘沙索菲特	272

One Farrer	263
Swissôtel The Stamford 史丹福瑞士	274
Orchard 乌节	264
Fort Canning	251
Carlton 卡尔登	246
Carlton City 卡尔登城市	247
Park Regis 柏伟诗	266
Pan Pacific 泛太平洋	265
The Westin 威斯汀	279
Conrad Centennial 康莱德	248
Mandarin Orchid 文华	258

New Majestic 大華	262
Vagabond	280
Naumi	261

Jen Orchardgateway 乌节门今旅	257

Amoy 华绣	244
Wanderlust	283

Bencoolen 明古连	245

243

UNIQUE 独特 MAP 地图 17/B-2

Amoy
华绣

Part boutique hotel, part museum, the very individual Amoy hotel is set around the former Fuk Tak Chi temple which is now home to an exhibition about Singapore's Chinese immigrants. Blending traditional architecture with new designs, the 'cosy singles' and 'deluxe doubles' spread around this historic building make good use of natural materials.

位处福德祠遗址,一半是精品酒店,一半是仍然保留了祠堂原貌、介绍本地华裔移民历史的博物馆,蛮有趣的一间酒店!大堂内还保留着寺庙原来的水井,不论是馨逸单人房还是豪华双人房,每间房间最少有一件古代工艺品作装饰,风格全是古旧中隐隐透着时代感。免费机场接送服务还附有博物馆导览。

TEL. 6580 2888
76 Telok Ayer Street
直落亚逸街 76 号
www.stayfareast.com

👤 = $ 238-318
👤👤 = $ 298-378
☕ = $ 20

Rooms 客房 37

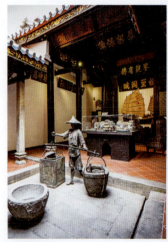

244

FUNCTIONAL 实用　　　　　　　　　　MAP 地图　17/B-2

Bencoolen
明古连

A simple hotel, not without a certain style, that's ideal for a short stay. Bedrooms come in a variety of categories – the 'Executive' rooms provide a little more space. Breakfast is help-yourself from the buffet in an area that doubles as the lounge and reception. For those staying a little longer there's a pantry in which to prepare meals and do washing.

从1968年便开始经营酒店业务的明古连家族旗下新开设的酒店。面积不大、设计简约却是五脏俱全，适合短期住宿的旅客。房间类型从普通的阁楼客房至奢华高尚的豪华房，切合不同客人需求。Level 6是屋顶阳台，其上附有按摩功能的小泳池。喜欢下厨的住客可自购食材在酒店的茶水间亲手炮制最爱餐点。

TEL. 6460 4933
47 Hong Kong Street
香港街 47号
www.hotelbencoolen.com

♦ = $ 163-400
♦♦ = $ 163-400

Rooms 客房　33

CONTEMPORARY 时尚 MAP 地图 17/B-1

Carlton
卡尔登

  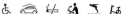

Business travellers will find the location ideal, especially as it is just a few minutes' walk to convention venues and three main MRT stations, along with large shopping centres and various restaurants. This is the largest independently-owned hotel in Singapore, with 930 bedrooms – these are bright, spacious and sufficiently well-equipped.

设有逾九百个房间的卡尔登酒店是新加坡最大的独立酒店，设施及服务均符合国际标准。其选址占尽地利，离会议展览场所及三条主要地铁线道仅数分钟步行距离，是商务停留的一流之选，附近亦有大型购物中心和众多食肆。房间光亮，空间充裕，室内设计时尚实用且设施齐全，床单的素质亦好。

TEL. 6338 8333
76 Bras Basah Road
勿拉士峇沙路76号
www.carltonhotel.sg

RECOMMENDED RESTAURANTS 餐厅推荐
Wah Lok 華樂 ✕✕

👤 = $ 230-600
👥 = $ 230-600
Suites 套房 = $ 2,500-6,030

Rooms 客房   920
Suites 套房   10

CONTEMPORARY 时尚   MAP 地图   17/A-3

Carlton City
卡尔登城市

This sister hotel to The Carlton in Civic is on the edge of the CBD and offers up to date facilities for business travellers. Bedrooms are bright and modern and offer either Chinatown or harbour views. There are also good views from the Graffiti bar on the 29th floor. 'Plate' serves international dishes and overlooks the pool and sun terrace.

卡尔登城市座落于中央商业区一角，靠近丹戎巴葛地铁站，不论是公干或旅游，其地点都很便利。酒店的建筑和设计风格时尚独特，客房能俯瞰醉人的港湾或繁华的牛车水景色。欲饱览狮城海岸美景可到位于Level 29的Graffiti喝一杯。行政楼层客房及设施是商务人士理想之选。

TEL. 6632 8888
1 Gopeng Street
高平街1号
www.carltoncity.sg

👤 = $ 220-350
👥 = $ 220-350
Suites 套房 = $ 500-650
☕ = $ 29

Rooms 客房 384
Suites 套房 2

TRADITIONAL 传统 MAP 地图 18/C-1

Conrad Centennial
康莱德

There's no doubt this hotel will satisfy anyone who is looking for a well run and comfortable hotel in a good location – one that offers large bedrooms, a good cocktail bar and a relaxing lounge. What really sets this place apart however, is the vast and impressive collection of paintings and sculptures that are scattered around the building.

得天独厚的地理位置、宽敞舒适的住宿环境和宾至如归的服务，都令旅客对这酒店趋之若鹜，俯拾皆是的博物馆级艺术藏品，更为旅客带来美妙的住宿体验。开阔的大堂吧富丽堂皇，是享用鸡尾酒和现场音乐的绝佳场所。中餐厅金牡丹提供的美食定能令旅客满意而归。

TEL. 6334 8888
2 Temasek Boulevard
淡马锡荫道2号
www.conradhotels3.hilton.com

👤 = $ 300-400
👥 = $300-400
Suites 套房 = $ 400-3,000
☕ = $ 43

Rooms 客房 482
Suites 套房 25

PERSONALISED 个性

MAP 地图 1/A-1

Equarius
逸濠

The most exciting bedrooms at this hotel – which is close to all the main attractions of Sentosa Island – are the 11 ocean suites: they offer spectacular views of Marine Life Park and make you feel you're living under the sea. The deluxe rooms are more soberly decorated but are spacious and well-equipped. If you want a tropical forest experience, book a 'beach villa'.

海景套房壮丽的海洋生物园景，令人心感震憾，感觉犹如身处水底世界。豪华客房以米色及浅棕色为主调，风格素净，简约舒适。置身热带雨林是什么感觉？便要试试围绕泳池而建的海滨别墅。ESPA水疗中心提供多种令你忘却烦忧的水疗和浸浴服务，饿了还能到附设的水疗膳食餐厅尝尝美味健康的菜式。

TEL. 6577 8888
Resorts World Sentosa,
8 Sentosa Gateway
圣淘沙桥门8号名胜世界
www.rwsentosa.com

RECOMMENDED RESTAURANTS 餐厅推荐
Forest 森 ❀ XxX

👤 = $ 450-3,000
👥 = $ 450-3,000
Suites 套房 = $ 800-3,000
🍽 = $ 28

Rooms 客房 185
Suites 套房 30

249

LUXURY 豪华　　　　　　　　　　　　　　　　MAP 地图　18/C-1

Fairmont
费尔蒙

It may be located in Raffles City but The Fairmont offers nothing but tranquillity, whether you're by the pool, having a snack at Alligator Pear or sitting on a balcony overlooking the Marina. Ask for a room in the North Tower – not only has it been renovated, with a new look that pays homage to Singapore's past, but it also has the best views.

位于喧闹的莱佛士城内，面向迷人的滨海湾，这座充满娘惹风貌的酒店，供给住客宁静的处所。不论是设备齐全的蔚柳溪水疗中心、或是宽敞舒适的客房，素质均在水准以上。悠闲的午后，到池畔餐厅品尝健康小食、享受水疗中心的服务或在阳台上欣赏海湾景色，皆是赏心乐事。刚修葺的北翼房间景观较佳。

TEL. 6339 7777
80 Bras Basah Road
勿拉士巴沙路 80号
www.fairmont.com/singapore

👤 = $ 290-830
👥 = $ 290-830
Suites 套房 = $ 800-4,600
☕ = $ 39

Rooms 客房　737
Suites 套房　32

CLASSIC 古典　　　　　　　　　　　　　　　　　MAP 地图　17/A-1

Fort Canning

The city may be on the doorstep but feels miles away when you're on the shady patio of this rather grand building, which was built in 1926 for the British army – little wonder it's a popular wedding venue too. Choose between a bedroom with a city view or with a more relaxing vista of Fort Canning Park. The Tisettanta Lounge is the place for a good cocktail.

建于1926年，原为英军行政大楼。虽位处市中心，然隐藏在绿树成荫的公园内，却予人宁谧之感。前排客房面向繁华市中心，后排客房是清幽园景、布置较前排的要华丽一点。幽雅的花园景色、清澈的泉水泳池加上完备的场地设施，是举办婚宴的热门场地。

TEL. 6559 6770
11 Canning Walk
康宁径11号
www.hfcsingapore.com

♂ = $ 300-530
♂♀ = $ 300-530
Suites 套房 = $ 750-1,000
🍽 = $ 28

Rooms 客房　84
Suites 套房　2

251

ELEGANT 典雅

MAP 地图 6/A-3

Four Seasons
四季

There aren't many city hotels with tennis courts – the very exclusive Four Seasons hotel has four, two of which are indoor. It also has two swimming pools, one of which offers sweeping views of the city skyline. The spacious bedrooms come equipped with every extra and amenity you'll ever need and the large marble bathrooms are particularly luxurious.

坐落于恬静优美、绿意盈盈的乌节林荫道，距离购物、娱乐和商业中心仅咫尺之遥。客房设计富现代气息，备有各式电子设施，云石浴室设备齐全。酒店设两个泳池，位于顶层的可饱览迷人天际线，另一个与水疗中心相连，感觉闲适写意。运动爱好者可尽情于健身室和网球场舒展筋骨。

TEL. 6734 1110
190 Orchard Boulevard
乌节林荫道190号
www.fourseasons.com/singapore

RECOMMENDED RESTAURANTS 餐厅推荐
Jiang-Nan Chun 江南春 XxX

♦ = $ 429-659
♦♦ = $ 429-659
Suites 套房 = $ 729-7,000
☕ = $ 49

Rooms 客房　199
Suites 套房　56

ELEGANT 典雅 MAP 地图 6/B-2

Goodwood Park
良木园

No roll call of Singapore hotels would be complete without Goodwood Park. Built in 1900 as the Teutonia Club for German expats, it became a hotel in the late 1920s and has been enlarged and improved over time since then, culminating in its Grand Tower becoming a National Monument in 1989. The charming bedrooms are dotted around the 6 hectares of garden.

酒店建于1900年，是本地历史最悠久的酒店之一，其塔楼于1989年获列为国立纪念物。它原是侨居当地德国商界名流聚集的条顿具乐部(Teutonia Club)，于30年代修缮成酒店。坐落市中心，四周是翠綠蔥蔥的園林，保留殖民地风貌的房间设计豪华，配备各式现代设施，为旅客提供远离烦嚣的休闲空间。

TEL. 6737 7411
22 Scotts Road
史各士路 22号
www.goodwoodparkhotel.com

RECOMMENDED RESTAURANTS 餐厅推荐
Alma ✽ ✕✕
Gordon Grill ✕✕✕
Min Jiang 岷江川菜馆 ✕✕✕

♦ = $ 300-1,125
♦♦ = $ 300-1,125
Suites 套房 = $ 520-1,425
☕ = $ 38

Rooms 客房 212
Suites 套房 21

253

MODERN 现代   MAP 地图 6/B-2

Grand Hyatt
君悦

It may be geared predominantly towards the business community but, thanks to a terrific state-of-the-art spa which boasts 11 treatment rooms as well as an impressive swimming pool, this international hotel is equally suited to those looking to spend time at more leisurely pace. The restaurants are varied and numerous and offer a huge range of different cuisines.

邻近乌节路和乌节地铁站的君悦酒店是商务和会议酒店，但亦适合休闲旅客入住。客房面积宽广，个别备独立起居室，房间设计时尚但不矫揉造作，便利设施应有尽有。水疗中心设有十一间理疗室，其中一间为双人房，并提供多种水疗护理。泳池被绿茵树木环绕，静谧怡人。设有两个室外网球场。

TEL. 6738 1234
10 Scotts Road
史各士路10号
www.singapore.grand.hyatt.com

RECOMMENDED RESTAURANTS 餐厅推荐
Mezza9 ××

♦ = $ 390-660
♦♦ = $390-660
Suites 套房 = $ 600-3,500
☕ = $ 35

Rooms 客房 637
Suites 套房   40

MODERN 现代   MAP 地图 6/A-2

Hilton
希尔顿

Not just a hotel, but a shopping destination as well – there are two floors of luxury boutiques attached to this corporate chain hotel. Bedrooms are much more contemporary than the somewhat tired looking '70s façade would suggest – ask for one with a balcony or one on a higher floor with a view. There's a rooftop pool on the 24th floor, next to the Italian restaurant.

位于熙来攘往的购物景点乌节路上，酒店也是国际品牌的集中地，商店占地两层，住客可尽享购物乐趣。客房设计富现代感兼具功能性，令酒店从七十年代起一直受商务旅客青睐。高层的住客更可从阳台望到美不胜收的景致。游泳池设于顶层Il Cielo餐厅旁，下一层亦可找到健身中心。

TEL. 6737 2233
581 Orchard Road
乌节路 581号
www.hilton.com

RECOMMENDED RESTAURANTS 餐厅推荐
Iggy's ××
Il Cielo ××

♦ = $ 280-580
♦♦ = $ 300-600
Suites 套房 = $ 500-800
☕ = $ 38

Rooms 客房 405
Suites 套房 16

ELEGANT 典雅　　　　　　　　　　　　　　MAP 地图　8/C-3

Intercontinental
洲际

It's not just its location in Bugis that makes this a worthy choice. A steady programme of improvement and refurbishment over the last few years has ensured its high standard of accommodation is maintained. The decoration cleverly blends Peranakan heritage with contemporary styles to create attractive and comfortable bedrooms – ask for one in the original building.

位于武吉士区的心脏地带，交通便利，再加上布置温馨的大堂、悦目的酒廊、舒适的客房及完善的餐饮设施，对旅客来说，确是极具吸引力。客房分布在十六层高，带有娘惹风情、设计时尚的主座大楼及充满殖民时代气息、娘惹风味更浓的小楼内，要时尚还是想怀旧?悉随尊便。

TEL. 6338 7600
80 Middle Road
密驼路 80号
www.intercontinental.com/singapore

RECOMMENDED RESTAURANTS 餐厅推荐
Ash & Elm ✗
Chikuyotei 竹葉亭 ✗✗
Man Fu Yuan 满福苑 ✗✗✗

♦ = $ 290-700
♦♦ = $ 290-700
Suites 套房 = $ 640-5,000
☕ = $ 40

Rooms 客房　340
Suites 套房　63

256

MODERN 现代   MAP 地图 7/A-3
Jen Orchardgateway
乌节门今旅

 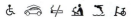

Opened in 2014 in the heart of Orchard Road, this hotel is directly connected to three different shopping malls as well as Somerset MRT station. There's cutting-edge technology throughout the hotel and bedrooms are bright, modern and functional. As their name suggests, the Panorama Club rooms have the best views. There are also three terrific rooftop pools.

酒店耸立于乌节路心脏地带，2014年开业，邻近索美塞地铁站和三个购物商场，占尽地利。酒店配备最尖端的设备，房间视野开阔，高级和豪华客房分别适合短期和长期旅客。欲饱览天际景致，不能错过顶级全景贵宾廊客房。酒店顶层设有三个别具一格的游泳池，让你静赏城市全景，更可享受按摩服务。

TEL. 6708 8888
Level 10, 277 Orchard Road
乌节路 277号 Level 10
www.hoteljen.com

♦ = $ 270-510
♦♦ = $ 270-510
☕ = $ 30

Rooms 客房 499

257

CONTEMPORARY 时尚　　　　　　　　　　　　MAP 地图　6/B-3

Mandarin Orchard
文华

An on-going refurbishment of the hotel is steadily making the spacious bedrooms more contemporary in looks. The hotel dates from 1971 and enjoys a good location on Orchard Road, with shopping centres and MRT stations on its doorstep. The rooms have good views but nothing matches the 360° vistas from the Meritus Club Lounge on the top floor.

这家于1971年已营业的酒店座落在繁忙的乌节路上，邻近各大购物商场，离两个地铁站也只是数分钟步行距离，非常方便。客房景观开扬，空间充裕。位于M楼座顶层环状的Meritus Club Lounge更可俯瞰全市美景。客房正陆续进行翻新工程，以换上更时尚的装饰。

TEL. 6737 4411
333 Orchard Road
乌节路 333号
www.meritushotels.com

RECOMMENDED RESTAURANTS 餐厅推荐
Shisen Hanten 四川饭店 ❀❀ ✕✕✕

- 👤 = $ 220-699
- 👥 = $ 220-699
- Suites 套房 = $ 355-4,500
- ☕ = $ 20

Rooms 客房　1,041
Suites 套房　36

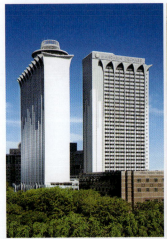

258

LUXURY 豪华　　　　　　　　　　　　　　　　　MAP 地图　18/C-1

Mandarin Oriental
文华东方

The Mandarin Oriental name is synonymous with luxury accommodation and impeccable service and this 'branch' of the international hotel group doesn't disappoint. Rising up from the fan-shaped courtyard are 21 floors of comfort and sophistication, with breathtaking views of Marina Bay. The colours, silks, linens and carvings all pay tribute to the hotel's unique setting.

欲享受新加坡的迷人气息，同时远离都市烦嚣，可考虑文华东方酒店。这幢有如酒店标志的扇子形建筑距离繁华的市中心只有数分钟路程，面朝滨海湾的醉人景致。大堂以大理石和木制雕刻布置，气氛奢华优雅。无论服务、装潢或便利设施都无可挑剔。旅客更可到泳池、室外瑜伽亭和水疗中心尽情放松身心。

TEL. 6338 0066
5 Raffles Avenue, Marina Square
莱佛士道 5号金沙购物商城
www.mandarinoriental.com

RECOMMENDED RESTAURANTS 餐厅推荐
Cherry Garden 樱桃園　✕✕✕
Dolce Vita　✕✕
Melt Café　✕✕

♦ = $ 710-740
♦♦ = $ 710-740
Suites 套房 = $ 930-5,500
🍽 = $ 46

Rooms 客房　487
Suites 套房　40

259

CONTEMPORARY 时尚　　　　　　　　　　　　　　MAP 地图　18/D-2

Marina Bay Sands
滨海湾金沙

 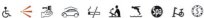

The three vast towers that make up this hotel, casino and conference centre are the city's most iconic structure. You'll need GPS to navigate through it, from the gambling tables to the vast array of shops and restaurants, to the pool and Observation deck, but it'll be an exhilarating journey of discovery. Thanks to their floor-to-ceiling windows, bedrooms have unobstructed views.

座落于滨海湾，三幢相连的宏伟时尚建筑，顶层是名闻遐尔的金沙空中花园及全球最大的无边际泳池，同楼层的观景台，让你将狮城景色尽收眼底。客房面积宽敞、环境舒适，设备齐全，还能欣赏窗外的壮丽景色。酒店内的购物城有逾百家包含零售和餐饮服务的店铺，让你足不出酒店也能享受购物和大快朵颐之趣。

TEL. 6688 8868
10 Bayfront Avenue
贝弗兰道 10 号
www.marinabaysands.com

RECOMMENDED RESTAURANTS 餐厅推荐
Cut ✿ ✕✕✕
Daniel Boulud Bistro & Oyster Bar ✕✕
Long Chim ✕✕
Punjab Grill ✕✕
Sky on 57 ✕✕
Spago ✕✕
Waku Ghin ✿ ✕✕✕

🕴 = $ 399-799
🕴🕴 = $ 399-799
Suites 套房 = $ 749-6,499
☕ = $ 43

Rooms 客房 2,381
Suites 套房 180

260

DESIGN 型格

MAP 地图 18/C-1

Naumi

There are a number of good reasons to choose this boutique hotel: its interesting architectural features and great location just behind Raffles hotel, its appealingly arty atmosphere, and the seductive décor and attention to detail of its bedrooms. If you want a larger room ask for one of the 'designer rooms' inspired by Andy Warhol or Coco Chanel.

有趣的建筑风格、艺术气息浓厚的大堂，会否令你驻足于此？设计时尚的客房精致小巧配合优质床具，感觉蛮舒服。私隐度高的天台泳池和附属的露天酒廊，是繁忙过后舒缓紧张情绪的最佳选择。欲选择面积较宽敞的客房，可以考虑灵感源自两位不同领域的设计大师安迪沃荷、可可香奈儿的Designer客房。

TEL. 6403 6000
41 Seah Street
余街 41号
www.naumihotel.com

👤 = $ 300-1,200
👥 = $300-1,200
☕ = $ 22

Rooms 客房 73

QUIRKY 奇趣   MAP 地图   17/A-3

New Majestic
大華

Built in 1928, the New Majestic is an iconic building on what was once called 'Mistress Street'. The bright white lobby with its art installations immediately alerts you to the fact that this unconventional hotel is all about individuality. Each room is styled by a different designer; some have tubs inside, some outside and some even have beds above the tubs!

建于1928年,是昔日Mistress Road的地标。黄包车、艺术作品看似随意地搁在大堂不同角落,稀奇的设计风格,格调非常独特的精品酒店。房间设计独立而各有特色:花园客房提供露天大浴盆、Aqua和Loft客房的大浴盆却在睡房内和睡床下面……古怪得来却蛮酷!

TEL. 6511 4700
31-37 Bukit Pasoh Road
武吉巴梳路 31-37号
www.newmajestichotel.com

- ♀ = $ 220-380
- ♀♀ = $ 220-380
- ☕ = $ 38

Rooms 客房 30

RECOMMENDED RESTAURANTS 餐厅推荐
Majestic 大華 XX

CONTEMPORARY 时尚　　　　　　　　　　　　　MAP 地图　8/C-1

One Farrer

 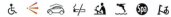

Some may consider this self-styled 'urban resort' hotel, which opened in 2014, a little too far from the city centre but Farrer Park MRT station is directly underneath the 20 storey building. The large spa and 50m swimming pool certainly add to its appeal, as do the many pieces of artwork. Longer staying guests should consider the Loft Apartments or Sky Villas.

酒店楼高二十层，位于花拉公园地铁站之上，邻近有许多景点名胜，地点非常便利。现代设计加时尚摆设的客房充满城市感觉，偌大的琉璃窗外是热闹且具有浓厚地方色彩的小印度街景，感觉蛮舒适。Level 6的奥运标准泳池、设备完善的健身中心及水疗设施，是一天繁忙后或空闲时最佳的消闲处。

TEL. 6363 0101
1 Farrer Park Station Road
花拉公园站路 1 号
www.onefarrer.com

♦ = $ 280-560
♦♦ = $ 280-560
Suites 套房 = $ 380-12,000
☕ = $ 30

Rooms 客房　169
Suites 套房　74

263

PERSONALISED 个性

MAP 地图 6/A-2

Orchard
乌节

Bedrooms in this large yet conveniently located hotel are divided between two wings: The Orchard Wing, opened in 1985, has the more functional rooms, although it also hosts the chic Signature rooms created by the interior designer Pierre Yves Rochon. Those in the newer Claymore Wing are larger, more contemporary in their design and certainly quieter.

从酒店步行至静谧的新加坡植物园或繁华的乌节娱乐购物地段都十分方便。房间分布于两幢楼翼，翻新过的Claymore设计时尚，房间面积较宽广，环境宁静舒适。Orchard的客房面积较小，时尚而富功能性，其中贵宾行政客房由著名室内设计师Pierre Yves Rochon精心设计，融合东方和欧洲元素，时尚豪华。

TEL. 6734 7766
442 Orchard Road
乌节路 442号
www.orchardhotel.com.sg

RECOMMENDED RESTAURANTS 餐厅推荐
Hua Ting 華廳 XxX

👤 = $ 230-270
👥 = $ 230-270
Suites 套房 = $ 400-800
☕ = $ 36

Rooms 客房 636
Suites 套房 20

ELEGANT 典雅   MAP 地图   18/C-1

Pan Pacific
泛太平洋

Immaculate upkeep ensures that this not-so-new kid on the block still gleams. It's a good option for business travellers and those on longer stays as its location is excellent – it's linked to Marina Square and Millenia Walk and all the boutiques and food courts you'll ever need. It also has two high-end restaurants of its own, along with a never-ending buffet.

客房空间感十足、整洁明亮、设施便利，是商务旅客或长期旅客的绝佳之选。酒店邻近购物热点滨海广场及美年径，满足购物和享用美食的欲望。若不想走得太远，酒店内也有不同餐厅任君选择，不论是印度菜馆Rang Mahal、中餐厅，或提供早、午自助餐的Edge，都能让你大快朵颐。

TEL. 6336 8111
7 Raffles Boulevard
莱佛士林荫道7号
www.panpacific.com/singapore

RECOMMENDED RESTAURANTS 餐厅推荐
Rang Mahal ✕✕✕

👤 = $ 340-450
👥 = $ 340-450
Suites 套房 = $ 650-900
☕ = $ 48

Rooms 客房   759
Suites 套房   31

CONTEMPORARY 时尚

MAP 地图　17/A-2

Park Regis
柏伟诗

A relative newcomer, this hotel is a couple of minutes' walk from Clarke Quay and suits both business travellers and tourists. The bright bedrooms are comfortable and contemporary; choose a Quay room and you'll have direct access to the 3rd floor pool from your own terrace. As well as an all-day café there's Royal Pavilion, a Cantonese restaurant on the ground floor.

距离克拉码头及河岸边只有数分钟路程的柏伟诗开业至今已有五年，装潢属于时尚舒适派，客房面积不大，但窗外的商业区或河岸景致却弥补了空间上的不足。选择Quay Room可以直接从房间的私人露台走到位于Level 2的小瀑布室外泳池，边欣赏美丽风光边畅泳或享受日光浴。

TEL. 6818 8888
23 Merchant Road
茂昌路23号
www.parkregissingapore.com

👤 = $ 200-300
👥 = $ 200-300
☕ = $ 28

Rooms 客房　202

LUXURY 豪华　　　　　　　　　　　　　　　MAP 地图　17/B-2

Parkroyal on Pickering
皮克林宾乐雅

One of the more original looking hotels in Singapore is made up of three glass towers linked by Sky Gardens. Its eco-credentials are very much in evidence throughout, with its use of natural materials and living walls of plants. All the stylish bedrooms have views of the city skyline. If you don't suffer from vertigo ask for a room on one of the Sky Garden floors.

装潢以木、石、水和植物等大自然元素作主题,更显环保意念。设计现代兼具个性的客房能观赏一望无尽的天际；水疗中心内的无边际泳池,景色更是扣人心弦。建议选择空中花园楼层的房间,闲来在房外的小径散步解郁,煞是美好！

TEL. 6809 8888
3 Upper Pickering Street
皮克林街上段 3号
www.parkroyalhotels.com

� = $ 300-460
♦♦ = $ 300-460
Suites 套房 = $ 480-1,800
☕ = $ 38

Rooms 客房　338
Suites 套房　29

267

TRADITIONAL 传统　　　　　　　　　　　　MAP 地图　18/C-1

Raffles
莱佛士

It may have changed hands many times over the last decade but Raffles, with its striking colonial architecture, remains an essential part of Singaporean identity. The gardens may need some TLC and the public areas of shops, restaurants and boutiques are packed with visitors but, once ensconced in the areas reserved for hotel guests, the mood changes and the pace slows.

这幢获列为国家历史文物的酒店在过去十年曾多次易手，犹幸其经典的殖民建筑风格仍得以完整保存。走过绿草如茵的花园，步入富丽堂皇的大堂，慑人的建筑和历经变迁的怀旧布置都叫人目眩神驰。所有房间均为套房。屋顶泳池是放松身心的上佳之选。购物廊行人如鲫，数十家商店叫人流连忘返。

TEL. 6337 1886
1 Beach Road
美芝路 1 号
www.raffles.com/singapore

Suites 套房 = $ 740-12,000
Suites 套房　103

RECOMMENDED RESTAURANTS 餐厅推荐
Long Bar Steakhouse ✕✕✕
Raffles Grill ✕✕✕✕

ELEGANT 典雅　　　　　　　　　　　　　　　　MAP 地图　6/A-3

Regent-Four Seasons
丽晶

From its marble bathrooms to its elegant bedrooms blending Asian and Western styles, it's clear this is a hotel that exudes sophistication and luxury. The location is also good, as it's within walking distance of both the Botanic Gardens and the shops of Orchard Road. Another striking feature is the Manhattan bar – a very glamorous space inspired by old New York.

酒店位处优越地段，步行即可抵达植物园或乌节路，设有各种会议设施。客房融合中西设计精髓，典雅中不失便利，套房更享私人露台。想尽情放松，可以到漩涡浴池、按摩浴池、蒸气浴室或桑拿房。嗜杯中物者不妨到访Manhattan酒吧，置身怀旧情调的酒吧中，细品匠心调制的香醇美酒，实是人生乐事。

TEL. 6733 8888
1 Cuscaden Road
卡斯加登路 1号
www.regenthotels.com

RECOMMENDED RESTAURANTS 餐厅推荐
Basilico XX
Summer Palace 夏宫 XXX

† = $ 299-599
†† = $ 299-599
Suites 套房 = $ 429-3,000
☕ = $ 40

Rooms 客房　394
Suites 套房　46

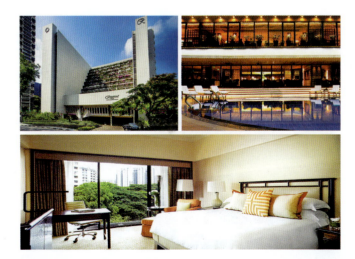

ELEGANT 典雅　　　　　　　　　　　　　　　　MAP 地图　6/A-2

Shangri-La
香格里拉

There are three different wings to this resort-style hotel: the Tower Wing, which is the oldest wing and whose floor-to-ceiling windows offer views of the city; the Garden Wing, ideal for those wanting to feel close to nature; and the Valley Wing, the most recent and most exclusive wing. The hotel is surrounded by 15 acres of tropical garden.

酒店外十五英亩的青葱园林、大堂内的大理石柱、螺旋型楼梯和落地窗，带来独一无二的豪华体验。房间分布于三个楼翼：塔翼充满现代美感，房间的落地窗能远眺城市或泳池美景。设私人阳台的花园翼掩映于热带园林之中，还有室外按摩浴缸。峡谷翼从大堂、餐厅以至房间均私密度高，深得商务旅客欢心。

TEL. 6737 3644
22 Orange Grove
柑林路 22 号
www.shangri-la.com

RECOMMENDED RESTAURANTS 餐厅推荐
Nadaman 滩万日本料理 XX
Shang Palace 香宫 XXX

♦ = $ 675-820
♦♦ = $ 675-870
Suites 套房 = $ 940-8,810
☕ = $ 43

Rooms 客房　712
Suites 套房　35

CLASSIC 古典

MAP 地图 6/B-2

Sheraton
喜来登

Opened in the mid '80s, this business hotel is usefully located and its bedrooms are fully equipped with all the necessary extras demanded by the modern business traveller; they are also pleasingly bright, thanks to the floor-to-ceiling windows. The Pool & Terrace rooms on the 5th floor come with private balconies which look onto the swimming pool.

这间于1985年开业的商务酒店予人温暖舒适之感。房间设计典雅明亮，大琉璃窗外是繁华的史各士路，配有便利齐全的现代化设施，满足商务旅客需要。Level 5的露台客房和泳池客房设有独立阳台，可将泳池景致尽收眼底。想让身体尽情流汗？可到健身中心或桑拿浴室去，绝对能让你整天精力充沛。

TEL. 6737 6888
39 Scotts Road
史各士路39号
www.sheratonsingapore.com

RECOMMENDED RESTAURANTS 餐厅推荐
Li Bai 李白 ✖✖✖

👤 = $340-800
👥 = $340-800
Suites 套房 = $640-2,500
☕ = $40

Rooms 客房 402
Suites 套房 18

271

PERSONALISED 个性　　　　　　　　　　　　　　MAP 地图　1/B-2

Sofitel Sentosa Resort & Spa
圣淘沙索菲特

It's all about relaxation at this resort hotel perched on the cliff top above Tanjong Beach. It's surrounded by a tropical garden and has a delightful outdoor pool. The SO spa offers an impressive range of treatments as well as a restaurant with a health-conscious menu. Bedrooms are not particularly big but, thanks to some French design flair, they are very charming.

酒店于2015年翻新，法籍设计师用花朵和叶片在墙身和地毯作装饰，加上柔和灯光及暖色调的客房，面积虽称不上很大，却很温暖舒适。浴室用的是法国名牌用品。座落于丹戎海滩之上，是其一大优点。面积偌大的So Spa内有逾二十个治疗室和户外水疗阁，还有瀑布泳池可供使用。酒店有专车往返水疗中心。

TEL. 6708 8310
2 Bukit Manis Road
武吉马尼斯路 2号
www.sofitel-singapore-sentosa.com

🚶 = $ 280-820
👫 = $ 280-820
Suites 套房 = $ 620-3,500
☕ = $ 35

Rooms 客房　183
Suites 套房　32

DESIGN 型格　　　　　　　　　　　　　　　　　　　　MAP 地图　17/B-3

Sofitel So Singapore
索菲特

This iconic building, built in 1927 and the former home of Singapore Telecommunications, now hosts this very stylish boutique hotel – some of its striking design elements are courtesy of Karl Lagerfeld. You can choose a So Cosy, So Hip, So Heritage or So Vip bedroom; all are beautifully furnished and original in looks. Hi So is the rooftop pool and trendy bar.

建筑物建于1927年，是新加坡电讯公司的旧址，为狮城地标，现已变成这间设计时尚别致、带有强烈个人风格的精品酒店。分布于两翼的房间，保留了建筑物原有风味配以时尚的家俬摆设，非常雅致。住客可到Level 7的天台泳池和酒吧舒展身心。位于大堂的咖啡店供应经典及渗入了亚洲风味的法国菜。

TEL. 6701 6800
35 Robinson Road
罗敏申路35号
www.sofitel.com/8655

♦ = $ 250-1,200
♦♦ = $ 250-1,200
☕ = $ 35

Rooms 客房　134

LUXURY 豪华

MAP 地图 18/C-1

Swissôtel The Stamford
史丹福瑞士

What was once the world's tallest hotel can still boast of having some of the city's largest bedrooms. It is also the hotel of choice for many fans of Formula 1 due to its coveted position on the circuit – there's even a heliport for ticket holders who are financially more fortunate. Service levels have always been high and there's a host of bars, cafés and restaurants.

全赖良好的定期维修，虽已开业二十九年，感觉仍然新净。客房宽敞舒适，窗外景致尤为动人。要欣赏最迷人景色，切记要求入住面向海景的房间，不光能欣赏幽美的落日景致，还能观看酒店举行的各样活动。酒店位于滨海湾跑道第九个弯处，欲观赏本年F1方程式大赛晚间赛事，这儿是不错的选择。

TEL. 6338 8585
2 Stamford Road
史丹福路 2号
www.swissotel.com/singapore-stamford

♦ = $ 270-720
♦♦ = $ 270-720
Suites 套房 = $ 700-4,200
☕ = $ 38

Rooms 客房　1,261
Suites 套房　29

LUXURY 豪华　　　　　　　　　　　　　　MAP 地图　18/C-2

The Fullerton
富丽敦

From General Post Office to National Monument, the story of the neo-classical Fullerton is one that's inexorably linked to the emergence of Singapore as a modern city of the world. This luxury hotel exudes sophistication without being stuffy or old fashioned. Each bedroom comes with thoughtful little touches and all have either city or water views.

这幢富历史意义的古典时尚建筑物在刚过去的十二月获政府列为国家古迹之一。宽敞的客房设计典雅时尚，窗外景色更是幽雅迷人。房间的设备很完善，能体贴客人的需要，例如衣橱内设有一个神秘柜子供住客摆放鞋子，特别的是住客把鞋子放进柜内，隔天再拿出来时会发现鞋子给擦得光光亮亮。

TEL. 6733 8388
1 Fullerton Square
富丽敦广场 1 号
www.fullertonhotel.com

RECOMMENDED RESTAURANTS 餐厅推荐
Jade 玉楼 XxxX
The Lighthouse XX

† = $ 700-820
†† = $ 700-820
Suites 套房 = $ 1,200-6,880
☕ = $ 45

Rooms 客房　372
Suites 套房　28

LUXURY 豪华

MAP 地图　18/C-2

The Fullerton Bay
富丽敦海湾

Its angled glass façade may make it another instantly recognisable hotel but what makes it really stand out is what's inside: four unique restaurants and a rooftop lounge, pool and garden as well as bedrooms whose contemporary decorative elements manage to also respect the past. And then there are the views, from every angle and in every direction…

座落于滨海湾码头之上，倾斜的琉璃外墙异常耀眼夺目！时尚中带着殖民时代气息的装潢:柔和的灯光、丝绒沙发、几何图案、华丽的水晶吊灯，气派典雅高贵，还有体贴细心、令人愉悦的服务和完善的设施，难怪吸引不少文人雅士到此住宿！

TEL. 6333 8388
80 Collyer Quay
歌烈码头 80号
www.fullertonbayhotel.com

RECOMMENDED RESTAURANTS 餐厅推荐
The Clifford Pier ✕✕

† = $800-1,210
†† = $800-1,210
Suites 套房 = $2,000-6,000
☕ = $38

Rooms 客房　92
Suites 套房　6

LUXURY 豪华

MAP 地图 18/D-1

The Ritz-Carlton, Millenia
丽思卡尔顿美年

A hotel for the worldly and the well-travelled. As soon as you walk through the doors of this classic, well-styled hotel you find yourself instantly switching to relax mode and your pace slowing. The location is central and great views are a given – what makes this hotel stand out is the quality of the service, the standards of comfort and the attention to detail.

踏进豪华精美的大堂，步伐自然会变慢，目光被四周充满视觉刺激的布置所吸引，弗兰克·斯特拉(Frank Stella)的雕塑和戴尔·奇胡利(Dale Chihuly)的琉璃艺术叫人凝神屏息，诸多艺术作品如星罗棋布。酒店占尽地利，景观耀眼，加上顶级的水疗服务……每个环节都天衣无缝，令人完全忘却外间的喧扰。

TEL. 6337 8888
7 Raffles Avenue
莱佛士道 7 号
www.ritzcarlton.com

RECOMMENDED RESTAURANTS 餐厅推荐
Colony ✕✕
Shiraishi 白石 ✕✕
Summer Pavillion 夏苑 ✿ ✕✕✕

👤 = $ 390-1,040
👥 = $ 390-1,040
Suites 套房 = $ 1,500-20,000
☕ = $ 45

Rooms 客房   529
Suites 套房   79

277

ELEGANT 典雅 MAP 地图 6/A-2

The St. Regis
瑞吉

Being within walking distance of both the Botanic Garden and Orchard Road mean this luxurious hotel certainly ticks all the right location boxes. But it is the impressive art collection around the public areas of the hotel that really sets it apart. The bedrooms come in chic designs and the beautiful bathrooms are bedecked with French marble.

金属琉璃外墙和豪华典雅的内部装潢，令酒店散发着奢华高雅的气派。四处陈列着顶级特色艺术品，包括国际知名艺术家的雕塑、绘画及版画，加上充满中国风情的布置，令客房格调雅致。房间备有一流的现代设施，旅客亦可到水疗中心、桑拿浴室、蒸气房、健身室和室内网球场，享受闲适的悠然时光。

TEL. 6506 6888
29 Tanglin Road
东陵路 29 号
www.stregissingapore.com

RECOMMENDED RESTAURANTS 餐厅推荐
Shinji (Tanglin Road)
Yan Ting 宴庭

👤 = $ 440-620
👥 = $ 440-620
Suites 套房 = $ 740-15,000
☕ = $ 47

Rooms 客房 262
Suites 套房 37

278

TRADITIONAL 传统   MAP 地图   17/B-3

The Westin
威斯汀

Smack in the middle of what locals refer to as 'the new frontier' sits this bright, modern hotel for global financial types. The neatly decorated bedrooms are on floors 36-46 so there's little noise to disturb a night's sleep, once all surrounding cranes are quietened. If you're a keen jogger new to the city you can engage the services of the Running Concierge.

酒店座落于新金融商业区心脏地带，客房位于36-46层，高耸的位置能隔绝地面噪音。房间宽敞、睡床舒适，能让你酣畅入睡。有运动习惯的旅客可轻装入住，酒店提供运动装备租借服务，更可跟随酒店的跑步礼宾一同路跑，尽情呼吸户外空气，重唤活力。酒店邻近地铁站，交通便捷。

TEL. 6922 6888
Asia Square Tower 2,
12 Marina View
滨海景12号亚洲广场2号塔
www.westin.com

♂ = $ 400-700
♂♂ = $ 400-700
Suites 套房 = $ 1,200-3,000
☕ = $ 45

Rooms 客房 284
Suites 套房 21

COSY 舒适   MAP 地图   8/D-2

Vagabond

When a hotel has its own artist in residence you know it's going to be a little different. This 1950s building has been transformed into a theatrically decorated and charming boutique hotel; it is full of original touches and comes with an atmosphere all of its own. The bedrooms may be somewhat compact but great care has gone into their decoration.

地点不在商业区，亦非便利，却位处小印度和十榜格南中间，令这家建于1950年、装潢时髦舒适的精品酒店多了点韵味。店主和设计师千挑万选出逾百幅油画、相片及原创作品；接待台前的犀牛和大堂的大象雕塑等令整间酒店生色不少。客房较密集和细小，但木家具和温暖的装饰布置却令人有家的感觉。

TEL. 6291 6677
39 Syed Alwi Road
赛阿威路 39号
http://hotelvagabondsingapore.com/

♦ = $ 198-598
♦♦ = $ 198-598
Suites 套房 = $ 398-798
☕ = $ 20

Rooms 客房   41
Suites 套房   1

DESIGN 型格

MAP 地图 1/C-2

W Singapore Sentosa Cove

Those familiar with the brand will recognise many of the elements of this W hotel, which is located on the East side of Sentosa Island. There's the moodily-lit bedrooms with names like Wonderful, Spectacular and Fabulous; there's the lounge music that gives the hotel and its lobby such energy; and a young client base who are more interested in partying than peacefulness.

喜欢潮流艺术和好凑热闹的人，大概会爱上这间给棕榈树环抱、能欣赏港湾景色的酒店。奢华偌大的户外泳池、音韵缭绕充满情调的大堂，让你倾刻受到其气氛感染。房间布置新颖细致，面向小港湾的客房景色较佳。能随意调校颜色的灯饰，让房间情调顿添。设有小型私人泳池的逍遥客房，特别悠闲舒适。

TEL. 6808 7288
21 Ocean Way
圣淘沙湾 21号
www.wsingaporesentosacove.com

♦ = $ 400-940
♦♦ = $ 400-940
Suites 套房 = $ 664-14,000
🍽 = $ 48

Rooms 客房   213
Suites 套房   27

If breakfast is included, the cup symbol ⌣ appears after the number of rooms.

在房间数目下面看到这个 ⌣ 茶杯图标表示需额外付款才能享用该酒店的早餐。

If you are looking for particularly pleasant accommodation, book a hotel shown in red: 🏠...🏘️.

欲享受特别舒适的留宿体验,请参考注有这个 🏠……🏘️ 红色酒店图标的推介酒店。

TRENDY 时髦　　　　　　　　　　　　　　　　MAP 地图　8/C-2

Wanderlust

A converted school from the 1920s in lively Little India is the setting for this charming and vibrant hotel with a look all of its own. What the bedrooms lack in space they more than make up for in their decoration; each floor has its own theme and each room is different. The ersatz-industrial looking restaurant has communal tables and a French menu.

这家与热闹的小印度相邻的酒店装潢时尚且别树一帜。客房面积较小，设计和布置倒是充满生气。以单色或鲜艳的色系如黄、红、紫、青等将客房区分，每个色系均有自己的歌曲，例如U2的Red Light；披头四的Yellow Submarine。想空间多点，可考虑Momo或Whimsical系列的客房。

TEL. 6396 3322　　　　　♦ = $ 129-309
2 Dickson Road　　　　　　♦♦ = $ 129-309
狄生路 2号　　　　　　　　 ☕ = $ 25
www.wanderlusthotel.com
　　　　　　　　　　　　　Rooms 客房　29

283

MAPS
地图

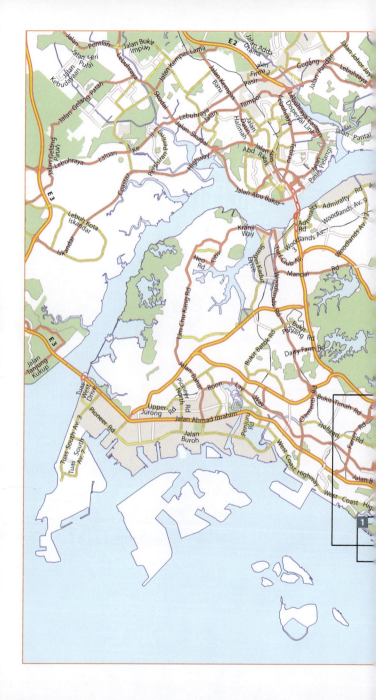

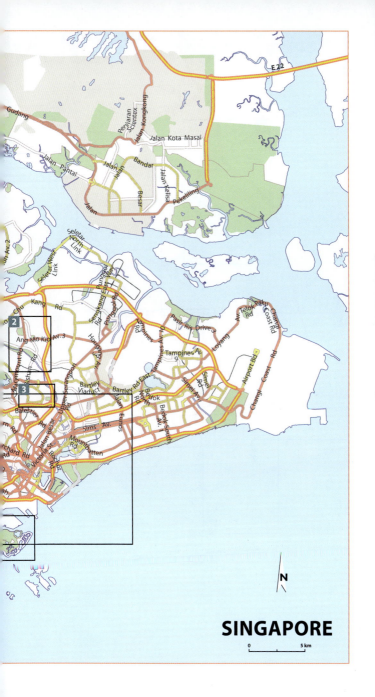

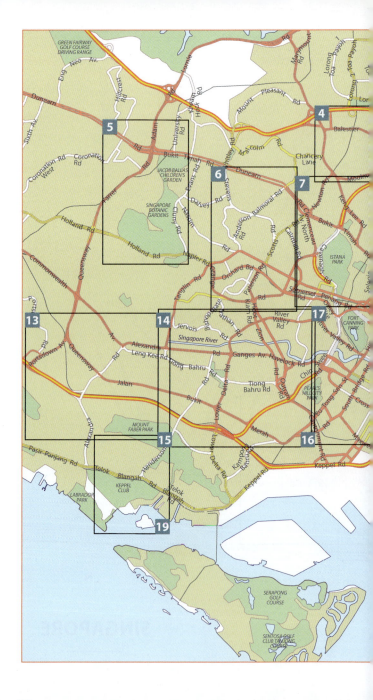

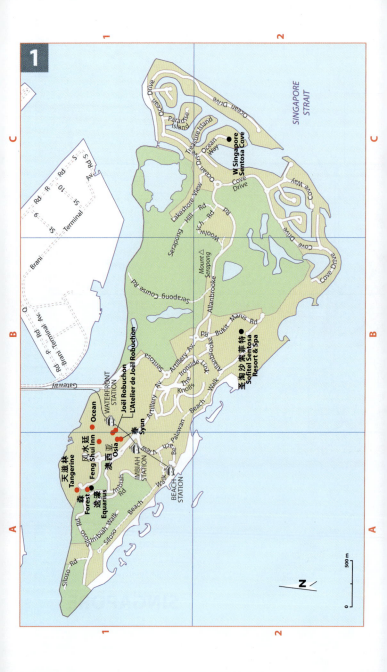

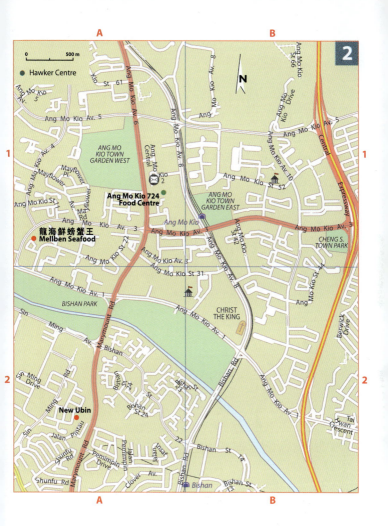

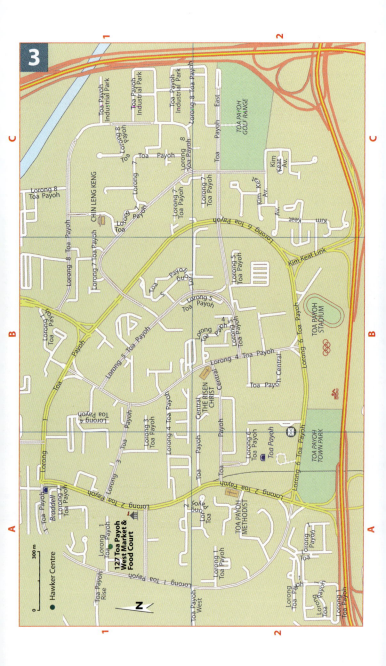

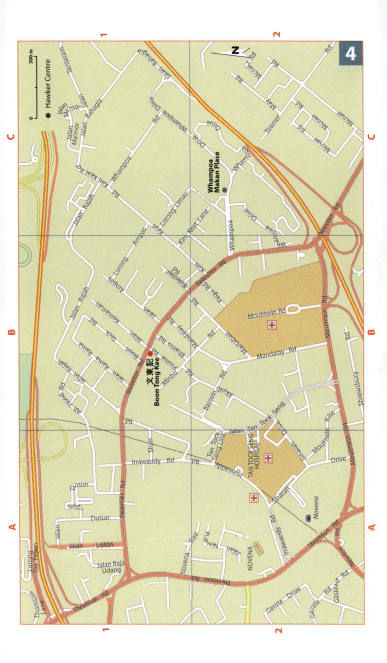

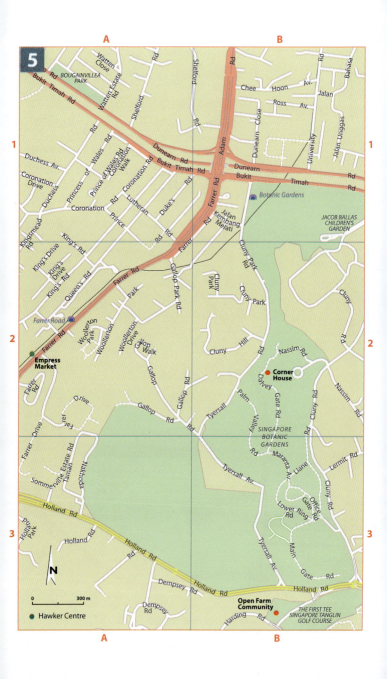

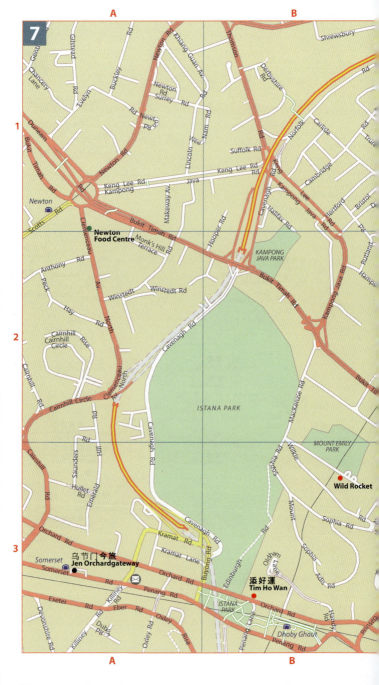

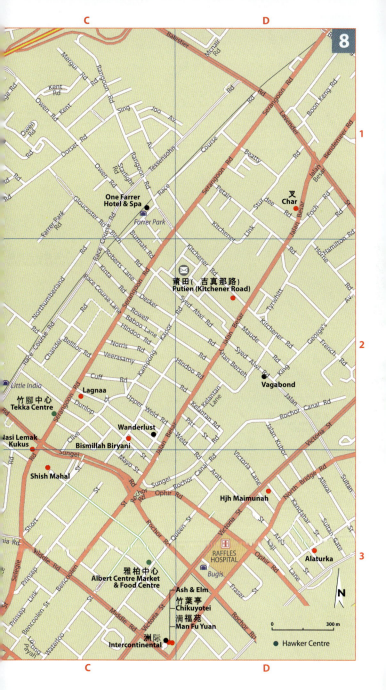

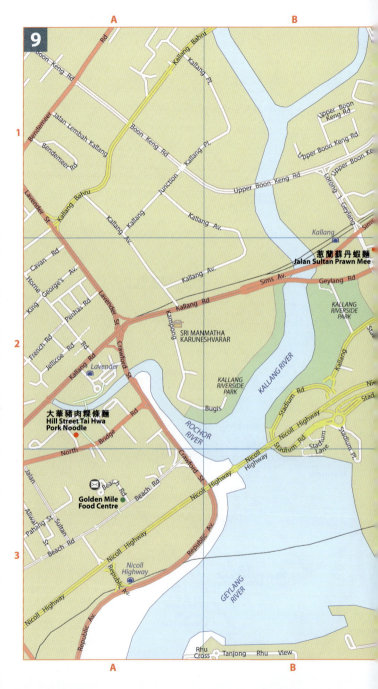

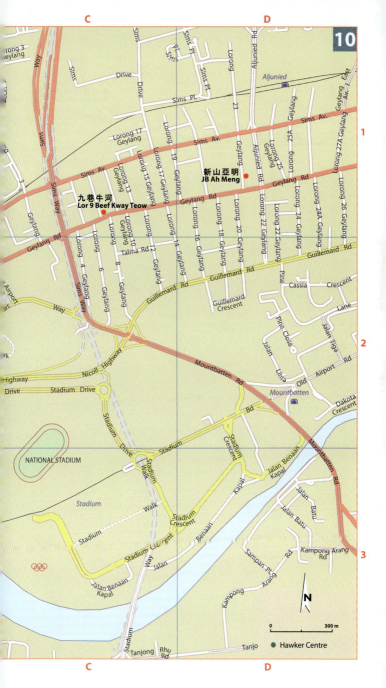

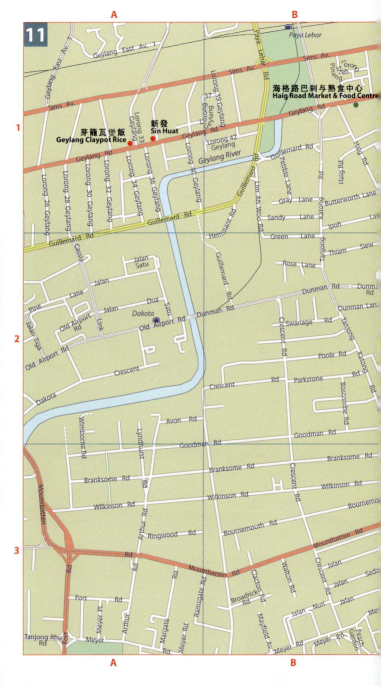

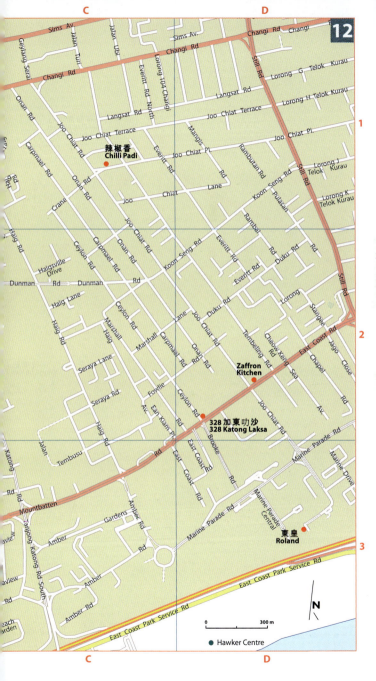

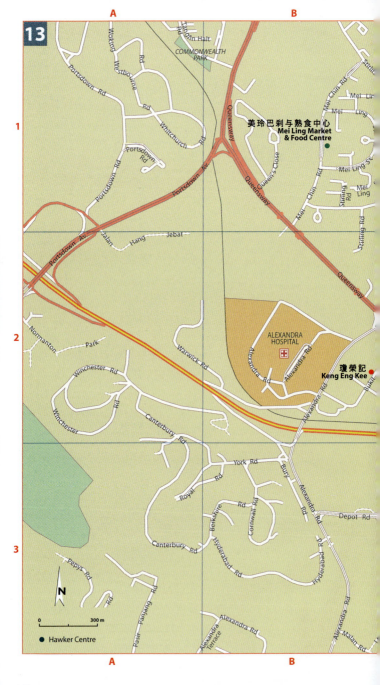

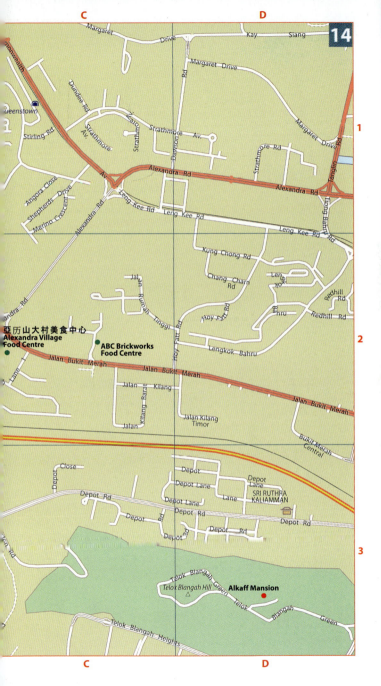

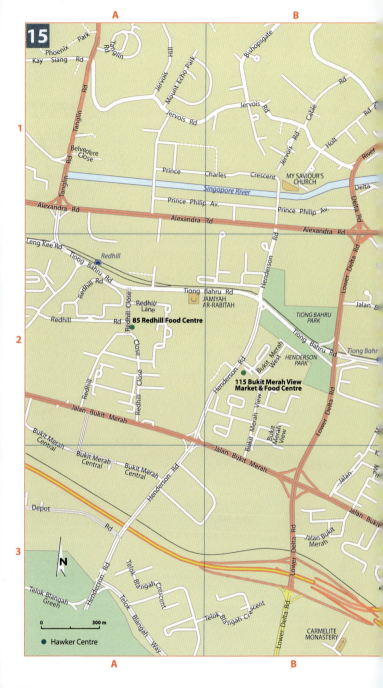

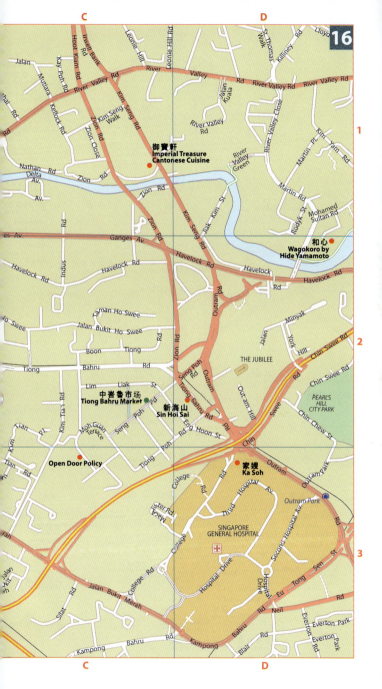

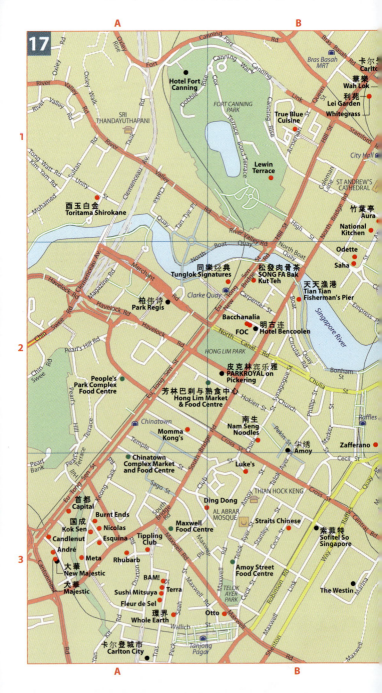

Symbols shown in red indicate particularly charming establishments.

红色图标 表示酒店和餐馆在同级别舒适程度的酒店和餐馆中较优秀。

Read 'How to use this guide' for an explanation of our symbols, classifications and abbreviations.

请仔细阅读"如何使用餐厅/酒店指南",当中的图标、分类等简介助你掌握使用本指南的诀窍,作出智慧的选择。

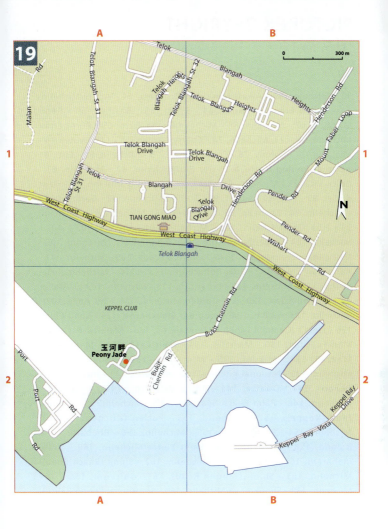

PICTURE COPYRIGHT
图片版权

58 - Michelin, 59 - Alkaff Mansion, 60 - Alma, 61 - Andre/Michelin, 62 - Ash & Elm, 63 - Aura, 64 - BAM!, 65 - Basilico, 66 - Béni/Michelin, 67 - Michelin, 68 - Michelin/Buona Terra, 69 - Burnt Ends/Michelin, 70 – 73, Michelin, 74 - Cherry Garden, 75 - Chikuyotei, 76 - Michelin, 77 - Colony, 78 - Corner House, 79 - Michelin, 80 - Cut , 81 - Daniel Boulud Bistro & Oyster Bar/Michelin, 82 - Michelin, 83 - Dolce Vita, 85 - Michelin, 86 - Fat Cow, 87 - Feng Shui Inn, 88 - Fleur de Sel, 89 - FOC, 90 - Forest, 91 - Forlino/Michelin, 92 - Garibaldi, 93 - Michelin, 94 - Michelin, 95 - Gunther's, 96 - Michelin, 97 - Michelin, 99 - Hua Ting/Michelin, 100 - Michelin, 101 - Il Cielo, 102 – 103 - Michelin, 104 - Imperial Treasure Super Peking Duck (Paragon), 105 - Michelin, 106 - Indocafe, 107 - Jaan, 108 - Jade, 109 - Michelin, 111 - Jiang-Nan Chun, 112 - Joël Robuchon , 113 – 114 - Michelin, 115 - Ki-sho, 116 - Michelin, 117 - Labyrinth, 118 - Michelin, 119 - L'Atelier de Joël Robuchon, 120 - Lei Garden/Michelin, 121 - Les Amis, 122 - Michelin, 123 - Li Bai, 124 - Long Bar Steakhouse, 125 - Long Chim, 126 - Luke's (Gemmill Lane), 127 - Majestic, 128 - Majestic Bay, 129 - Man Fu Yuan, 130 - Michelin, 131 - Melt Café, 132 - Meta, 133 - Mezza9, 134 - Mikuni, 135 - Min Jiang, 136 - Nadaman, 137 - Michelin, 139 - National Kitchen, 140 - Michelin, 141 - Nicolas, 142 - Ocean , 143 - Odette, 144 – 145 - Michelin , 146 - Osia, 147 - Michelin, 148 - Palm Beach Seafood, 149 - Michelin, 151 - Peony Jade (Keppel), 152 - Michelin, 153 - Putien (Kitchener Road)/Michelin, 154 - Raffles Grill, 155 - Michelin, 156 - Rhubarb, 157 - Roland, 158 - Michelin, 159 - Saint Pierre/Michelin, 160 - Shahi Maharani, 161 - Shang Palace/Michelin, 162 - Shinji (Beach Road)/Michelin, 163 - Shinji (Tanglin Road), 165 - Shiraishi, 166 – 167 Michelin, 168 - Shoukouwa/Michelin, 169 - Sin Hoi Sai (Tiong Bahru), 170 - Sky on 57, 171 - Michelin, 172 - Spago, 173 - Michelin, 174 - Summer Palace, 175 - Summer Pavillion, 176 - Sushi Ichi, 177 - Sushi Mitsuya, 179 - Syun/Michelin, 180 - Tambuah Mas, 181 - Tangerine, 182 - Michelin, 183 - The Clifford Pier, 184 - Michelin, 185 - The Lighthouse, 186 - 187 - Michelin, 188 - Michelin, 189 - Tim Ho Wan (Plaza Singapura), 190 – 192 - Michelin, 193 - Michelin/Tunglok Signatures, 194 - Umi+Vino, 195 - Michelin/Wah Lok, 197 - Waku Ghin, 198 - Whitegrass, 199 - Whole Earth, 200 - Wild Rocket, 201 - Yan Ting, 202 - Yhingthai Palace, 203 - Michelin, 205 - Zaffron

Kitchen (East Coast), 244 - Amoy, 245 - Michelin, 246 - Carlton, 247 - Michelin, 248 - Conrad Centennial, 249 - Equarius, 250 - Fairmont, 251 - Fort Canning, 252 - Four Seasons, 253 - Goodwood Park, 254 - Grand Hyatt, 255 - Hilton, 256 - Intercontinental, 257 - Jen Orchardgateway, 258 - Mandarin Orchard, 259 - Mandarin Oriental, 260 - Marina Bay Sands, 261 - Michelin, 262 - New Majestic, 263 - One Farrer, 264 - Orchard, 265 - Pan Pacific, 266 - Park Regis, 267 - Parkroyal on Pickering, 268 - Raffles, 269 - Regent-Four Seasons , 270 - Shangri-La, 271 - Sheraton, 272 - Sofitel Sentosa Resort & Spa, 273 - Sofitel So Singapore, 274 - Swissôtel The Stamford, 275 - The Fullerton, 276 - The Fullerton Bay, 277 - The Ritz-Carlton, Millenia, 278 - The St. Regis, 279 - The Westin, 280 - Vagabond, 281 - W Singapore Sentosa Cove, 283 - Wanderlust

Michelin Travel Partner
Société par actions simplifiées au capital de 11 288 880 EUP
27 Cours de L'Ile Seguin - 92100 Boulogne Billancourt (France)
R.C.S. Nanterre 433 677 721

© Michelin et Cie, Propriétaires-éditeurs
Dépôt légal July 2016

Printed in China: June 2016

No part of this publication may be reproduced in any form without the prior permission of the publisher.

Although the information in this guide was believed by the authors and publisher to be accurate and current at the time of publication, they cannot accept responsibility for any inconvenience, loss or injury sustained by any person relying on information or advice contained in this guide. Things change over time and travellers should take steps to verify and confirm information, especially time sensitive information related to prices, hours of operation and availability.

E-mail : michelinguide.singapore@michelin.com

Maps : (C) 2012 Cartographic data Universal Publications, Ltd / Michelin
Printing and Binding: Book Partners China Ltd.

Welcome to RobertParker.com!

For more than 38 years,
Robert Parker Wine Advocate has established itself as the independent fine wine guide on the international scene and is seen today as the most influential wine review globally.

Receive the WINE ADVOCATE bi-monthly digital review and access over 10 years of archives with a fully searchable database of 285,000 tasting notes, scores, articles and reviews.

Enjoy the member's benefits brought to you by our Global Membership Programme that will reward you with special gourmet and wine experiences offered by our retail and F&B partners, and provide you a privileged access to our worldwide series of events *"Matter of Taste"*.

To activate your free one-year online membership *(valued at USD99)* to The Wine Advocate and MICHELIN guide Singapore, simply use the code below and register on RobertParker.com and guide.michelin.sg.

MSGDawsxH

Partners of
The 2016 MICHELIN Guide Singapore

Title Partner
Resorts World™ Sentosa

Official Card Partner
American Express

Supporting Partner
Singapore Tourism Board

GOLD PREMIER PARTNERS

Credit Suisse	Official Premium Partner
Lexus	Official Car

SILVER PREMIER PARTNERS

Tiger Beer	Official Beer

PREMIER PARTNERS

Chope	Official Reservation System Provider
Classic Fine Foods	Official Fine Food Supplier
Badoit & Evian	Official Waters
Deliveroo	Official Food Delivery Partner
Ruinart	Official Champagne
Hennessy	Official Cognac
Nespresso	Official Coffee

PATRONAGE
Angliss Singapore